D1826572

GLOBAL SECURITY WATCH
TURKEY

GLOBAL SECURITY WATCH

TURKEY

A Reference Handbook

Mustafa Kibaroğlu and Ayşegül Kibaroğlu

Foreword by Talât S. Halman

PRAEGER SECURITY INTERNATIONAL

Westport, Connecticut · London

Library of Congress Cataloging-in-Publication Data

Kibaroğlu, Mustafa, 1962–
   Global security watch—Turkey : a reference handbook / Mustafa Kibaroğlu and Ayşegül Kibaroğlu ;
foreword by Talât S. Halman.
     p. cm. — (Global security watch, ISSN 1938–6168)
   Includes bibliographical references and index.
   ISBN 978–0–313–34560–9 (alk. paper)
   1. Turkey—Foreign relations—1980– 2. Turkey—Strategic aspects. I. Kibaroğlu, Ayşegül. II. Halman,
Talât Sait. III. Title.
DR477.K53   2009
327.561—dc22   2008040400

British Library Cataloguing in Publication Data is available.

Library of Congress Catalog Card Number: 2008040400
ISBN: 978–0–313–34560–9
ISBN: 978–1–4408–3615–2 (pbk.)
ISSN: 1938–6168

First published in 2009

Praeger Security International, 88 Post Road West, Westport, CT 06881
An imprint of Greenwood Publishing Group, Inc.
www.praeger.com

Printed in the United States of America

Contents

Foreword

Security has been a constant in human history—an instinct for the individual, a concern for the community, an aspiration for each nation. It has instigated unfriendly fences and hostile defenses. Its apparatus has ranged from slings and arrows to outrageous nukes. Its principles are certainly positive, even hallowed; but, tragically, it has also fomented distrust, hatred, and destruction. Because of the ravages wreaked by morbid feelings of insecurity, the martial spirit has come to dominate some societies. Pathological fear often breeds wrath, anxiety, and angst—sometimes leads to annihilation.

Peace, as humanity's noble ideal, is still a far cry from reality. The ancient Latin dictum *si vis pacem, para bellum* continues to admonish nations, large and small, to "prepare for war if you wish peace." Even now, the shibboleth inspires nations and shapes their foreign policy as well as institutions. It has served as the *spiritus movens* for ideologies evolved and alliances created.

Security, once a distinct concept, now functions as a versatile, multipurpose term. Its spectrum of senses ranges from a person's psychological confidence about safety to a nation's feeling of freedom, from danger to systematic protection against aggression. The term accommodates both "social security" and "national security affairs," not to mention the economically crucial "securities and bonds."

The noun security in English dates only from the fifteenth century. Its vital connection with real or fictive peril was already sensed in the seventeenth century when the English clergyman Thomas Fuller wrote: "Security is the mother of danger and the grandmother of destruction." This wry observation presaged the anomalous link that developed between animosity and security in the succeeding centuries. Fears about threats against security bred psychopathological strategies of war and totalitarian repressive measures. Security as the twin brother of militaristic expediency not only led to warmongering at times but also created in certain societies (at least sporadically) an atmosphere of state terrorism, espionage, and oppression.

Security is certainly justified in its passive or defensive stance. Yet, in recent history, it has sometimes been forced to resort to the devices and vices of the forces that create the circumstances of insecurity.

Global security is a phenomenon of the modern age. History has witnessed innumerable wars: they have all been local, regional, internecine, civil, limited. The so-called world wars of the first half of the twentieth century were not total in the real sense of the term. World War I was territorially confined to Europe with ripple effects in a few other regions. World War II took place in Europe, Asia, and North Africa. In both wars, there was decisive U.S. participation but no combat in continental America.

There has never been a truly global war—only its horrendous possibility looming ahead. In early twentieth century, total war was an imaginary event, a literary phenomenon, for example, in H. G. Wells's *War of the Worlds*. Humanity felt the panic of a global war, of total annihilation only from the mid-twentieth century onward. The sinister idea behind the Latin expression *bellum omnium contra omnes* rears its head, two millennia later, with a compelling force: war of all against all.

The present book by Dr. Mustafa Kibaroğlu and Dr. Ayşegül Kibaroğlu, a young couple, ranking as two of the most successful analysts of Turkey's foreign and security policies during the Republic's first 85 years, provides a provocative account of this highly complex topic. Tracing the highlights of the history of a *sui generis* nation that often defies comparison with others, it narrates a remarkable diversity of political experience from nomadic confederacies to sedentary principalities, from tribal rule to sovereign states and an enduring empire (the Ottoman Empire that lasted from the end of the thirteenth century until 1922), and finally a modernizing republic.

Culturally, few nations have experienced exposure to a greater variety of orientations. Few have had a more extensive geographic spread in less than 15 centuries—from the environs of China almost to the shores of the Atlantic Ocean. The Turkish language was written in at least five different scripts—Göktürk, Uygur, Arabic, Cyrillic, and (since 1928) Latin-type. Turkish communities of different eras and territories have belonged to many creeds (for instance, pagan beliefs) and major religions (Judaism, Buddhism, Manichaeanism, Christianity, and Islam).

From the standpoint of sovereignty and security, two historical facts stand out: The Turks have held sway continuously on the present-day territory of the Republic for almost a thousand years now and they constitute the only Muslim nation that was never colonized. Their early peripatetic life, their sprawling empire, and their staunch control of their present homeland endowed in them certain capabilities that are crucial in dealing with security affairs: emphasis on military prowess, openness to cultural and technological change, and flexibility in the conduct of foreign affairs.

Since its establishment in 1923, the Republic has consistently avoided military adventure designed for territorial expansion, while it has maintained a full commitment to powerful defense. Through diplomatic dexterity, caution, and restraint, it managed to escape entry into World War II, succeeded in not yielding to Soviet demands of territory in eastern Turkey or to U.S. pressure for participation in the U.S. action against Iraq. Its only military involvements in an 85-year period since 1923 have been the bloodless annexation of Hatay, Turkish troops joining the UN forces in Korea, the military action in Northern Cyprus, and numerous forays into northern Iraq recently. Most of these were short-lived or away from the Turkish mainland, and many were defended on the grounds that compatriots were being threatened or victimized (as in Cyprus) or Turkey's own territorial integrity was being menaced by terrorists with help from the outside (as in PKK in northern Iraq).

During the Cold War and since then, investments of countless billions into socalled deterrents have actually deterred development in scores of countries. The circumstance that force Turkey to maintain huge armed forces (the second largest in NATO, the largest in Europe) has deprived the country of resources that might have been used for economic development. Yet, this military capability coupled with the country's strategic location might prove advantageous for Turkey's eventual admission to membership in the European Union.

The Turkish Republic is the prototype, perhaps the paragon, of a state whose foreign policy is, or must be, dictated by security constraints. Few countries, if any, are comparable to it in terms of external threats and internal instabilities. Turkey stands virtually unique the way it is surrounded by real or potential enemies, some of whom have historical grievances and/or current animus. Part of the territory of each neighboring state once belonged to Ottoman Turkey and existed under its suzerainty. Syria, Iraq, Iran, Russia, Armenia, Bulgaria, and Greece, even if some of them have no present-day conflict with Turkey, all harbor less than friendly feelings for Turks. The geopolitical situation of the country is such that it is exposed to danger from all directions and from diverse configurations of power. One must always bear in mind that Turkey is not only on two continents (Asia and Europe) but also an integral part of the Middle East, a component of the Islamic bloc, a member of NATO, a southernmost extension of the Balkans, an opening to North America and to the Caucasian region. This multiplicity has numerous advantages but creates some difficulties and dangers as well.

The Kibaroğlus, brilliant scholars of international relations as they are, dissect and discuss these issues with compelling clarity. Their insights, objectivity, and fair-mindedness are admirable. The world should watch out for how Turkey fares with its security affairs. This book is an excellent guide to the Turkish component of the Global Security Watch.

The Turkish Republic stands threatened by internal and external pressures some of which continue unabated. It miraculously escaped what might have been disastrous consequences of involvement in World War II. Also, it masterfully bypassed the ill effects of the Cold War and the Soviet greed for Turkish territory. It has managed to remain intact despite rampant sedition, domestic unrest, and secessionism. It remains a checkerboard of conflicting interests and an arena of interference by several Western powers. It is often convulsed by terrorist organizations, some presumably aided and abetted by outsiders. Its geopolitical location is such that it is not likely to be immune to anxiety about possible trouble along its borders in the foreseeable future.

If global security (in a positive sense) is ultimately achieved, the world, and certainly beleaguered Turkish Republic, will reap the benefits of freed economic resources that could be channeled into health, employment, and education. Security, if reduced, could help create a stronger and economically sound Turkey.

Professor Talât S. Halman
Dean
Faculty of Humanities and Letters
Bilkent University
Ankara, Turkey
July 28, 2008

Preface

The idea of writing a book on matters pertaining to Turkey's foreign and security policies has long been in our minds. However, our pressing agendas, being scholars who wanted to meet the demands coming from various circles such as journals to submit articles and/or opinion pieces, think tanks to present papers, institutions to give lectures, and the like, forced us to postpone the idea, which was indeed an *ideal*. However, an e-mailed letter from Mrs. Alicia Merritt, the consulting acquisitions editor for reference books working with Praeger Security International, in which she kindly extended an offer to write a book on Turkey, excited us a lot and made us reconsider our agendas for the following months and years. The aspect that excited us the most in Mrs. Merritt's letter was the perfect correlation between our preliminary thoughts about the content and the scope of such a book, and the expectations as well as the recommendations of the editor of Praeger Security International. Hence, we decided to seize the moment and to make our contribution to the literature as best as we could.

It goes without saying that Turkey is an important actor in the international arena. There are a number of factors which elevate Turkey to the league of key players in world politics and more so in its region (i.e., Eurasia and the Middle East). As a long-standing member of the Western world, a candidate country to the European Union, a "staunch" ally of the United States, and a frontline state in the fight against terrorism, Turkey is too important to be studied superficially. Proper understanding of how decisions regarding foreign and security issues are being taken within the state apparatus in Turkey is crucially important, especially when "unexpected" developments take place.

The making of Turkey's foreign and security policies is indeed not a very complex matter to monitor, provided that the analysts and researchers know where to look at, whom to talk to, and more importantly, what factors make up the mind-sets of the decision-makers. There were, and still are, a number of factors that shaped the mind-sets of the makers of Turkey's foreign and security policies which, however, may not be understood or even noticed easily from a distance. Hence, misreading of the intentions may be the case especially for nonexperts.

Therefore, the information that will be supplied in this book and our views as the authors based on our academic backgrounds and our rich accumulation of knowledge through our contacts with political, military, and diplomatic circles over the years are hoped to provide not only meaningful explanations into the past events but also useful insights into the current and future developments that take place in and around Turkey. As such, this book may be used as a template by its readers, ranging from high school and college students to think-tank analysts, civil and military bureaucrats, and even business people who at times have to deal with Turkey, with its in-depth analyses of the world events from Turkey's perspective that may facilitate their proper understanding of complex foreign policy issues.

We strongly believe that the specific knowledge and the academic expertise about foreign and security policies pertaining to Turkey and other countries that we built over the years, which we tried to reflect to the content of the book to the extent possible, is primarily a result of our hard work inside and outside of Turkey benefiting from research opportunities thanks to a number of fellowships that we earned and exploited to the most. Hence, we would like to acknowledge the invaluable contributions to our careers of these fellowships, such as the Jean Monnet fellowship and the Turkish Academy of Sciences fellowship earned by Ayşegül and spent at the University of Amsterdam and at the University of Dundee, respectively; and the United Nations Institute of Disarmament Research fellowship, the International Atomic Energy Agency fellowship, Center for Nonproliferation Studies' postdoctoral fellowship, and the Belfer Center's sabbatical fellowship earned by Mustafa and spent at the United Nations Offices in Geneva, at the University of Southampton, at the Monterey Institute, and at Harvard University, respectively.

We would also like to acknowledge that we benefited greatly from our active presence in the deliberations at the numerous academic meetings and brainstorming sessions organized by the leading research centers of Turkey, such as the Foreign Policy Institute (FPI), the Eurasian Center for Strategic Research (ASAM), the Center for Strategic Research (SAM) of the Turkish Ministry of Foreign Affairs, and the Center for Strategic Research and Study (SAREM) of the Turkish General Staff. Our advisory positions at the Southeastern Anatolia Project Regional Development Administration (GAP RDA) and the Center of Excellence Defence Against Terrorism (COE-DAT) have enabled us to enhance our understanding of the sensitivity and the importance attached to some foreign policy–related matters by the civil and military bureaucracy in Turkey. We are most grateful to the confidence entrusted to our academic competence by those who have been involved in these circles.

Our academic institutions, namely Bilkent University and the Middle East Technical University, have provided us with the most stimulating academic environments being two of the best universities in Turkey in all respects. We would like to acknowledge the various forms of inputs provided by our colleagues in our respective departments through our formal and informal discussions and debates since our first encounters with them. Our special thanks should go to Professor Jack Kangas, former Academic Dean at the National Defense University in Washington, D.C., and a visiting senior lecturer at Bilkent University, who kindly recommended us to Praegers for commissioning this book. We feel indebted to him.

Professor Talât Halman, Dean of the Faculty of Humanities and Letters at Bilkent University and Turkey's first and the founding Minister of Culture, has been extremely kind to accept reading our manuscript and to write a "Foreword" to this book. His invaluable contribution to our work is above all appreciation.

Finalizing the typing phase of this book coincided with the summer semester at Bilkent. We kindly asked from some of our students to share their views about the latest draft of the manuscript before sending it to the series editor. Hence, we would like to acknowledge the comments and suggestions of our students, namely Emine Demir and Mehmet Emir Karataş, as well as of our former student Captain Olcay Denizer from COE-DAT. We would also like to acknowledge the contribution of Aylin Gürzel, doctoral student at Bilkent. Without her assistance, compilation of some of the data would certainly take much longer time for us.

Our greatest appreciation should go to our families who have made who we are now with their incessant love and generous support of all sorts for literally decades. Our son Onat, our greatest love and a unique source of joy and happiness for us, has boosted our morale with his very useful and timely comments and suggestions about the content of our work. He has been our firsthand editor, as a ninth grade student, and he guided us throughout the writing of the manuscript. We very much hope that this has been a wonderful opportunity for Onat to discover the genius and the talent he has in social sciences.

We very much enjoyed writing this book. With the contributions of Adam Kane, our series editor, to the construction of the initial frame of the book, and Christy Anitha, our project manager, who supervised the amazing precision of the copy editing process, we believe the readers of our book will enjoy even more reading it.

Mustafa Kibaroğlu and Ayşegül Kibaroğlu
Bilkent, Ankara
November 29, 2008

Abbreviations

AKP	*Adalet ve Kalkınma Partisi* (Justice and Development Party)
ANAP	*Anavatan Partisi* (Motherland Party)
ASALA	Armenian Secret Army for the Liberation of Armenia
AWACS	Airborne Warning and Control System
BSEC	Black Sea Economic Cooperation
BTC	Baku-Tbilisi-Ceyhan oil pipeline
CENTO	Central Treaty Organization
CFE	Conventional Forces in Europe
CHP	*Cumhuriyet Halk Partisi* (Republican People's Party)
CIS	Commonwealth of Independent States
CSCE	Conference on Security and Cooperation in Europe
DSP	*Demokratik Sol Parti* (Democratic Left Party)
DYP	*Doğru Yol Partisi* (True Path Party)
EC	European Community
ECO	Economic Cooperation Organization
EEC	European Economic Community
EOKA	*Ethniki Organosis Kyprion Agoniston*
ESDI	European Security and Defense Identity
ESDP	European Security and Defense Policy
EU	European Union
FP	*Fazilet Partisi* (Virtue Party)
GAP	Southeastern Anatolia Project
GAP RDA	Southeastern Anatolia Project Regional Development Administration
GOLD	General Organization for Land Development
IAEA	International Atomic Energy Agency
ICJ	International Court of Justice
ICO	Islamic Conference Organization
IFOR	Implementation Force

IRBM	Intermediate Range Ballistic Missile
ISAF	International Security Assistance Force
JTC	Joint Technical Committee
KRG	Kurdistan Regional Government
MHP	*Milliyetçi Hareket Partisi* (Nationalist Action Party)
MNP	*Milli Nizam Partisi* (National Order Party)
MOU	Memorandum of Understanding
MSP	*Milli Selamet Partisi* (National Salvation Party)
NATO	North Atlantic Treaty Organization
NBC	Nuclear, Biological, Chemical
NIS	Newly Independent States
NPT	Nuclear Nonproliferation Treaty
NSC	National Security Council
NWFZ	Nuclear-Weapons-Free Zone
OPEC	Organization of the Petroleum Exporting Countries
OSCE	Organization for Security and Co-operation in Europe
PASOK	Pan-Hellenic Socialist Party
PfP	Partnership for Peace
PJAK	*Partiya Jiyana Azad a Kurdistanê*
PKK	*Partiya Karkerên Kurdistan* (Kurdistan Workers Party)
RCD	Regional Cooperation for Development
RP	*Refah Partisi* (Welfare Party)
SDI	Strategic Defense Initiative
SFOR	Stabilization Force in Bosnia-Herzegovina
TAF	Turkish Armed Forces
TGNA	Turkish Grand National Assembly
UNPROFOR	United Nations Protection Force in Bosnia-Herzegovina
UNSC	United Nations Security Council
WMD	Weapons of Mass Destruction

CHAPTER 1

From the Khanates in Central Asia to the Republic in Anatolia

Thousands of years ago Turks were living thousands of miles away from where they live now as the citizens of the Republic of Turkey. Turks have their homeland in Central Asia where they have established the Great Hun Empire as early as 204 BC, which was spread over a vast portion of land extending from Siberia in the north and Tibet and Kashmir in the south to the Caspian Sea in the west and the Pacific Ocean in the east. The Göktürk Empire, which was founded around AD 550, is the first state to use the word "Turk" in its official name. Since then the Turks have steadily moved mostly westward for various reasons, including, among others, the desire to discover new lands as well as to escape the atrocities of Mongol warriors who have conquered large territories in Central Asia and in the Caucasus. Turks have arrived in Anatolia, their *new* homeland for almost a thousand years now, and founded the Seljuk Empire in AD 1040. The Ottoman Empire, which was founded in 1299, can be said to be an offspring of the Seljuks.

From the Great Hun Empire to the Ottoman Empire, Turks have established sixteen states in history.[1] The seventeenth Turkish state, namely the modern Republic of Turkey, was proclaimed on October 29, 1923 as a sovereign state in the aftermath of the War of Liberation fought under the command of Mustafa Kemal (Atatürk) against Great Britain, France, Italy, and Greece that had occupied what was left from the Ottoman Empire after the end of World War I mostly on the Anatolian peninsula.

Most authors use the term "war of independence" for defining the period of a series of military campaigns of the Turks against the occupying powers from 1920 to 1922. One may see no difference between a "war of liberation" and a "war of independence" so long as they both lead the way to the liberation of a territory from foreign occupation. Yet, "war of independence" is a more suitable term for people fighting for their freedom against colonial powers who ruled their territories for extended periods such as decades, if not centuries.

In the case of the Turkish War of Liberation, one must bear in mind that the Turks, who have built empires, have never been colonized or ruled by outside powers throughout the history with the exception of a very short period of foreign occupation on the last pieces of the Ottoman lands mostly in Anatolia as a result of the surrender of the defeated Ottoman Sultan Mehmed VI (Vahdeddin) at the end of World War I.

The decision of Sultan Vahdeddin was by no means accepted by Mustafa Kemal and his like-minded comrades and followers who had launched a national resistance and liberation movement and an all-out offensive over the Turkish territory that was portioned with the Treaty of Sèvres dated August 10, 1920. Successive military victories that were gained in the battlefields against the occupying powers paved the way to the peace conference that was convened in Lausanne, Switzerland from November 1922 to July 1923, and ultimately to the emergence of the modern Republic of Turkey.

The journey of the Turks extending from the Central Asian steppes on the east to Central Europe on the west and settling somewhere in between in the Anatolian peninsula, spanning over thousands of years, is an interesting story that is worth remembering briefly with its most significant milestone events, especially since the foundation of the Ottoman Empire, which is the ancestor of the present-day Republic of Turkey.

JOURNEY STARTS IN CENTRAL ASIA

Throughout history the Turks have established numerous states in various geographical regions on the continents of Asia, Europe, and Africa. According to Chinese records, Turkish political history in Asia commenced with the Huns. The Hun State, which first appeared in the third century BC, became a significant and powerful state during the reign of its founder, Mete Khan. Having a defined and special strategy, Mete Khan defeated the Mongols and then the Yuechis, and after having taken the western gates and trade routes of China under his control, gained significant economic power. When Mete Khan died, the Great Hun Empire was at its peak due to its military organization, domestic and foreign policies, religion, army, war strategies, and arts.

After the collapse of the Asian Hun State, a new state called the Göktürk Empire was founded at the foot of the Altay Mountains. The Göktürks, who were the first to employ the word "Turk" in their official state name, chose Ötüken, the former capital of the empire, as a base and established Khanates. Later they spread out and became an Empire. They professed that a khanate could not be ruled by means of war and bravery alone and that wisdom was very important. Bilge Khan and Kül Tegin are noted as the wisest and most heroic figures among Turkish statesmen in history. Göktürk Khans immortalized their accomplishments with Orkhun inscriptions, which are the first written texts of the Turkish language.

The Uygur Turks established the third great Turkish state in 741. They later were dispersed by an attack of the Kyrgyz Turks in the northwestern part of the capital. The West Huns, descendents of the Asia Huns who lived in the Turkistan region and around Lake Aral, left their homeland due to the pressure exerted by the Uars and migrated west of the Volga. In 434, Atilla assumed control of the West Hun Empire which is the first known Turkish state established in Europe. During Atilla's reign, the barbarian tribes of Europe were defeated, even Byzantium and Rome submitted, and the borders of the West Hun Empire expanded from the shores of the Rhine river to those of the Volga river. With Atilla's death in 453, the incursion of Turks into Europe subsided. The West Huns were pioneers in opening up the way to Europe for the Turks, who not only took their culture and civilization to Europe but also protected those civilizations that were threatened by barbarian tribes in Europe. This resulted in a migration from Asia to Europe that would last for 900 years.

Another Turkish tribe that was respected and feared in Europe was the Avars who followed the West Huns. The Avars, who left their homeland in Central Asia and escaped toward the West when the Göktürk State was founded in 552, played an important role in European history. They first came to Caucasia and the north of the Black Sea. They went all the way to the banks of the Danube river. They frequently went to the Balkans. They founded a civilization that spanned from present-day Yugoslavia to Germany. They reigned over the Slavs in the Danube area and the Bulgarians living on the shores of the Black Sea. The first Turks in history to lay siege to İstanbul were the Avars. The constant attacks of the French Emperor Charlamagne, which began in 791 and lasted 15 years, diminished the power of the Avars. They wished to settle in the plateau between the Danube and the Tizsa rivers. The French attacks continued and the Avar group dispersed in the Balkans. In 805, they lost their national identity.

After the Avar existence in Europe came to an end, a new Turkish state called the Khazars came into being. The Khazars, who were considered the continuation of the Göktürks, appeared after the Avars defeated the Sabir State in the east of Europe. Between the seventh and eighth centuries they founded a strong state that spanned from the Volga to the Dnieper and to Kiev. The Khazars established a period of peace in East Europe during the seventh thru ninth centuries. The Khazar State was extremely tolerant regarding the religious beliefs of the people living under its domination, and it is considered one of the first and few states that showed religious tolerance. The Khazars were not able to withstand the attacks of the Russian forces on the Khazar cities for long. The Russian army

captured most of the Khazar lands and their political existence as a state came to
an end in 968.

After the decline of the Uygur State in 840, the Karakhanli State was founded
by the Karluks. The reign of the Karakhanlis is considered to be a turning point
in Turkish history, because Islam was adopted as the official religion. The foundations of a historical development referred to as Turkish-Islamic culture and
civilization were laid in this period. During the rule of the Karakhanlis, there
was another Turkish state, the Gazneli Sultanate (936–1187), the capital city of
which was Ghazi in Afghanistan. Mahmud of Ghazna was the first to use the title
of "Sultan" and laid the foundation for today's Pakistan. The Ghaznelis had to
retreat to India after the Dandanakan War with the Seljuks in 1040 and finally
came under the sovereignty of the Seljuks.

Another great Turkish state, the Seljuk State (1040–1157), was founded by
Selçuk Bey who was a member of the Kinik tribe of the Oghuz Turks. The
borders of the state spanned from the Marmara Sea to Lake Balkhash in Central
Asia and from the Caucasus, the Caspian Sea, and the Aral Sea to the borders of
India and Yemen. The Seljuks entered into a struggle of hegemony with the two
Turkish states, the Karakhanlis and the Ghaznelis, and succeeded in establishing
Turkish unity. Tuğrul Bey, the Sultan of the Seljuks, entered Baghdad, the
Abbasid Caliphate capital, and ended the domination of the Buwayhids, a Persi
Shiite dynasty, in 1055. Therefore, the Caliph bestowed upon Tuğrul Bey the
title of "Ruler of the World." During the reign of Sultan Alparslan, the successor
and son of Tuğrul Bey, the territories of the country expanded significantly.
Sultan Alparslan defeated the Byzantine army which was led by Romanus
Diogenes at Manzikert (*Malazgirt*) in 1071. This victory literally opened up
the gates of Anatolia to the Turks. During the reign of Sultan Malik Shah, the
Seljuk State experienced its most successful period.

After Sultan Malik Shah died, the country was divided into small states. The
Syrian Seljuks (1092–1117), Iraq and Khorasan Seljuks (1092–1194), Kirman
Seljuks (1092–1187), and Anatolian Seljuks (1092–1194) were among the small
states. Moreover, the Kharezm Shah State (1097–1231) was established by
Mohammed Kharezm Shah, the son of Anushtegin, the palace servant of Sultan
Malik Shah, on the territories of the Great Seljuk State where Lake Aral inter-
sected the Ceyhun river in the southern region.

One of the most important states of the fourteenth century was the Tamerlane
State (1370–1507). Tamerlane expanded the borders of the state from the Volga
river to the Ganges river in India and from the Tanri Mountains to İzmir and
Damascus in a short period of 35 years. The Empire disintegrated after the death
of Tamerlane just as rapidly as it had been established.

The Turkmen group of the Karakoyunlu founded the Karakoyunlu State
(1370–1507) between Irbil and Nakhichevan. The Akkoyunlu State (1350–
1502) was founded by Turkmen tribes who settled around Diyarbakir-Malatya

during the collapse of Mongol rule. During the most powerful period of the Akkoyunlu State, the borders of the state extended from the Caspian Sea to Syria and from Azerbaijan to Baghdad. However, defeat in the Otlukbeli Battle in 1473 by Sultan Mehmed *the Conqueror* paved the way for the founding of the Safavid State (1501–1736) by Shah Ismail, who established political unity in Iran. His activities in Anatolia and also his attempts to annex Anatolia provoked the reaction of the Ottoman Sultan Selim. Shah Ismail's army was seriously defeated at the Battle of Chaldıran in 1514.[2]

THE OTTOMAN HERITAGE

Foundation

The Ottoman Empire was founded by Osman Bey who was the son of Ertuğrul Ghazi, head of one of the Seljuk principalities, which were spread all over Anatolia toward the demise of the Seljuk Empire. In 1299 Osman proclaimed his independence from the Seljuks and sowed the seeds of the Ottoman Empire in Söğüt, a region east of modern-day Bursa, which was the first seat of the Empire that would survive for over six centuries. In the century after the death of Osman Bey, the Ottoman rule began to extend over the eastern Mediterranean and the Balkans. The victory at the Battle of Kosovo in 1389 marked the beginning of the Ottoman expansion into Europe.

With the conquest of Constantinople, the seat of the Byzantine Empire, in 1453 by Sultan Mehmed II *the Conqueror,* the Ottoman Empire took over the control of nearly all of the former Eastern Roman Empire territories. Constantinople became the new capital city of the Ottoman Empire by the name of İstanbul. The Ottoman Empire has soon become the preeminent power in Southeastern Europe and in the eastern Mediterranean during a long period of conquest and expansion that followed. Thanks to the conquests on land and the advanced naval power controlling the major trade routes between Europe and Asia, the Ottoman Empire has also become a great trading power, which quickly flourished economically as well.

Expansion

The Empire also prospered under the rule of Sultan Selim I (1512–20) who further expanded the Empire's eastern and southern frontiers. Selim first defeated Shah Ismail of the Persian Empire at the Battle of Chaldıran and then he established the Ottoman rule in Egypt. Selim also assumed the Caliphate title, the leader of the Islamic world.

The Ottoman Empire lived its heydays during the sultanate of Süleyman *the Magnificent* (1520–66), who further expanded the Ottoman territories. He first captured Belgrade in 1521 and then conquered the Kingdom of Hungary after the Battle of Mohacs in 1526, which paved the way to establishing the Ottoman rule in Central and Eastern Europe. Süleyman *the Magnificent* is well known in history for his attempts to take the city of Vienna, the heart of the Austrian Habsburg Monarchy, in 1529 and in 1532, but failed to do so. During the reign of Süleyman, Transylvania and Moldavia became the principalities of the Ottoman Empire. In 1535, the Ottoman Empire expanded its rule toward the east by taking Baghdad from the Persian Empire and gaining control of Mesopotamia enabling access to the Persian Gulf.

In addition to the conquests on land, the Ottoman Empire has also become a dominant naval power in the Mediterranean, especially during the rule of Sultan Selim and Sultan Süleyman. The Ottoman admiral Barbaros Hayrettin Pasha, who commanded the Turkish navy during the reign of Sultan Süleyman, had a number of victories over the European navies. He conquered Tunisia and Algeria, which were under the Spanish rule. Barbaros is also known for his role in the evacuation of the Jews as well as the Muslims who were being persecuted by the Spanish inquisition. Barbaros also defeated Andria Doria, naval commander of the Holy League of Charles V, at the Battle of Preveze in 1538. He then captured Nice from the Holy Roman Empire in 1543.

The opposition of the Ottoman Empire to the rule of the Habsburgs in Southern and Central Europe paved the way to an alliance with their rivals such as France, England, and the Netherlands all of which were great trade powers and thus became the trade partners of the Ottomans. The Ottoman sultans have started to grant privileges to these countries, meaning the right to making trade within the Empire with tax exemptions. As such, the Ottoman Empire has become one of the key actors in European politics and economy of the time.

Stagnation

The Ottoman influence on the trade routes between Europe and Asia, thanks to its powerful naval presence and superiority in the Mediterranean, forced the Europeans to discover new ways and means to overcome the blockade. In addition to a series of naval warfare in the Mediterranean, the preoccupation of the Ottomans in military campaigns in Austria in the west and in Persia in the east put a lot of strain on the administration of the Empire in terms of the logistics of maintaining lines of supply and communication across two distantly separated war theaters. Such a situation had serious consequences for the Ottoman navy, which eventually degraded when compared to the renovated and upgraded naval capability of the European powers.

The death of Süleyman *the Magnificent* also marked the beginning of the end of the era of expansionism with great lapses on three continents. The efforts of the European powers to upgrade their naval capabilities with a view to circumventing the Ottoman blockage on the trade routes between Asia and Europe as well as the discovery of alternative routes started to cause serious damage to the Ottoman trade and economy. Deterioration of the economic situation that resulted in significant decreases in revenues put strain on the treasury, which in turn caused serious difficulties in sustaining an effective administrative mechanism. The victory of the coalition of Catholic powers led by Spain at the Battle of Lepanto in 1571 challenged the primacy of the Ottoman Empire in the Mediterranean.

Against all the odds, territorial gains were still possible, thanks to the momentum that was gained in the previous decades. However, the Battle of Vienna in 1683 has been a landmark event that heralded the end of Ottoman expansionism into the European territories. The defeat in Vienna also signified how much overstretched the Ottoman army's capabilities were. The distance between two major theaters, namely the Habsburgs of Austria in the west and the Safavids of Persia in the east, was so big that allocating resources to both fronts, while the naval strength in the Mediterranean had started to deteriorate, required leadership skills in the Ottoman sultans who have succeeded Süleyman *the Magnificent*. This difficult period, however, also coincided with less competent Ottoman sultans coming to power some of whom have never displayed any ambition to keep pace with the developments in world affairs. One particular exception was Sultan Murad IV who recaptured Yerevan and Baghdad from the Safavids in 1635 and 1639, respectively, of which the latter paved the way to the signing of the Treaty of Kasr-ı Shirin, which determined the Turkish-Iranian borders ever since.

Added to the difficulties in sustaining the Ottoman rule on three continents were the technological and scientific developments and innovations taking place in Europe as a result of the Renaissance and the Reformation processes. But, the Ottoman Empire could not keep pace with these developments that had direct bearings on the military strengths as well as the economic welfare of the states that were in the same political arena.

Scientific developments and innovations in the military technologies have also affected the tactics used in the battlefields. The supremacy of fire power, which had once helped the Turks in the siege and then the conquest of the Byzantine capital Constantinople, and its extensive use by the European armies in their encounters with the Turks resulted in successive losses of territories that used to be under the Ottoman rule.

Much of the late sixteenth and early seventeenth centuries was characterized with revolts, rebellions, and the inability of the Ottoman administration to properly control local communities in faraway places even though they were still nominally under the weakening Turkish rule. That was also the period when the Ottoman dynasty was preoccupied with intriguing relations among the elite who were blinded with the ambition to seize power of the sultanate.

All of these developments were indeed the powerful signals of the stagnation that was experienced in the imperial rule. The net effect of stagnation has been the beginning of dramatic losses of vast territories, especially in Eastern Europe and in the Balkans. Moreover, the Ottoman territories in North Africa and the Middle East were entering the *de facto* rule of the British and the French.

Decline

Lagging behind the scientific and technological developments that were taking place in Europe has usually been acknowledged as the prime reason behind stagnation of the advances of the Ottomans both in the economic and in the military domains. The impact of the religious elite on the ruling elite has been significant in yielding such an outcome. A typical story told among the historians to illustrate such a situation has been the denunciation of the printing press by the religious elite arguing that it was the "Devil's invention."

The need to catch up with the European powers was felt dearly after consecutive defeats in the battlefields on almost all fronts, especially in the wars with the Austrians and the Russians. The Black Sea was used to be known as a Turkish lake for the last three centuries since the conquest of Kila and Aqkirman (Cetatea Alba/Belgorod) in 1484, important ports on the right bank of Dniester. But, the defeat of the Ottomans in the hands of the Russians in the Russo-Turkish War of 1768–74 resulted in the signing of the Treaty of Küçük Kaynarca. Then, Ukraine, the Crimean Peninsula, and Northern Caucasus were brought into the Russian sphere of influence.

Sultan Selim III (1789–1807) is known for his reformation efforts, especially in the military organization. Military commanders from the Prussian Army were invited to the Ottoman Empire for this purpose. Such an initiative, however, has shaken the fundamentals of the Ottoman military establishment that resulted in the revolts among the elite warriors, namely the Janissaries, costing the throne and the life of Sultan Selim III.

His successor Sultan Mahmud II abolished the Janissary Corps in 1826 that had become over the years an almost autonomous organization within the Ottoman administration, which was not obeying the rules if they were not pleased by them and not willing to fight wars. Sultan Mahmud II was succeeded after his death by his son Sultan Abdülmecid I who launched the Reform and Reorganization (*Tanzimat*) movement in 1839, with a view to introducing reforms to the Ottoman administration and the society.[3]

Under the *Tanzimat* movement, the Ottoman army was reorganized on the Prussian model, the taxation system was overhauled, and representative assemblies from the provinces were created. As part of the reforms, French criminal and commercial laws inspired the Ottoman administration to introduce a penal code applicable in the new state courts, which were separate from the religious courts. Moreover, minorities and non-Muslims were granted certain rights and immunities that have eventually become subject to abuse and exploitation by great powers.

Neither the reforms nor the reorganizations that the Ottoman society and the administration have undergone as a result of the *Tanzimat* movement could be of any help to revitalize the Empire. Furthermore, decades of inability to keep up with the scientific and technological developments, due to various reasons extending from the impact of religion on governance to the indifference of some of the sultans to the events going on outside of the imperial palace, coincided with the uprisings resulting from the fast spreading nationalistic movement in Europe have paved the way to the decline of the Ottoman Empire.

The nineteenth century was characterized with the rise of nationalism that affected the entire world, not only the Ottoman Empire. However, the impact of nationalism on the Ottoman Empire has been one of acceleration of the decline because of the ineffectiveness in the administration of large territories and populations of different ethnic and religious origins. Of these, the Greek launched their war of independence from the Ottoman administration and managed to proclaim independence a decade later in 1829. Greece was followed by the Danubian principalities, Serbia, Montenegro, Bosnia, and Moldova who declared their independence from the Ottoman Empire. As a result of the war with the Russians in 1877–78, Ottoman administration was left with no choice but to recognize the independence of these states. In addition to them, Bulgaria was granted autonomy.

The reforms and reorganizations were followed with arrangements in the legal domain culminating in the inception of the Constitutional Era (*Meşrutiyet*) which was signified with the Basic Law (*Kanun-i Esasi*) written by members of the Young Ottomans. The Basic Law, which was promulgated in 1876, established freedom of belief and equality of all citizens before the law. Nevertheless, only after two years of staying in force, Sultan Abdulhamid II (1876–1909) suspended the Ottoman Parliament.

As a consequence of the defeat in the hands of the Russians in the 1877–78 war, Ottomans let Cyprus to the British rule in 1878. The Abdulhamid period was characterized with the search of balance of power by forming alliances with European countries such as Great Britain, France, and Russia, rather than entering conflicts alone. One can argue that the balance of power strategy helped retard disintegration of the Ottoman Empire, because the British and the French wanted to keep the Ottoman territories for themselves instead of letting Austria and Russia partition them and to expand their spheres of influence toward the eastern Mediterranean and the Middle East.

Demise

The early twentieth century was dominated by the politics of the Committee of Union and Progress (*İttihat ve Terakki Cemiyeti*), led by the Young Turks. The Young Turk Revolution began in 1908 and spread throughout the Ottoman territories, resulting in the announcement by the Sultan Abdulhamid II of the restoration of the 1876 Constitution and the reconvening of Parliament, which he had suspended in 1878 under the pretext of the Russo-Turkish War. This period is known as the Second Constitutional Era, which ended with the Sultan Abdulhamid II being deposed and sent to exile in Saloniki in Greece.

The Young Turk Revolution gave the opportunity to the Austria-Hungarian Empire to officially annex Bosnia and Herzegovina, which was under its occupation since the Russo-Turkish War of 1877–78 and the Congress of Berlin in 1878. Soon after, benefiting from the Italo-Turkish War in 1911–12, Greece, Bulgaria, Serbia, and Montenegro declared war on the Ottoman Empire. As a result of the Balkan Wars, new independent states emerged, such as Macedonia and Albania, out of the Ottoman provinces in the Western Thrace.

With the breaking out of World War I, the Ottoman Empire sided with the Germans. Even though important victories were won at the initial stages of the war, the most remarkable of which was the Battle of Gallipoli (or the Dardanelles) in 1915, the Ottoman Empire was not capable of conducting wars on all fronts extending from North Africa to the Arabian Peninsula and from the Middle East to the Caucasus. The Arab communities that were under the Turkish rule were provoked by the British and the French to revolt against the Ottoman Empire to facilitate their task to take over the control of these territories from the Ottomans. On the Caucasian front, Russians defeated the Ottomans. Even though much of these territories were recovered by the Ottomans benefiting from the chaotic situation in Russia due to the Bolshevik Revolution in 1917, since the German-Ottoman Alliance lost the Great War together, Russian rule soon returned to the Caucasus with the end of World War I. The Armistice of Mudros was signed on October 30, 1918 between the Ottoman Empire and the Allied powers in the Greek island Lemnos. The Armistice was followed by the occupation of İstanbul by the Allied powers.

NATIONAL WAR OF LIBERATION

At the end of World War I, the Paris Peace Conference convened with the participation of some 30 countries with a view to establishing a lasting peace in the world. A number of treaties were produced from the Paris conference most significant of which were the Treaty of Versailles signed between the German Empire and the Allied powers on June 28, 1919 and the Treaty of Sèvres signed on August 10, 1920 between the Ottoman Empire and the Allied powers, which partitioned the Ottoman territories among the British, French, Italians, and Greek that had already occupied large portions of lands in Anatolia and the Thrace region. Occupation of the Ottoman territories triggered the resistance and liberation movement of the Turks who have never accepted such a fate.

Mustafa Kemal Steps Up

While the Paris Peace Conference that would yield tragic outcomes from the standpoint of the Ottoman Empire was going on, Turks had already launched a national liberation movement under the leadership and command of Mustafa Kemal. Despite sporadic attempts to resist the occupation in the then capital city İstanbul, a much more comprehensive, large-scale, and well-organized movement was necessary. The landing of Greek soldiers in İzmir on May 15, 1919 prompted the first step in the Turkish War of Liberation with Mustafa Kemal leaving İstanbul to go to Samsun, a small city on the Black Sea. Indeed, Sultan Vahdeddin had sent Mustafa Kemal to Samsun for the purpose of eventually disbanding the Ottoman Third Army in Anatolia. Instead, Mustafa Kemal defied the orders given by the Sultan and engaged in organizing a nationwide resistance movement against the foreign occupying forces all over Turkey without delay. Due to his noncompliance with the orders of the Sultan, Mustafa Kemal was officially dismissed from his military position and was also declared an outlaw.

Mustafa Kemal had no more an official capacity to issue orders for an all-out resistance movement. But, because of the trust of the Turks on his military capabilities and leadership, which he had displayed unequivocally during the Battle of Gallipoli in 1915, he did not encounter much difficulty in mobilizing the masses. What was necessary at that stage was to display determination to liberate the country from foreign occupation that would lend confidence to the Turks to keep their heads up and to volunteer keen support to the national movement.

The resolve of Mustafa Kemal and his like-minded followers, a small group of community leaders drawn from all corners of the countryside, was declared to the world with the Amasya Circular on June 22, 1919. The Amasya Circular was significant in the sense that it was the first of such declarations that underlined that the national sovereignty would be regained at all cost with the determination of the Turkish population to fight back the occupying powers.

Popular Support Grows

The Circular gave a big boost to the morale of the Turks who seemed at the beginning desperate due to being under the rule of foreign forces. Then, a large congress was convened in the eastern Anatolian city of Erzurum between July 23 and August 9, 1919. At the end of the Erzurum Congress, the Association for the Defense of Rights of Eastern Anatolia (*Müdafa-i Hukuk Cemiyeti*) proclaimed the political objective of the national resistance and liberation movement launched by Mustafa Kemal. Among the decisions taken at the Erzurum Congress, the most significant ones were the following:

The country must remain unified within the national borders;

...The entire nation will be mobilized to defend the country and resist foreign occupation because of the inability of the Ottoman Government in İstanbul to do so under the pressure of occupying powers;

...A temporary government will be formed in Anatolia if necessary to conduct the national liberation movement;

...The national will must be exercized uniquely with national forces;

...Mandate or protectorate of foreign countries will not be accepted;

...The Chamber of Deputies (*Meclis-i Mebusan*) of the Ottoman Parliament should reconvene.

The political objective that was pronounced at the Erzurum Congress would later be known as the National Pact (*Misak-i Milli*) with which the borders of the state that would be created after the liberation of the country were identified. The Erzurum Congress was a clear indication of the resistance against the partition and foreign occupation of Anatolia. Even though the Congress was convened with the participation of mostly the regional representatives, the decisions had a nationwide appeal. A Representative Committee (*Heyeti-i Temsiliye*) headed by Mustafa Kemal was elected, which would act as the executive organ to oversee the implementation of the decisions taken during the Congress. The resolve of the Turks to liberate the country was reiterated at the Congress of Sivas, which was convened between September 4 and 11, 1919. Despite the efforts of the İstanbul Government, which had become a puppet of the occupying powers, to prevent the convention of such a congress in the central-eastern Anatolian city of Sivas, the Representative Committee that was expanded both in number and in terms of representation gathered the Congress. The significance of the Sivas Congress was, among others, its reaffirmation of the decisions taken in the previous Erzurum Congress, as well as the unification of the Associations for the Defense of Rights of Eastern Anatolia and Rumelia (northwestern districts of Turkey mostly on the Thrace region) under one roof.

Nationalists at Par with the Sultanate

The national liberation movement was brought under the effective oversight of the extended Representative Committee and the command of Mustafa Kemal who was treated as a national heroic leader. First thing Mustafa Kemal did was to delegate the decisions taken at the Erzurum Congress as well as the Sivas Congress to the İstanbul Government and to advise the Government not to take decisions that would bind the entire nation without prior consultations with the Representative Committee and until the convening of the Chamber of Deputies. Negotiations were held in these respects between Mustafa Kemal and Salih Pasha, then Minister of the Navy and a special envoy of the İstanbul Government, between October 20 and 22, 1919 in Amasya. The net result of the negotiations was the recognition, both *de facto* and *de jure,* of the national resistance and liberation movement that was launched and conducted under the leadership of Mustafa Kemal by the İstanbul Government, which was under the control of the occupying powers and, therefore, not capable of representing the true will of the Turkish population.

On December 27, 1919, Mustafa Kemal arrived in Ankara, which he chose as the seat of the national resistance and liberation movement. Ankara's geographical location in central Anatolia was very suitable to serve such a purpose. Around the same time the Assembly of People's Deputies wanted to reassert itself following the elections in December 1919. Mustafa Kemal planned to become the President of the Chamber of Deputies, and the members of the Chamber would adopt the National Pact. When on January 12, 1920 the Chamber of Deputies convened a plenary meeting, things did not go according to plan and the deputies failed to elect Mustafa Kemal as the President of the Chamber. But, the decisions of the Erzurum Congress and the Sivas Congress were adopted. On January 28, 1920, Ottoman Chamber of Deputies developed the National Pact, which proclaimed the following:

> The future of the territories inhabited by an Arab majority at the time of the signing of the Armistice of Moudros will be determined by a referendum. On the other hand, the territories which were not occupied at that time and inhabited by a Turkish-Moslem majority will remain the homeland of the Turkish nation;
>
> ...The status of Kars, Ardahan, and Batum may be determined by a referendum;
>
> ...The status of Western Thrace will be determined by the votes of its inhabitants;
>
> ...The security of İstanbul and Marmara must be provided for. Transport and free-trade on the Straits of the Bosphorus and the Dardanelles will be determined by Turkey and other concerned countries;
>
> ...The rights of minorities will be issued on condition that the rights of the Moslem minorities in neighboring countries were protected.
>
> ...In order to develop in every field, the country must be independent and free; all restrictions on political, judicial and financial development will be removed.

Turkish Grand National Assembly Opens

As such, the National Pact adopted by the Chamber of Deputies of the Ottoman Parliament was indeed a consolidation of the cause of the national resistance and liberation movement launched by Mustafa Kemal, which, however, contradicted with what was planned by the occupying powers. Hence, the British in particular and the other occupying powers put pressure on Sultan Vahdeddin to dissolve the Ottoman Parliament, a decision which soon took effect on April 11, 1920. In less than two weeks, on April 23, 1920 the Turkish Grand National Assembly (TGNA) was formed and convened its first plenary session and elected Mustafa Kemal as the Speaker of the TGNA.

Soon after, the Paris Peace Conference resulted in the signing of the Treaty of Sèvres, which envisaged the partitioning of what was left from the Ottoman

Empire among the British, French, Italians, and Greek. The İstanbul Government signed the Treaty. But since the Ottoman Parliament was already dissolved by Sultan Vahdeddin, the Treaty was never ratified by the Turks and therefore never entered into force. According to the Treaty of Sèvres, the British were given the mandate of the Mosul, Basra, and Baghdad districts of the Ottoman Empire, what is now known as Iraqi territory. The control of the Straits and Sea of Marmara were given to the Allied powers as an international zone. The French, on the other hand, was given the mandate of Syria and Lebanon by the League of Nations having already occupied large areas in southeastern Anatolia adjacent to Syria. The Italians also occupied vast areas of southern and western Anatolia, the Aegean and Mediterranean shores and inlands as well as the Dodecanese islands. In addition to the Ottoman territories partitioned among these three members of the Triple Entente, almost the entire Thrace region was left to Greece together with İzmir and its environs as its protectorate. The Treaty of Sèvres also recognized the creation of an independent Armenian state carving significant amount of territories out of Turkey's eastern Anatolian districts. Similarly, eventual creation of an independent Kurdish state was also envisaged in the Treaty. Indeed, the Treaty of Sèvres was literally nothing but the execution of the secret deal between France and Great Britain, with the acquiescence of Russia, which was signed in 1916. That secret deal was also known as the Sykes-Picot Agreement after the names of the British diplomat Mark Sykes and the French diplomat François Georges-Picot.

Diplomatic Maneuvers

Mustafa Kemal pursued a very wise and sophisticated strategy to achieve the goals that were set out in the National Pact. Kemal greatly benefited from the divergences of opinions between the great powers of the period. He took advantage of the Bolshevik Revolution in Russia, first for arms procurement to sustain the armed struggle especially against the Greek, and then to consolidate the eastern borders. Following the victory of Colonel İsmet against the Greek in the Battle of İnönü in January 1921, the Treaty of Moscow was signed on March 16, 1921 between the Nationalists in Turkey who were represented by the TGNA and the Soviet Union. According to the Treaty of Moscow, the Soviets recognized the new Turkish state, the TGNA, and the National Pact while also consolidating Turkey's eastern borders.

The Soviet revolutionary leader Viladimir Ilyic Ulyanov (Lenin) sympathized with the revolutionary movement of the Turkish Nationalists against the imperial powers who had occupied the Turkish territories. More important than the sympathy of Lenin with the cause of the Turks was his strategic calculation about the future of the region. Lenin would prefer to see a new and probably weak Turkish state in Anatolia that could eventually enter its sphere of influence, rather than Western imperial powers. Hence, any support that would be provided to Mustafa Kemal was thought by Lenin to bear fruit later once the Western powers were driven out of Anatolia.

Having secured the eastern borders with the Treaty of Moscow, Mustafa Kemal turned to the French and the Italians. With the French, a deal was cut and the Treaty of Ankara was signed on October 20, 1921. According to the Treaty, in return for economic privileges that France would receive from Turkey, it would recognize the TGNA as the representative of the Turks, and the French military would soon evacuate the territories that it had occupied since the end of World War I. That was not only a huge diplomatic success for Mustafa Kemal but also a huge blow to the Triple Entente.

Mustafa Kemal did carefully exploit the cracks in the Triple Entente that have become very obvious with the signing of the Ankara Treaty. He adopted a similar strategy toward the Italians who were also in an uneasy situation within the Entente because of the British approach favoring the Greek. Not only did the Italians cease their occupation, but they have also provided significant amount of arms supplies as well as munitions. Moreover, Italians also provided military aircraft to the Turks, which have been extremely vital in intelligence collection and aerial reconnaissance operations against the Greek forces that were advancing toward the new capital city Ankara.

Grand Offensive and Decisive Victory

Only the British, which was controlling İstanbul and its environs, but not in military confrontation with the Nationalist Forces (*Kuvvay-i Milliye*), and the Greek were left to deal with. Mustafa Kemal concentrated all his efforts and the capabilities of the Nationalist Forces on the Greek offensive with a view to achieving a decisive victory in the fight that was going on since the first Battle of İnönü in January 1921. Hence, with a series of battles fought around the western Anatolian cities like Kütahya, Eskişehir, and Sakarya, first the Greek military's advances were stopped, then pushed back to the shores of the Aegean Sea with a new offensive between August 26 and 30, 1922. The Greek were forced to leave the Turkish territories, and İzmir was liberated on September 9, 1922.

Mustafa Kemal's next target was the liberation of the Straits and İstanbul, which were under the occupation of the British, as well as the Eastern Thrace that was occupied by the Greek. Being left alone in the Triple Entente, the British chose to call for an armistice first and then to launch peace negotiations, rather than to fight the Turks. The decision of Great Britain was also accepted by Mustafa Kemal. Then, the Armistice of Mudanya was signed according to which the Greek would also evacuate the Turkish territories in the Eastern Thrace. Britain extended invitations on October 22, 1922 both to the İstanbul Government to represent the Ottoman Empire and to the victorious Nationalist Turks to attend the peace negotiations to be convened in Lausanne, Switzerland. Hence, Mustafa Kemal took a radical decision and abolished the sultanate so as to prevent a double-headed representation of the Turks that could damage their interests.

The leader of the victorious Turks, namely Mustafa Kemal, appointed his closest friend İsmet (İnönü), a brother-in-arms and a deputy throughout the War of Liberation, to preside over the Turkish delegation. İsmet was mandated to achieve an extremely demanding task to ensure the recognition—by the great powers of the period such as Great Britain and France—of the full independence and the undisputed sovereignty of the new Turkish state that would born out of the ashes of the Ottoman Empire. In addition to these basic claims, there was a long list of *conditio sine qua non,* which would shape the future of the new Republic, such as abolition of the capitulations (i.e., privileges) that were granted to the British, French, and other European powers by the war-weary Ottoman administrations, especially during the period of decline of the Empire since the eighteenth century. The capitulations were given to the Europeans in return for their loans that, however, served nothing but sustaining the sultanate in power rather than improving the quality of life in the countryside or modernizing the army, which was not capable of putting down the revolts that broke out almost everywhere in the territory of the Empire that was once spread over three continents.

Lausanne Peace Negotiations

Comprehensive negotiations started in Lausanne on November 20, 1922 with the participation of the representatives of Turkey (successor to the Ottoman Empire) on one side and of Britain, France, Italy, Japan, Greece, Romania, and the Kingdom of Serbs, Croats, and Slovenes (Yugoslavia) on the other. The conference, which lasted approximately nine months, was held with intermissions due to deep divergences of views between the Turkish delegation and especially the British delegation headed by Lord Curzon over a number of fundamental issues about the characteristics of the new Turkish state that was about to born. Intensive negotiations took place on Turkey's stubborn request of lifting the capitulations.

One particular reason behind the concerns of the Western powers with the lifting of capitulations was their suspicions about whether the new Turkish nation would enter under the Soviet influence. Mustafa Kemal sensed such a concern of the West and convened the İzmir Economics Congress between February 17 and March 4, 1923 in which he delivered a long speech emphasizing the fact that the new Turkish state would adopt a Western-style economic and political regime. The peace negotiations resumed in April, and after intense negotiations that lasted nearly four months in this second round, the Lausanne Peace Treaty was signed on July 24, 1923.

The Lausanne Treaty recognized the boundaries of the modern Republic of Turkey. Eastern Thrace, several Aegean islands, a strip along the Syrian border, the Smyrna district were recovered. The internationalized Zone of the Straits was to remain demilitarized and remain subject to an international convention and would be open to all shipping. Outside the Zone of the Straits, no limitation was imposed on the Turkish military establishment. The Allies dropped their demands of autonomy for an independent Kurdish state and Turkish secession of territory to Armenia. They also abandoned claims to spheres of influence in Turkey and imposed no controls over Turkey's finances or armed forces. Turkey recovered full sovereign rights over all its territory, and foreign zones of influence and capitulations were abolished. No reparations were exacted. In return, Turkey renounced all claims on former Turkish territories outside its new boundaries and undertook to guarantee the rights of its minorities. Turkey also recognized British possession of Cyprus and Italian possession of the Dodecanese islands. A separate agreement between Greece and Turkey provided for the compulsory exchange of minorities. After all these developments, the Republic of Turkey was proclaimed on October 29, 1923.

NOTES

1. The official Web site of the Turkish Presidency (http://www.cankaya.gov.tr/eng_html/gunes.htm) presents the 16 Turkish empires with the following sentence: "The sixteen yellow stars on the Presidential insignia represent the sixteen Turkish states in history, and the sun at the centre represents the Republic of Turkey." The 16 Turkish empires that were built throughout history are the following: (I) Great Hun Empire, 204 BC–AD 216; (II) Western Hun Empire, AD 48–216; (III) European Hun Empire, 375–454; (IV) White Hun Empire, 420–552; (V) Göktürk Empire, 552–743; (VI) Avar Empire, 562–796; (VII) Hazar Empire, 602–1016; (VIII) Uygur State, 740–1335; (IX) Karahanli State, 932–1212; (X) Gazneli Sultanate, 962–1183; (XI) Greater Seljuk Empire, 1040–1157; (XII) The Kharezm Shah State, 1077–1231; (XIII) The Golden Horde, 1224–1502; (XIV) Greater Timur Empire, 1369–1501; (XV) Babür Empire, 1526–1858; (XVI) Ottoman Empire, 1299–1922.

2. http://www.turkeyforunsc.org/tr_history_3.php.

3. The *Tanzimat* movement (1839–71) was first introduced by Sultan Abdülmecid I (1839–61) and then by Sultan Abdülaziz (1861–76). See Edhem Eldem, "Ottoman Financial Integration with Europe: Foreign Loans, the Ottoman Bank and the Ottoman Public Debt," *European Review* 13, no. 3 (2005): 431–45.

CHAPTER 2

Foreign Policy of the Young Republic under Atatürk and İnönü: The *Interwar* Period

The foreign policy of the young Turkish Republic was devised and conducted under the leadership of Mustafa Kemal Atatürk, the founder and the first President of the Republic, from 1923 until his passing on November 10, 1938. Then, İsmet İnönü, Atatürk's brother-in-arms during the War of Liberation and the first Prime Minister of the Republic of Turkey, took over the driver seat as the second President of the Republic elected by the TGNA on November 11, 1938, where he served until May 22, 1950. The making and the conduct of the foreign and security policies of the young Republic was a challenging task due to a number of structural as well as conjunctural reasons.

First and foremost, the necessary institutions of the newly created state were either not in place or in severe shortage of a cadre of professionals who could carry out the foreign policy decisions of the leadership. Decades of consecutive bloody wars had decimated the human stock of the Ottoman Empire. Most of the best educated pupils of the Turkish population were sent to the battlefields on all fronts, many of whom could not return. Only a handful of skilled people survived the ultimate War of Liberation who had to undertake heavy-duty tasks in the establishment of the republican institutions, including the ministries, state enterprises, banks, schools, universities, hospitals, and the like. Under these circumstances, those who could speak foreign languages were hired by the Ministry of Foreign Affairs without much regard to their professional or educational adeptness.

Secondly, even though the Lausanne Treaty of July 24, 1923 paved the way to the proclamation of the Republic of Turkey on October 29, 1923, several issues could not be resolved during the peace negotiations, such as the sovereignty of the Straits of Bosphorus and the Dardanelles, the status of the Sancak of

Iskenderun (Hatay) and the Mosul province of the Ottoman Empire, the liabilities of Turkey emanating from the Ottoman debts, and the exchange of populations between Greece and Turkey. The Turkish delegation headed by İsmet Pasha (İnönü) who conducted the painstaking negotiations in Lausanne aimed at attaining a delicate balance between achieving the recognition by the Western powers of the creation of a new nation out of the ashes of the Ottoman Empire and achieving all of the objectives set out in the National Pact prior to the start of the negotiations. Once it turned out during the heated negotiations that insisting on the latter goal would endanger attaining the former as well, namely the creation of the Republic of Turkey as a new and sovereign member of the international community, Turks have decided to have their republic first and to look forward to the resolution of the remaining issues in due course. Hence, the first fifteen years of the foreign policy of Turkey were busy with dealing with the residues of the Lausanne negotiations.

The third reason why the making as well as the conduct of Turkish foreign policy during the "Interwar" period was a challenging task was because of the very rapid and unanticipated developments that were taking place in the international arena due to the policies pursued by Italy under Mussolini and Germany under Hitler. Turkey, as a newly formed state lacking both human and material resources for economic and political development, and also heavily preoccupied with the inception as well as the consolidation of social, economic, political, and cultural reforms in the country, was in pursuit of establishing zones of friendship and peace in its immediate neighborhood, namely the Balkans, the eastern Mediterranean, and the Middle East. The rapidly changing conjuncture resulted in challenges and opportunities that required timely and appropriate decisions to be taken so as to avoid risks and to benefit from emerging opportunities.

Against this background, because of the challenges extending from the lack of human resources to the rapidly changing international conjuncture, one might expect a series of failures in the implementation of the foreign policy of Turkey in attaining its goals. However, this was not the case thanks to the leadership of Atatürk who proved himself to be not only a very successful commander in the battlefields but also a great statesman in the political domain. Turkey achieved many of its foreign policy goals during the difficult Interwar period, much of which also coincided with the prolonged effects of the "Great Depression" of 1929 that had started with the "Black September" collapse in the stock markets in the United States followed by others around the world. After the passing of Atatürk, İnönü's leadership was Turkey's luck because Atatürk and İnönü had long fought shoulder to shoulder for the liberation of the country and the two had also shared perfectly the same ideals as well as the same vision for the future of the Turkish Republic. Hence, İnönü's takeover at probably one of the most difficult periods in history and his impeccable leadership qualifications helped Turkey pass through the devastation of World War II all over the world without getting serious wounds or bruises. Therefore, one of the most exciting periods of Turkish foreign policy between 1923 and 1945 is worth studying in detail.

THE ATATÜRK ERA IN TURKISH FOREIGN POLICY: 1923–38

The guiding principle in the formulation of the foreign policy of Turkey has been "peace at home, peace in the world" as laid out by Atatürk since the creation of the Republic. This motto says a lot in few words in the sense that it empha-sized, in the particular case of Turkey, the need to strike a delicate balance between achieving the goals set in domestic politics, by way of introducing reforms and revolutionary changes in the regime within the Turkish society, and in the foreign policy area. Atatürk was well aware of the difficulties of trans-forming an entire society, which was exhausted by endless wars for decades and left backwarded by all means, including the economical and social conditions. What Atatürk did achieve was literally a regime change from sultanate that was ruled by Sheri'a to a republic that would be secular by Constitution. Creating a "nation" from what was left from a cosmopolitan Ottoman *ummah* society would only be possible by taking revolutionary decisions in the legal and political frameworks, introducing a series of reforms in public and private life that such a transformation would require, and also implementing them rather swiftly. All of this transformation process would also necessitate a conducive atmosphere in domestic politics, given the fact that there was also a significant amount of opposition and resistance to the reforms that were introduced one after another in various circles within the Turkish society.

In addition to achieving peace and harmony in the process of nation-building at home, Turkey also needed peaceful and harmonious relations with its neigh-bors as well as the great powers of the period. The war-weary and backwarded Turkish society of the 1920s could not afford getting into conflicts with other states any more. Such a development would not only endanger peace and stabil-ity in the international arena but most probably lead to a disturbance within the country. Therefore, while Turkey had to work hard at home in consolidating the new republican regime through political, legal, social, and cultural reforms as well as rapid economic and industrial development, it would also need to care-fully exploit the merits of diplomacy in achieving its goals in the foreign policy area to resolve the residual conflicts without resorting to military option. Achiev-ing peace through diplomacy was the key principle in devising policies both at home and abroad.

Residual Issues from the Lausanne Conference

The fundamental tenets and the grand objectives of the foreign policy of the young Turkish Republic were laid out in the National Pact, which was drawn up during the War of Liberation. Natural boundaries of the new Turkish nation-state that would be created out of the ashes of the Ottoman Empire stretching from Western Thrace and the Straits to the Sancak and Mosul provinces were identified in the National Pact. Extensive interpretation of the National Pact assigned priority to the presence of Muslim Turkish community including the Western Thrace and Mosul in terms of delineation of the boundaries of the new Turkish state, while the narrow interpretation assigned priority to military-strategic considerations and emphasized the significance of the Straits and the Sancak province. Hence, during the Lausanne Conference, Turkish diplomacy did strategic retreat in two of its targets, namely the Western Thrace and Mosul, and tactical retreat in the other two, namely the Straits and Sancak that were assigned highest priority. History shows that the foreign policy objectives of the Republic of Turkey were not based on irredentist or ethno-religious considerations, but they were rather motivated by rational, realistic, and strategic considerations. Due attention was paid to the conjectural developments and changes in the international arena with a view to taking advantage of windows of opportunities that were rarely opened.

The Question of Mosul

The Mosul province of the Ottoman Empire has been subject to a stiff competition between France and Great Britain even before World War I. But these two great powers of the period had agreed among themselves to leave the region to France with the Sykes-Picot Agreement signed on May 16, 1916 as the ultimate collapse of the Ottoman Empire was seen on sight. However, in the San Remo Conference on April 24, 1920, France waived its claims on Mosul in return for receiving 25 percent share of Mosul oil revenues and Britain's evacuation of Syria. The San Remo Conference was significant in that it determined the allocation of the League of Nations mandates for the administration of the former Ottoman territories between France and Britain. Iraq and Palestine were left to the British mandate, while Syria and the present-day Lebanon would be administered by the French mandate.[1]

Mosul has soon become a bone of contention between Turkey and Britain. The parties had divergent positions vis-à-vis the future of the region. For the British, Mosul was an important strategic point in protecting the stable route to India, obtaining the rich oil reserve, and securing a bridgehead to pursuit the successful Middle Eastern policies. British delegation led by Lord Curzon, then British Foreign Secretary, argued persistently that Mosul should be under the British rule and remain within the boundaries of Iraq.[2] According to the British view, the Mosul issue was so related to the boundary dispute that the plebiscite, which the Turkish delegation had offered, was not needed. Also, Kurds and Arabs not only had never asked for a plebiscite but also had not known what really it meant.

According to the Anglo-Iraqi Treaty of 1922, both Britain and Iraq had the duty to protect the territorial integrity of Iraqi land. Therefore, Britain could not withdraw from Mosul due to its commitments to Arabs, to the people of Iraq, and to the League of Nations. Moreover, the British argued that based on their statistics, the population of the Turks in the world constitute only 1/12 of the entire Mosul population.[3] Therefore, concession of Mosul to Turkey would ignore the opinions of the Kurds and Arabs who not only did not have the same origins with the Turks but also did not support the Turks during World War I. In addition, it was asserted that all the economic relationships of the Mosul province relied upon Syria and Iraq mainly, not upon Turkey. Moreover, the Christian minority living in Mosul could not be left under the rule of Turkey. Also, considering the close distance from Mosul to Baghdad, Turkey could challenge Iraq's security if Turkey gained Mosul.

For Turkey, it was essential to keep Mosul in the boundaries of the National Pact due to the ethnographic, political, geographical economic, and military-strategic reasons. Based on the Turkish statistics, the rate of the Kurds and the Turks who had lived in Mosul, Kirkuk, and Suleymaniyah was constituting the 4/5 of the entire Mosul population.[4] In addition, because there were about 170,000 Turkish, Kurdish, and Arab migrant tribes who moved from season to season, it was impossible to calculate their exact number. As the National Pact did not involve any difference between Turks and Kurds in terms of race, religion, and tradition, Turks responded to the British claim that Kurds were of Persian origin by saying that Kurds were Turanian in race.

The British claim that the Kurds did not want to live together with the Turks was a totally unfounded allegation. Mosul was under Turkish rule since the eleventh century, and the British army occupied Mosul after the Mudros Armistice was signed. Thus, there was no legal basis for a mandate in Iraq because it has been a part of Ottoman Empire. In addition to that, Mosul was part of Anatolia in terms of its climate and the structure of its land. With the respect of its economics, Mosul relied more upon Anatolia rather than Iraq because of the railway line that connected Mosul to the Mediterranean. Finally, the British argument that the boundary offered by Turkey was only 60 miles from Baghdad and that it would threaten Iraqi security was unreasonable because capitals of many countries were located close to each other's boundaries and the Turks were at peace with Arabs for centuries. Turkish arguments were more reasonable than those of British in various aspects. First of all, even though Sèvres Treaty had envisaged the creation of an independent Kurdish state in southeastern Anatolia and northern Iraq, Kurds fought alongside the Turks in the War of Liberation. This would support the legitimacy of the Turkish argument in terms of the racial reasons. In other words, the vast majority of both Turks and Kurds still identified themselves primarily through religion rather than any concept of race or nation argued by British.[5]

Due to the deep disagreements between the Turkish and the British delegations over the "Turkishness" of the Mosul and Suleymaniyah districts, the delineation of the Turkish-Iraqi border would not be possible during the Lausanne
negotiations. Article 3 of the Lausanne Treaty stated that the Turks and the
British would discuss the issue separately at a later time so as to finalize it within
nine months. No agreement was reached either during the İstanbul meeting of
the parties from May 19 to June 5, 1924. In addition to its request for Mosul
and Suleymaniyah to be left to Iraq, Britain also asserted that Hakkari should
also be within the Iraqi territory due to the majority of Assyrian population of
the city, many of whom had already migrated to Iraq.

Should there be no solution within the time frame that was envisaged in the
Lausanne Treaty, the parties had previously agreed to bring the issue before the
League of Nations. The Council of the League started to look into the issue in
September 20, 1924. In the meantime, the dispute was shifted by Britain to the
matter of fixing the Iraqi border. However, the Turks were adamant that the
question mainly concerned the fate of the Mosul province rather than the border
issue. The League of Nations set up an inquiry commission consisting of three
members. Border dispute between Turkey and Britain led to military skirmishes
because the failure to reach a consensus between Turkey and Britain became
tense. Britain was accused by the Turks of staging provocations in Turkey's
southeastern districts so as to destabilize the region in order to force the Turks
to come to its terms regarding the dispute over the Mosul province. In order to
avoid the increasing tension between two sides, Turkey applied to the League of
Nations on October 29, 1924 for a temporary border to be fixed between Turkey
and Iraq, which came to be known as "the Brussels Line."[6]

The special commission established by the League of Nations was tasked with
investigating the local conditions and opinions about whether the people of
Mosul wanted to remain in Iraq or in Turkey. The members of commission were
Count Pal Telki, the former Prime Minister of Hungary, Carl Einar af Wirsen,
former Swedish Ambassador to Bucharest, and Colonel Albert Paulis, a Belgian
veteran officer. Some members from Turkey and Britain would be appointed to
help and counsel the commission. Just after ending its missions, the commission
submitted a report to the Council in September 1925 that Mosul should be
under the rule of British mandate for 25 years and that the border between
Turkey and Iraq should be the line which had been drawn in Brussels. According
to the Brussels Line, Mosul was left to Iraq, while Hakkari was left to Turkey.
However, this report had several significant contradictions. First of all, it was
based on the last census carried out by the Iraqi authority that could not be
understood with common sense. The censuses of Britain, Turkey, and Iraq were
displaying contradictory results.[7]

The indication of this table that Turkish population was about 38,000, even
lower than 61,000 of Christians, could be considered as the evidence that the

Ethnic background	Turkish census: statistics submitted in Lausanne	Estimate made by British political officers in 1921	Census by Iraq (1922–24)
Kurds	263,830	424,720	494,000
Arabs	43,210	185,763	166,941
Turks	146,960	65,895	38,652
Christians	31,000	62,225	61,336
Jews	–	16,865	11,897
Yezidis	18,000	30,000	26,257
Nomads	170,000	–	–
Total	673,000	785,468	799,083

commission wanted to support the British view. Also, the report stated that it was indisputable that Turkey retains its legal sovereignty over the disputed territory so long as it does not renounce her rights. According to this view, Mosul should have remained within the boundary of Turkey because Turks had never given up Mosul. Furthermore, the report mentioned that if a plebiscite had been made, the residents of Mosul would have wanted to stay in Iraq. However, the Turkish proposal of plebiscite was not accepted and the report involved that Mosul had to stay under the mandate of Britain for an additional 25 years. Turkish strong rejection against the decisions of the commission that had many self-contradictory factors was an expected result. As a result of Turkey's objections, the Permanent Court of International Justice gave an advisory opinion to the League of Nations on September 19, 1925. After receiving the opinion of the Court, the Council of the League took a decision in its meeting on December 16, 1925 requesting that the border between Turkey and Iraq be the Brussels Line and that Mosul be placed in Iraq under British mandate due to an Anglo-Iraqi Treaty. The Turkish committee did not take part in that session of the Council.

The reactions against the decision of the League of Nations came from all segments of the society in Turkey. The first reaction came with the letter of the Foreign Minister Tevfik Rüştü Aras, which was submitted to the meeting of the Council where Turkish representatives were absent on December 16, 1925. In the letter, Foreign Minister Aras claimed that "the sovereign rights of a state over a territory can only come to an end with its consent and that, therefore, our sovereign rights over the whole of the province of Mosul remain intact in response to the decision of League of Nations."[8] It is interesting to note that Turkey signed with the Soviet Union the Treaty of Neutrality and Friendship on December 17, 1925, only one day after the League made its final decision.

In the Turkish public domain, the popular reaction was severe. It was written in *Cumhuriyet* on December 17, 1925 that

> the decision proved once more that the League of Nations is the servant of the strongest, namely Great Britain. Only in the medieval ages do we encounter such unjust and tyrannical decision. As the case was during our campaign for nationhood, so now the rights of the Turks are safe under the sharp bayonets of the Turks, and we know perfectly well how to take back with our hands "Turkish Mosul"—given to Great Britain by the League of Nations—just as we saved Adana, Bursa, İzmir and İstanbul.[9]

However, the strong reactions of Turkey were not connected to the practical actions, including military operations. The reasons why Turkish government could not take such decisions despite the strong reactions from Turkish politicians and public may be speculated as relating both to external and to internal factors. As regards the external factors, Turkey was still isolated from the international society militarily and diplomatically. Therefore, Turkey needed British friendship for several reasons such as the improvement of relationship with the Western nations, especially France; the doubtful trust about the Soviet Union; and the concerns of military operations by Italy and Greece in the Aegean. As for the internal factors, Turkey did not have enough military capability to engage in a war with the British due to the fatigue of the wars of the last 10 years from 1911 to 1922. In order to recapture the modern civilization based on the Western values and recover from the damage of wars, Turkey needed peace and stability. Moreover, the Sheikh Said revolt, which was said to be a reaction to the abolition of the Caliphate, weakened the Turkish claims on the Mosul region. These reasons restricted the likelihood of using force against the British and thus Turkey believed that Britain would consider going to war over the Mosul dispute since it was of vital importance for its interest. Therefore, Turkey abandoned the aim of the National Pact and followed a realistic and non-adventurist policy.

The Ankara Treaty was signed on June 25, 1926 among Britain, Turkey, and Iraq. The Treaty was composed of three parts, namely the Borders, Good Neighborly Relations, and General Provisions, including 18 articles. According to this Treaty, the Brussels Line became the border line between Turkey and Iraq as the League of Nations decided and Turkey had the right to take a 10 percent share from the revenue of Mosul petroleum for 25 years.

The "Établi" Problem and the Relations with Greece

During the Lausanne Conference, a protocol was signed on January 30, 1923 concerning the exchange of the Muslim/Turkish population in Greece and the Greek Orthodox (Rum) population in Turkey. According to the protocol, the Rum population who used to reside within the metropolitan boundaries of İstanbul before October 30, 1918 and the Turks of Western Thrace would be exempt from the population exchange. However, divergence of viewpoints arose between the Turkish and the Greek representatives within the international commission that would supervise the population exchange. The disagreement was over the meaning and the scope of the term "établi" that would refer to the "established" Rums in İstanbul. While on the one hand Turkey wished to limit the number of the Greek Orthodox population who would remain in Turkey and, therefore, assigned very much importance to the precise determination of who were actually the residents of İstanbul prior to October 30, 1918, the Greek policy was to have as many Rums as possible to remain in İstanbul and pushed for lifting the requirement of being a resident (établi) of İstanbul prior to the given date so as to be exempt from population exchange. As the disagreement of the parties persisted over the meaning as well as the scope of the term "établi," the issue was taken to the Permanent Court of International Justice of the League of Nations. The opinion of the Council that was presented to the parties in February 1925 did not help resolve their differences over the issue. At the origin of the dispute during and after the Lausanne negations on the issue of population exchange were the concerns of the Turkish delegation to ensure the "homogeneity" of the newly built Turkey. After all, the new Turkey was founded as a result of the successful fight against the Greek armies that marched into Anatolia with the *Megali Idea,* the Greek dream of reconstituting the Byzantine Empire that was lost to the Ottomans in 1453, in mind.

The founders of the new Turkey wanted to create a nation and a nation-state different from the multinational system of the Ottomans. The expulsion of the Rums/Greeks, who were the largest Christian population that remained from the Ottoman Empire, was both an important step toward the realization of the desired nation-state and an important measure to prevent irredentist discourses in the future. Indeed, with the population exchange decided during the Lausanne Conference, the expulsion of the last major Christian population remaining from the Ottoman Empire from Anatolia was secured. In 1913, within the geography of today's Turkey, one-fifth of the population was Christian; at the end of 1923, the proportion had decreased to one-fortieth. As a result of the population exchange, Greece also gained a population that was more homogenous than it had ever been in its history. It was made legitimate for Greece to incorporate the largest Rum-Orthodox population living outside Greek borders and at the same time expel a significant number of Muslims living within the borders of Greece, with the exception of Western Thrace. The ratio of the Muslim population in Greece, at 20 percent in 1920, decreased to 6 percent in 1930.[10]

In addition to the "établi" problem, two major issues also remained problematic between Turkey and Greece in the same period. These were the status of the Patriarchate in İstanbul and the indemnities to be paid for the Greek assets that would be left behind as a result of the population exchange. The Patriarchate had been both a political and a social organization of the Rum-Orthodox community in the Ottoman Empire and it had also been influenced by Greek nationalism and the *Megali Idea* during the turbulent years. Consequently, the Patriarchate was an unwanted organization, the existence of which was regarded with mistrust and skepticism by the Turkish authorities, who had even abolished the Muslim Caliphate. Greece claimed, however, that the Patriarchate had become a solely religious organization after the foundation of "New Turkey" and requested the recognition of its status as such. As for the indemnities to be paid in return for the assets that were left behind, probably this was the most important of the three Articles 8 and 9 of the Greek–Turk Population Exchange Protocol envisaged the payment of an indemnity to emigrants for the assets they left behind. The immigrants to Greece, who constituted one-fourth of the population in Greece and were represented by approximately 60 deputies in the Greek Parliament, believed that they should be paid an indemnity by Turkey for the assets they left in "Asia Minor" (Anatolia). They claimed that there were many highly valuable immovable assets that were left behind in Turkey. As a response to the Greek claims, Turkey countered that the lands that had been the scene of battles, especially on the western Anatolian coast, were ruined, and therefore, no valuable Greek assets were left on those lands. It claimed further that the Muslim immigrants who came to Turkey had assets that were well-cared for and arable fields; therefore, their assets were more valuable than those left behind in Turkey by the Greeks.[11]

The so-called "établi" problem and the related issues remained on the agenda of the two nations for the next five years also poisoning the bilateral and regional relations. In the meantime, however, the prime ministers of both countries exchanged letters with a view to building confidence first and then to find ways to solve the problem through diplomatic ways. These letters, which were exchanged between Venizelos and İnönü in August and September of 1928, respectively, started a new period of negotiations between the two countries paving the way to the signing of the Ankara Convention on June 10, 1930. The first part of the Ankara Convention was prepared on the issue of immigrants' assets. That was the most challenging problem between Turkey and Greece, and the most delicate issue for the immigrant population and public opinion in Greece. Under this heading, a decision was taken to accept that the assets left by the immigrants in both countries were to be the assets of the departed country. In other words, Turkey and Greece agreed to accept the assets of the immigrants as equal and erase them. Another issue cleared up by the Ankara Convention was the issue of the definition of "établi": anyone in the region at the time when the pact was signed would be accepted as "établi." After the Ankara Convention, a visit by Venizelos to Turkey was organized for October 27–31. During this visit, Venizelos signed agreements that were succinctly named as Friendship Agreements, and he became the first Greek prime minister to visit both Ankara and the Patriarchate in İstanbul.[12]

Dispute Over the Turkish Straits and the Way to the Montreux Convention

During the Lausanne negotiations, the question of the Straits was subject to three rival theses. The thesis of the Western powers, which was already enshrined in the Treaty of Sèvres, proposed the establishment of demilitarized zones on the straits, and the formation of an International Commission that would consist of Britain, France, Italy, and Japan to regulate the regime of the Straits. Against the thesis of the Western powers, the thesis of the Soviet Union, which would derive from Article 5 of the Turco-Soviet Friendship Treaty of March 1921, suggested that the Straits should be open to all nations to facilitate commercial relations and also guaranteed that the military security of the Straits should be formulated by conferences restricted to the riparian states of the Black Sea. Finally, the Turkish thesis proposed that the full sovereignty over the Straits should be given to Turkey. İsmet Pasha, as the head of the Turkish delegation, sought support from the Soviet delegates but failed. He also failed to impose Turkey's thesis upon the Western powers all by himself on such a strategic issue, and leaned toward the Western thesis hoping that sooner or later Turkey would have the opportunity to modify the regime of the Straits.[13]

The window of opportunity that Turkey was looking for was opened about a decade later when the international political conjuncture started to change radically with the invasion of Manchuria by Japan in 1931, invasion of Ethiopia by Italy in 1935, and the heavy armament of Germany at about the same time. All of these developments proved the ineffectiveness of the international order that was hoped to have been established with the creation of the League of Nations in 1920. Italy's policy toward the Aegean and the eastern Mediterranean raised the threat perception of Turkey significantly. Under these conditions, arguing that the guarantee system concerning the Turkish Straits that was envisaged to operate under the auspices of the League of Nations would not be possible, Turkey started to raise the issue at the League of Nations as well as other international forums. By doing so, Turkey hoped to bring the concerned parties back to the negotiation table to conclude a new convention on the Straits that would carry more favorable terms from Turkey's perspective.

On May 23, 1933, Turkey brought the issue up during the Disarmament Conference in London. Turkey's request was refused on the grounds that the issue of the Straits had no relevance to the issue disarmament, which was being debated. Turkey iterated its attempt two years later on April 17, 1935 during an emergency meeting of the Council of the League of Nations concerning the rearmament of Germany. Turkey argued that the demilitarized status of the Straits weakened its national security and that the existing convention that was reached during the Lausanne Conference had to be modified in such a way to accommodate Turkey's serious security concerns. Despite the support given by the Soviet delegation to the Turkish proposal, which was presented by the Foreign Minister Tevfik Rüştü Aras, Britain, France, and Italy objected to the idea of negotiating a new convention. Having failed to get support of the Western powers, Turkey brought the issue before the members of the Balkan Entente at its meeting in Romania's capital Bucharest on May 3, 1935, but to no avail. Soon later, upon Italy's invasion of Ethiopia, the Council of the League of Nations convened an emergency meeting in October 1935, where Turkey made another attempt to raise its unhappiness with Lausanne Convention on the Straits of 1923. Finally, on April 11, 1936, Turkey decided to give a note to all the signatories of the Lausanne Treaty, through the Secretary-General of the League of Nations. In the diplomatic note it was indicated that Turkey was prepared to enter into negotiations with a view to arriving in the near future at the conclusion of agreements for regulations of the regime of the Straits under the conditions of security, which were indispensable for the inviolability of Turkey's territory. The note was received mostly favorable by the parties concerned. The leading powers of the period, including France, Britain, and the Soviet Union, attended the meetings convened in Montreux, Switzerland, which started on June 22, 1936 and ended with a new convention regarding the regime of the Turkish Straits on July 20, 1936.

With the entry into force of the Montreux Convention, the International Straits Commission was abolished. Turkish sovereignty and military control over the Straits and the refortification of the Dardanelles were fully resumed. Turkey was authorized to close the Straits to all foreign warships in wartime or when it was threatened by aggression. Turkey was also authorized to refuse transit from merchant ships that would belong to countries at war with Turkey. In addition to these, a number of highly specific restrictions were imposed on what type of warships are allowed passage.[14] This was a big diplomatic success for Turkey, which was a result of Atatürk's diplomacy pursued carefully and patiently by taking the right steps at the right time.

About a decade later, the Montreux Convention has become one of the topical issues during a series of conferences convened in Yalta and Potsdam with the participation of the leaders of the Allied powers. All three leaders of the United States, which had not sent even an observer to the Montreux Convention due to its "isolationist" policy, the United Kingdom, and the Soviet Union have agreed that the 1936 Convention had to be adjusted to the requirements of the new conjuncture that emerged at the end of the Great War. Having agreed on the need for a change, however, the Allied powers have failed to agree on how to amend the terms of the Convention. The Soviet Union that had backed up Turkey in its request to replace the old regime on the Straits starting from the mid-1930s changed its position drastically with the end of World War II. Stalin's request for establishing bases on the Straits combined with his further territorial claims on the Turkey's eastern provinces, namely Kars and Ardahan, which were ceded to Turkey with the Moscow Treaty of 1921, were found by the United States and Britain as far-reaching claims that could not be accepted. Hence, the ensuing political developments that pushed the wartime allies away from each other and that would eventually pave the way to the East-West divide in the international arena helped the Convention prevail at all times ever since.

The Sancak (Hatay) Question

The Treaty of Ankara that was signed between Turkey and France on October 20, 1921 granted a special status to the Sancak of Iskenderun (formerly Alexandretta), which was in the Syrian territory under the French mandate. But, the Turks remaining there would still be able to entertain their cultural rights. In 1936, France decided to give Syria and Lebanon their independence. Turkey did react to such a development by issuing a diplomatic note to France in October 1936 asking the same treatment for the Sancak of Iskenderun as well. In its response to the Turkish note, France declined to act along the lines that Turkey expected, on the grounds that giving independence to the Sancak of Iskenderun would mean partitioning Syria and that France would not have the authority to take such a decision as a mandate power. There has been another round of exchange of notes between Turkey and France regarding this issue, but to no avail. Hence, France suggested Turkey to take the issue before the Council of the League of Nations. Turkey subscribed to the French proposal. The Council of the League of Nations granted a special status to the Sancak of Iskenderun on January 27, 1937. According to this special status, Sancak would be recognized as a distinct entity ("entité distincte") having full autonomy in its domestic affairs, while it would still be dependent on Syria in its foreign relations. The state of affairs in the Sancak of Iskenderun, which would soon change its name to Hatay, would be observed by the League of Nations.

The League of Nations established a commission to draft a Constitution for Hatay. The Constitution, which was drafted also through consultations with France and Turkey, was finally adopted by the League's Council on May 29, 1937. On the same day, Turkey and France signed a protocol that would make them the guarantor powers for the security and territorial integrity of Hatay. The Constitution of Hatay would enter into force in November 1937 and the first thing that had to be done was to carry out general elections. However, there were demonstrations both in Turkey and in Syria as well as in Hatay. Due to the political atmosphere that was very tense, the elections could not be carried out. The League undertook the task of preparing bylaws for the electoral process. France and Turkey could not converge on the fundamental principles and the bylaws of the electoral system. Yet, the list of the electorate was started to be prepared by May 1938. Nevertheless, the tension in and around Hatay, especially on the Syrian side, compelled Turkey to deploy some 30,000 troops along the border. Taking this development as well as the pace of events in Europe into consideration, France started to soften its stance toward Turkey on the Hatay issue. As an indication of its changed attitude, France withdrew the French governor, who was partly responsible for the rising tension with his tough stance toward the Turks living in Hatay, and appointed a Turkish governor, resulting in a relaxation in the tension.

There is no doubt that the invasion of Austria by Germany in March 1938 has deeply affected the stance of France toward Turkey on the Hatay problem. The emergence of the Berlin-Rome axis in Europe underlined the strategic significance of the Turkish Straits as well as the stability in the eastern Mediterranean. On July 3, 1938, France and Turkey signed an agreement that reiterated their guarantorship for the territorial integrity and the commitment to the protection of Hatay jointly by France and Turkey. To this aim, the parties agreed to deploy 2,500 troops each to Hatay. Turkey started the troop deployment the next day. On July 4, 1938, Turkey and France also signed a Friendship Treaty.

The general elections in Hatay were held in August 1938 and the Turks won 22 out of 40 seats in the Parliament. The Parliament was opened on September 2, 1938 and proclaimed independence by the name of Republic of Hatay. Even though Turkish and Arabic were the two official languages, all the deputies sworn in in Turkish. During a little less than a year of independence, the Republic of Hatay always expressed its desire to annex to Turkey. While Turkey welcomed this desire of Hatay, the consent of France was also needed because of the agreement of May 29, 1937 that was signed between Turkey and France guaranteeing Hatay's territorial integrity jointly. As of the early 1939, the winds of war were gusting again in Europe. Turkey's intensified relations with the Western powers elevated Turkey to the position of a potential partner in the eyes of French politicians in a war against the German-Italian axis. France finally accepted the desire of Hatay to annex to Turkey and gave its consent with an agreement signed on June 23, 1939, in return for Turkey to agree to respect the independence and the territorial integrity of Syria. On July 23, 1939, Hatay finally annexed to Turkey.

Regional Foreign Policy of Turkey during the Interwar Years

For the most part of the first couple of decades of the young Turkish Republic, the makers of foreign policy found themselves in constant deliberations trying to find favorable solutions to the disputes that were not resolved during the Lausanne negotiations. The same period, namely the Interwar years, also witnessed a series of rapid developments in the international arena that raised the stakes for almost every country in terms of security considerations. Turkey was one of them, which was in the process of consolidating the legal and constitutional reforms at home as well as the revolutionary changes in all aspects of public life. In line with Atatürk's guiding principles that favored diplomacy over military instruments in the resolution of conflicts, Turkey has managed to attain many of its objectives regarding the residual conflicts. In addition to the issues remaining from the past, Atatürk's foreign policy objective regarding the emerging security situation in the world was to create zones of peace and stability in Turkey's immediate neighborhood. The sources of threat were Italy and Germany.

The Balkan Entente

While an axis was slowly but steadily emerging between Italy and Germany, Turkey's concerns about its security in the Aegean and in eastern Mediterranean as well as in the Balkans increased. With these in mind, one of Turkey's priorities was to enhance the stability in the Balkans by way of improving good neighborly relations in the region. The resolution of the major problems between Turkey and Greece with the Ankara Convention of June 10, 1930 helped foster these ideas. From Turkey's, and also Greece's, point of view, it was essential to preserve the status quo that was reached after years of painstaking deliberations. To further consolidate the bilateral relations, Turkey and Greece formed the Entente Cordial on September 13, 1933 and also invited Bulgaria to join in. But, because of the unsettled problems between Bulgaria and its neighbors, including territorial claims as well, Bulgaria was not warm to the idea of maintaining the status quo. On the contrary, Bulgaria turned out to be a source of challenge to the status quo. Yet, the purpose of Turkey in inviting Bulgaria to join the Entente Cordial was not to form a military pact, but it was rather to prevent Bulgaria from joining another country (Italy in this case) in an offensive against Turkey.

On February 9, 1934, Turkey and Greece, together with Romania and Yugoslavia, established the Balkan Entente. This was not a military pact. However, all four countries were heavily concerned with the threats posed by the activities of Italy in the eastern Mediterranean and its ambitions toward the Balkans. Turkey's primary objective in forming the Balkan Entente was the same, as has been the case with the Entente Cordial, which was to prevent the possibility of an alliance formation between Italy and the neighbors of Turkey in the Balkans that would lead to its isolation.

In addition to military-strategic considerations, the political motivations behind the Entente were also important. The Balkan Entente did not aim to challenge or parallel the international system that emerged with the establishment of the League of Nations. On the contrary, the fundamental political goals of the Entente were perfectly compatible with those of the League, especially with its emphasis placed on the good neighborly relations and respect to borders and territorial integrity. The Balkan Entente was not formed against Germany or the Soviet Union. No corollary could be established with the Little Entente that was formed by France in order to contain Germany. In order to provide assurances to the Soviets that the Balkan Entente was in no way against them, Turkey attached a reserve note to the Entente document that it would not be part of a military operation against the Soviet Union. A similar assurance was given to Italy by Greece.

The togetherness of Turkey, Greece, Romania, and Yugoslavia helped constrain the ability of Italy to find large rooms to maneuver in the Balkans and helped mitigate each other's security concerns. As such, the Balkans were pacified and prevented from becoming a springboard of an offensive to one or more of the countries in the region by outside powers. It would not be wrong to argue that the Balkan Entente was a product of successful diplomacy that aimed to prevent escalation of local disputes to hot confrontations. The Entente achieved its goals for several years. However, with the consolidation of the Rome-Berlin axis, especially since 1937, some members of the Entente, namely Romania and Yugoslavia, started to lean toward Italy and Germany due to their raised security concerns. Yugoslavia signed bilateral treaties of friendship with Bulgaria and Italy. Even though Yugoslavia sought the consent of the other Entente members before signing a treaty with Bulgaria, such a move would run counter to the spirit, if not the letter, of the Balkan Entente. Eventually, growing Italian military profile caused concerns in Greece, which led that country to soften its stance vis-à-vis Italy. Finally, a series of developments in 1939, such as the Munich Conference and the partitioning of Czechoslovakia, put an end to the Balkan Entente.

The Mediterranean Pact

Just like the Balkans, the eastern Mediterranean was another region where Turkey perceived threats to its security, again from Italy. Turkey had experienced the Italian occupation from 1919 to 1923 in the immediate aftermath of World War I. Italy was in pursuit of expanding its sphere of influence toward the eastern Mediterranean and North Africa, in accordance to what was promised by the other great powers Britain and France during the London Conference of 1915. However, the British policy toward the region that favored Greece over Italy after the war made Italian policies more aggressive, especially following the coming of Mussolini to power in 1922 with the ambition of returning to the glorious days of the Roman Empire. In addition to this, the presence of Italians on the Dodecanese islands in the Aegean Sea increased the level of threat perception from Italy. Hence, Turkey searched for ways of establishing a defense pact against Italy in the eastern Mediterranean. Considering the options, such a pact would only be possible with Great Britain and France, and also maybe with the Soviet Union. Nevertheless, France and Britain were neither receptive to the idea of collaborating with the Soviet Union in the eastern Mediterranean nor have they given their consent to forming a pact with Turkey against Italy. Instead, France and Britain considered Italy to be in competition with Germany both in the Balkans and in the Mediterranean. They, therefore, believed that Italy was indeed balancing the expansionist ambitions of Germany.

However, Italy's invasion of Ethiopia raised concerns not only in Turkey but also and particularly in Britain because invasion of a country in the Horn of Africa across the Mediterranean was seen as a clear indication of both the intentions as well as the capabilities of Italy as to what it could do. This was a clear threat to the British interests that heavily depended on the strategic trade routes to India in the eastern Mediterranean. Moreover, Italy's threatening attitude to the reaction of the League of Nations to the invasion and its decision to impose sanction according to Article 16 of the Covenant also heightened the tension in the region. Turkey and Britain were among the countries who had voted for the imposition of sanctions. The commonality of the threat perceived from Italy brought Britain and Turkey even closer. Britain issued guarantees to the states in the Mediterranean such as Turkey, Greece, Spain, and Yugoslavia that had agreed to impose sanction in case they were attacked by Italy. Spain rejected the offer, but Turkey, Greece, and Yugoslavia accepted who in turn issued similar guarantees to Britain. This system of exchange of guarantees is also known as the Mediterranean Pact against the common threat, namely Italy.

The Sadabad Pact

Italian aggression in the Horn of Africa and its ambitions toward the eastern Mediterranean pushed the Middle Eastern nations to consider ways of protecting their interest with a concerted action. With the initiative of Iran, Turkey, Iraq, and Iran signed an agreement in Geneva on October 2, 1935. Even though Turkey was very enthusiastic in its support to the initiative, putting the document that was signed into effect would not be possible for a while due to the border dispute between Iran and Iraq over the Shattul Arab in the Gulf region. Once the two countries got closer to resolving their differences, Turkey, Iran, Iraq, and Afghanistan came together in Tehran on July 8, 1937 to sign an agreement known as the Sadabad Pact because of the venue of the signing ceremony, which was the Sadabad Palace.

The Sadabad Pact cannot be categorized as a typical military pact that would require the involvement of the parties in a conflict that one or more of the others would be involved. The Pact was more of an expression of mutual guarantees and respect to each other's territorial integrity, noninterference in each other's internal affairs, and a declaration of non-aggression. These were extremely important items given the fact that Iran and Iraq had a border dispute, and the presence of the Kurds in each of the regional countries could provide leverages to use them against one another. Similarly, the presence of the Turks and Turkic nationalities who were spread across the region could be another potential source of instability in case they were used (by Turkey) as an instrument of interference in other countries' internal affairs. By signing the Sadabad Pact that would prohibit any such attempt by any of the regional countries, Turkey had displayed its sincerity in its policy of noninterference, and that it had no irredentist or expansionist ambitions toward its neighbors. Hence, it is safe to say that the cardinal aim of the Sadabad Pact was to achieve peace and stability among the countries in the northern tier of the Middle East.

Turkey's policy toward the Balkans, the eastern Mediterranean, and the Middle East could be summarized as a pursuit of concerted action with the involvement of regional states against the threats emanating from outside the region. In doing so, Turkey has both achieved the recognition of its borders as a newly emerged nation-state by its neighbors and also become capable of allocating much of its time, energy, and resources to the consolidation of the reforms and to rapid economic growth and social development. Achieving this dual objective in regional politics and solving the unresolved residual disputes from the Lausanne negotiations in favor of Turkey, with the exception of the Mosul question to a certain extent, can be regarded as a great diplomatic success in the overall. Whether losing Mosul to the British first and then to Iraq was a diplomatic failure or was it simply an inevitable outcome of the conjunctural developments of the period is a question even the competent historians cannot agree upon. Given the realities on the ground at present day, one must also bear in mind whether insisting in keeping the Mosul province within the borders of Turkey at all cost would help consolidate the republican regime in the country or not.

WORLD WAR II AND İNÖNÜ'S FOREIGN POLICY: 1939–45

The passing of Atatürk on November 10, 1938 meant the closing of an era in the history of the Turks. There is no doubt Atatürk was one of the most important leaders in world history as much as he was for the Turks. Hence, one would expect Turkey to encounter serious deficiency in the making as well as the conduct of its foreign policy at a very difficult time in history. Hopefully, the leadership skills of İnönü who was also known as the "National Chief" helped Turkey overcome many of the difficulties that it would have possibly undergone otherwise. İnönü's impact on Turkish foreign policy can be studied in two phases. First, his first year in office after an abrupt takeover of Presidency in the most turbulent days in the run up to World War II. Second, his policy during the Great War from which he persistently tried to stay away.

Turkish Foreign Policy in 1939

When Italy invaded Albania, France and Britain have given guarantees to Greece and Romania on April 13, 1939. Britain extended a similar guarantee to Turkey as well. Turkey accepted the guarantee but also asked for a detailed account of what that guarantee would mean politically and what it would cover militarily. Hence, Turkey and Britain started to negotiate the scope and the content of the guarantee. Germany, Italy as well as the Soviet Union were concerned about the negotiations between Turkey and Britain. Turkey did not want to give an image of establishing a pact that would be seen as being against a specific country. The scope and the content of the Turkish-British guarantee system was made public on May 12, 1939 in which it was stated that Turkey and Britain would help each other in case a war that would break out in Europe would spread to the Mediterranean. The British initially suggested to Turkey that mutual guarantees should cover the Balkans as well. However, Turkey declined. Because, if Britain had to be involved in the war on the side of Romania, it would have to send its navy to the Black Sea, which would have to pass through the Turkish Straits. For this to happen, Turkey had to let the British fleet go through the Straits. However, according to the Montreux Convention, this could only be possible if Turkey were in war as well. But, İsmet İnönü was determined to pursue a policy of "nonbelligerency," meaning noninvolvement in the war, in case war broke out. Since Turkey could not afford such a war, any proposal regarding future commitments that would constrain Turkey's room for diplomatic maneuver to stay outside of the war would not be acceptable to İnönü. Soon after, a similar declaration was signed between France and Turkey on June 23, 1939 upon the French acceptance of the annexation of Hatay to Turkey.[15]

These declarations raised concerns in Germany and in the Soviet Union. Germany stated that such initiatives would increase the probability of a war by 40 to 60 percent. Germany went even further to say that it would cut off its trade with Turkey considerably or even totally. Germany and the Soviet Union signed a Treaty of Non-Aggression on August 23, 1939. This was received in Turkey with surprise because Turkey was expecting to see the Soviet Union in the Western pact instead, as there were negotiations between the Soviet Union and France and Britain. These negotiations were also seen as incentives for Turkey to sign the declarations of guarantee with Britain and France. Now, Turkey would be left alone with these two countries, and the Soviet Union with which Turkey had collaborated on many occasions would be on the other side. To avoid such an eventuality, Turkey and the Soviet Union were engaged in separate negotiations to see if the two could find ways to mend their differences concerning the mutual guarantees extended to Turkey by Britain and France and vice versa. Talks on this matter went on in Moscow from September 26 to October 16, 1939, but to no avail. The requests of the Soviet Union were not compatible with the commitments that Turkey had made to France and Britain. Moreover, the Soviet demands on the Straits were contrary to Turkey's sovereign rights as well as its liabilities stemming from the Montreux Convention.

As a result of no progress in the talks with the Soviets, Turkey went on to sign a trilateral declaration with France and Britain on October 19, 1939, which emphasized essentially what was stated in the bilateral declarations among the three states. What was slightly different in the trilateral declaration was that, in case Britain and France were attacked by a European state, Turkey would remain a "benign neutral" state. But since the trilateral declaration of guarantees expanded its scope to cover the Balkans as well, in case France and Britain had to be involved in the war because of their individual guarantees given to Greece and Romania, Turkey would have to get involved as well. This particular clause was previously rejected by Turkey on the grounds that it would jeopardize its rights and liabilities stemming from the Montreux Convention, which rested on a very delicate balance. To avoid such an eventuality, a protocol was annexed to the declaration, which stated that the liabilities of Turkey would be written off in case they could pave the way to a confrontation with the Soviet Union.

At a time when the winds of war were gusting again, in the lack of perfect information that very much constrained one's ability to make forecasts about the future pace of events, İnönü was trying, on the one hand, to take necessary precautions by getting powerful assurances from the great powers of the period, such as Britain and France, so as to be able order to protect Turkey by forming a series of alliances in case war could not be avoided; and on the other hand, to stay out of the war, bearing in mind the degree of possible devastation that Turkey would have to endure in case it would be compelled to get involved in the war. In the absence of Atatürk in this extremely difficult time in the Turkish diplomatic history, only a great leader like İnönü—who had seen both sides of the truth, namely the blood and tears of the battlefields and the maze of diplomatic negotiations—could carry such a huge responsibility on his shoulders. So he did.

Turkish Foreign Policy during the Great War

Because of Turkey's geostrategically important location, both the Axis powers and the Allied powers wanted to have Turkey on their sides. But, Turkey was seeking for ways to stay outside of the Great War. When in May 1940 Germany attacked France and the other Axis powers, Italy declared war on France. According to Article 1 of the trilateral agreement that was signed in Ankara on October 19, 1939 among Turkey, France, and Britain, Turkey had to side with France. But Turkey did not because Turkey had to consult such an event with the Soviet Union according to the Friendship and Non-Aggression treaty of 1925 between the two countries. And, when in October 1939 Italy attacked Greece, Turkey again was called upon to honor its commitment at an early date according to Article 3 of the trilateral agreement, namely the Ankara Pact. But, under pressure of Germany and the Soviet Union, Turkey did not act the way the British and the French expected. In the face of the threat posed by the presence of Germany and also Italy in the Balkans, Britain was heavily concerned with the security of the oil fields and the Suez Canal in the Middle East as well as the trade routes to India. Therefore, British Premier Winston Churchill increased the pressure on İnönü to have Turkey on the side of the Allied powers actively involved in the war. Britain also suggested that Turkey, Greece, Yugoslavia, and even Bulgaria form a pact in the Balkans against Germany. Turkey suggested in return that the Soviet Union should also be included in the pact and the United States should endorse the pact militarily as well. In February 1941, U.S. President Franklin Delano Roosevelt sent his representative to Ankara in order to discuss Turkey's military requests. Ankara's insistence in having the active military endorsement of the United States was stemming from İnönü's belief that Britain would not be able to provide enough military equipment to Turkey anyway. The United States, in the meantime, found Turkey's procurement list to be exaggerated, especially in terms of the number of aircraft requested. One could read İnönü's intentions twofold: either he was overcautious, as a leader coming from the battlefields, or he was trying to find valid excuses for staying away from the war.

In the meantime, Hitler wished to transfer troops and military equipment to Iraq through the Turkish territory, in return for which he promised to İnönü land from Western Thrace and the Aegean islands. Anticipating the consequences of such a permission, İnönü rejected the offer. Turkey and Germany signed a Treaty of Non-Aggression on June 18, 1941. Only four days later, on June 22, 1941 Germany launched an offensive on the Soviet Union. The non-aggression pact between Turkey and Germany raised serious concerns in the United States as well as Britain. The United States ceased the economic aid that it used to give Turkey as part of the "lend and lease" policy. Contrary to what was believed in the United States, Turkey's non-aggression pact with Germany indeed served the interests of the Allied powers because Turkey had stood firm against the German request to transfer its military to Iraq through Turkey. Thus, Turkey helped protect the Middle East against German military presence. Moreover, it would be unfair to expect Turkey to resist Germany all by itself.

There was no single summit meeting among the leaders of the Allied powers in which their desire for Turkey's involvement in the war was not mentioned. Following the Casablanca summit between Churchill and Roosevelt in which the two leaders have agreed to open a front against the Germans in the Balkans and also decided to invite Turkey to side with them, Churchill paid a rush visit to Turkey on January 30–February 1, 1943 to meet with İnönü in Adana in order to convince him to join the war. İnönü's response was not positive again. Later in the year, during the summit meeting of the Allied powers in Tehran in November 1943, Roosevelt and Churchill were accompanied by Stalin in their request to Turkey to side with the Allied powers against Germany. The three leaders invited İnönü to the Cairo summit which took place on December 4–6, 1943. This time they weighed in heavily so as to break the stubborn attitude of İnönü, who in turn felt compelled to agree "in principle" to join the war provided Turkey received enough military equipment, arms, and munitions. Churchill agreed to the request of İnönü. Hence, a committee composed of Turkish and British officers started to work on the procurement list in January 1944, but ceased to negotiate in early February because the British argued that supplying the military equipment that Turkey wanted would take a very long time and would not be completed before the end of the war. This could be another tactical move of İnönü, who was determined to stay out of the war, to make such requests that could not be met and thus create excuses for Turkey's reluctance to get involved in the war.

Because of dragging its feet, Turkey's relations with the United States and Britain became tense. Churchill made comments here and there that Turkey would also stay out of the peace conference once the war would be over. In the summer of 1944, Germany's deteriorating situation in the war started to become more obvious. Hence, Turkey cut off its diplomatic relations with Germany in return for assurances from France and Britain that Turkey would take its seat in the peace conference after the war. While Turkey managed to improve its relations with these two leading powers of Europe, relations with the Soviet Union started to cool down. As of the early 1945, Turkey's primary concern was the Soviet ambitions, given the fact that the entire Central Asia and the Balkans had entered into the Soviet influence during the war. Two major conferences that took place just before and immediately after World War II, namely Yalta and Potsdam, respectively, have been significant for Turkey's security and territorial integrity as regards the claims of the Soviet Union on Turkey.

The significance of the conference that was convened in Yalta on February 4–11, 1945 emanates from the Soviet claims that the Montreux Convention was now obsolete and thus it had to be amended by taking the changes in the international arena. The Soviet argued that the Convention was negotiated at a time when the Soviet-British relations were not in good terms and that the situation has since changed dramatically. The United States stood against the Soviet claims and supported Turkey's sovereignty on the Straits. Britain as well supported this position and also suggested that Turkey should be given assurances about its territorial integrity. Hence, the Soviet Union was left alone on this issue. In the meantime, Turkey declared war on Germany and Japan on February 23, 1945 in order to be able to take its seat in the San Francisco Conference that would soon be convened to shape the postwar international order. Soon after, the Soviet Union declared that the Treaty of Friendship and Non-Aggression of March 19, 1925 was no longer valid. When Turkey asked for the renewal of the Treaty, the Soviet Union replied with a note on June 7, 1945 requesting Kars and Ardahan, two cities in Turkey's eastern province, as well as bases on the Straits.

With the end of World War II, the Soviet Union, being one of the victorious powers, wanted to benefit from the vacuum that emerged from the nonexistence of Germany and Italy on the world political stage. During the Potsdam Conference which was convened on July 17–August 2, 1945 in Potsdam, Germany, the Soviet Union made claims on the Straits of Turkey and on the islands in the eastern Mediterranean, which were under the Italian control. These claims were seen by the Western powers as clear indications of the Soviet desire to project power to the Mediterranean region. Britain once more iterated its support to Turkey's security and sovereignty on the Straits and also criticized the Soviet Union for threatening Turkey. In response to the criticisms, the Soviets argued that they only wanted back what was extracted from Russia back in 1921 when it was weak. On the issue of the Straits, the Soviet argument to substantiate its request for bases was that the claims on the Straits were simply a repetition of what the Turks had agreed with the Russians back in the early nineteenth century. However, Britain stated that it would not force Turkey to yield to the claims of the Soviet Union.

When the Great War came to a close, many of Turkey's worries were not materialized thanks to the wisdom of İnönü who managed to stay out of the war against all the pressure coming from the Western powers. And, once Turkey faced challenges from the Soviet Union, its geopolitical and geostrategic value for the West greatly helped avoid any confrontation with its northern neighbor.

NOTES

1. Ömer Kürkçüoğlu, *Türk-İngiliz İlişkileri* [Turkish-British Relation] (Ankara: Ankara Universitesi Siyasal Bilgiler Fakültesi Yayınları, 1978), 42.

2. Kemal Melek, *İngiliz Belgeleriyle Musul Sorunu 1890–1926* [The Mosul Question in British Documents 1890–1926] (İstanbul: Üçdal Neşriyat, 1983), 42.

3. According to British statistics, the population of Mosul was composed of 66,000 Turks, 455,000 Kurds, 186,000 Arabs, 62,000 Christians, and 17,000 Jews and totally 786,000. Kwangsoo Choi, "The Original Turkish Concerns about Developments in Northern Iraq" (master's thesis, Bilkent University, May 2008), 15.

4. According to Turkish statistics, the population of Mosul was composed of 146,960 Turks, 263,830 Kurds, 43,210 Arabs, 18,000 Yezidis, and 31,000 Mon-Moslems and totally 503,000. Choi, "Original Turkish Concerns," 18.

5. Choi, "Original Turkish Concerns," 19.

6. Nevin Coşar and Sevtap Demirci, "The Mosul Question and the Turkish Republic: Before and After the Frontier Treaty, 1926," *The Turkish Yearbook*, 35 (2004): 43–59.

7. "Question of the Frontier between Turkey and Iraq," Report Submitted to the Council by the Commission Instituted by the Council Resolution of September 30, 1924 (Lausanne: League of Nations, 1924), 33.

8. Zeynep Ö. Alantar, "Türk Dış Politikası'nda Milletler Cemiyeti Dönemi" [The Period of League of Nations in Turkish Foreign Policy], in *Türk Dış Politikası'nın Analizi*, ed. Faruk Sönmezoğlu (İstanbul: Der Yayınları, 2001), 83.

9. Henry A. Foster, *The Making of Modern Iraq* (Oklahoma: University of Oklahoma Press, 1935), 176.

10. Damla Demirözü, "The Greek-Turkish Rapprochement of 1930 and the Repercussions of the Ankara Convention in Turkey," *Journal of Islamic Studies* 19, no. 3 (2008): 309–24, Advance Access published on March 18, 2008.

11. Ibid.

12. Ibid.

13. Mustafa Türkeş, "Atatürk Döneminde Türkiye'nin Bölgesel Dış Politikaları 1923–1938" [Turkey's Regional Foreign Policy During the Atatürk Era 1923–1938], *Atatürkçülük ve Modern Türkiye,* Uluslararası Konferans, October 22–23, 1998, Ankara, 123–41.

14. Şule Güneş, "Türk Boğazları" [Turkish Straits], *ODTU Gelişme Dergisi,* no. 34 (December 2007): 217–50.

15. Fahir Armaoğlu, *20. Yüzyıl Siyasi Tarihi, Cilt 1–2: 1914–1995* [20th Century Diplomatic History, Volumes 1–2: 1914–1995] (İstanbul: Alkım Yayınevi, Genişletilmiş 13. Baskı, 2004).

CHAPTER 3

Cold War Period and Turkey's Place in the West

The roots of Turkey's orientation to the West, and the process of Westernization, go back to the *Tanzimat* (Reorganization and Reformation) movement in the early nineteenth century. The Westernization process was primarily conceived as a way to contribute to the improvement of security at home and abroad.[1] This inherent security-driven mentality becomes evident when one considers the fact that the Ottoman Empire had launched a reformation and restructuring process when it was militarily and economically outpaced by the European powers.

In the Republican era, as early as the 1920s, Atatürk set into motion comprehensive reforms that were perfectly compatible with the process of Westernization in accordance with the goal of elevating the young Turkish Republic to the rank of highly civilized nations in the world. These reforms, however, were so radical and intensive that they have shaken the foundations of traditional Ottoman/Turkish society and injected a strong ideational soul into the initially fear-driven Westernization process. Since then, the assertion of a Western identity has greatly affected the logic of Turkish foreign policy formulation.

It was mainly because of this particular reason that Atatürk had recognized the decision taken by the League of Nations concerning the status of the Mosul district, once an Ottoman *Vilayet* (governorate), which was left to Iraq with the Ankara Treaty of June 5, 1926. The decision of the League of Nations was largely believed among the Turks to be unfair and taken under the pressure of Great Britain, the superpower of the period. Yet, Atatürk, who laid out the foundations of the foreign policy of the young Turkish Republic, wished to avoid a confrontation with the West for the sake of intensifying the political, economic, and cultural ties that would altogether contribute to the eventual consolidation of a

Western-style secular democracy in the country. Because thus far Turks have not been successful in becoming an integral part of Europe politically or economically, let alone culturally, despite centuries of encounters between the Ottoman Empire and the Western powers such as the British and the French.

A series of wars between the Ottomans and Europeans have resulted in the deterioration of the image of the Turks (and of Turkey, eventually) in the West.[2] Even half-a-millennium after the siege of Vienna, the heart of the Austrian Habsburg Monarchy, by the Ottoman Sultan Süleyman *the Magnificent* in 1529 and 1532, bitter memories are still observed to be vivid in many circles in Europe today. Therefore, Turkey's place in the West has always been a controversial issue for both political scientists and historians to talk about.

EMERGENCE OF WESTERN SECURITY STRUCTURE

Turkey's institutional ties with the West, which were established only after World War II, have a much shorter life span when compared to its history in the West. In order to understand and to properly locate Turkey's place in the West, it is necessary first to comprehend the emergence and the evolution of the Western security structure in the immediate aftermath of World War II within which Turkey had a significant role to play for almost half-a-century. The role that Turkey assumed within the Western institutional frameworks was mainly an outcome of the entry of the United States into the picture. Prior to that, for the Turks, West was mainly understood as Europe where Turkey was not usually considered to be an integral part of it.

United States Enters the Picture

In the aftermath of World War II, anticipating the threats rising on the horizon, the Truman administration in the United States decided to have a foothold in Western Europe in order to build a forward defense capability against the possibility of forced expansion of communism toward the Eastern European nations that were liberated from the Nazi occupation by the Soviet Union. For the United States to have a foothold in Europe, an alliance system had to be successfully established among the Western European powers who had fought among themselves for centuries.

In the history of Europe, there have been countless attempts to achieve integration among the major powers. But, divergences of opinions have in most cases prevailed over the convergence of the ideals, which have unfortunately resulted in long-lasting and highly destructive wars. Even the League of Nations, which was created following World War I, has not been successful in maintaining peace and stability in the continent that was thought to have been achieved with the Treaty of Versailles, which officially ended World War I on June 28, 1919.

It is possible to distinguish two fundamental reasons in the failure of the League to meet the expectations of especially the Europeans who have long been living in a constant state of war. One reason was the lack of an enforcement capability of the League to achieve the fulfillment of the responsibilities of member states. As such, the League could not prevent Japan's invasion of Manchuria in 1931 or Italy's invasion of Ethiopia in 1935 or Germany's rearmament in the run up to World War II.

The second reason was the isolationist policy that the United States pursued after the end of World War I. It is interesting to note that it was President Wilson of the United States who had a particular weight in the initiative taken to establish the League of Nations, in conformity with his *Fourteen Points,* which were a culmination of his progressive ideas that underscored the necessity to help the creation of new nations out of the collapsing imperial powers around the world.

The decision of the U.S. Congress not to be a member of the League was a reflection of its desire to stay away from the world politics. That was understandable if taken into consideration the fact that President Wilson could no longer pursue his own ideals due to a debilitating stroke that he suffered in 1919. Besides, the domestic political as well as economic situation in the United States had started to deteriorate in the post–World War I period. On top of these, the U.S. decision-makers were confident that a major threat to the security as well as the vital economic interests of the United States, namely the rise of the Central powers that would control the entire Europe, was eliminated with a decisive victory of the Entente powers paving the way to the Treaty of Versailles.[3]

Even though the Wilson administration had decided at first to stay out of the war that was going on in Europe, eventually the unrestricted submarine warfare of the German Empire causing serious disruption of the trade routes on the Baltic Sea, the North Sea, and the Atlantic Ocean was started to be perceived as posing a grave threat to the security and the economic interests of the United States. The effect of disruption of the supply routes that were used by the merchant ships sailing to and from the United States mounted to a degree that was equal to causing damage to the American interests as if it was in war with the Germans. Hence, the U.S. President Wilson declared war on the German Empire in 1917 when it became clear that diplomatic initiatives would not yield the desired outcome.

The sensitivity of the United States on the principle of keeping the supply routes open at all times emanates from its geographical position, which at times has been a natural barrier against incursions from outside, thanks to the Atlantic and the Pacific oceans on both sides of the continent. The geographical position of the United States was also a source of vulnerability due to its isolation from the rest of the world. Therefore, it was essential for the Americans to prevent any power across the oceans from rising to such a level that could have the upper hand in the control of the lines of communication. This was one particular reason why the United States was compelled to enter World War I on the side of the Entente powers against the German Empire. A similar threat was seen on the horizon toward the end of the 1930s and urged the United States to turn back to Europe after two decades of isolationist policy in its international relations. The rise of Hitler to power in Germany, who then started to arm his country to the teeth, sent powerful signals across the Atlantic Ocean that the winds of war were gusting in Europe again.

As has been the case before, the United States entered World War II in its subsequent stages. It goes without saying that the unanticipated air raid of Japan against the American naval base in Pearl Harbor has been one particular cause for the Roosevelt administration to declare war on Japan. Another cause was the possibility of Great Britain to fail in stopping the expansion of the Nazi Germany to the shores of the Atlantic Ocean, France having already surrendered at the outset of the War. Such a development would be nothing but the recurrence of a nightmare for the United States: watching the rise of a power that could tamper with the lines of communication over the Atlantic Ocean while Japan was attempting to do the same on the Pacific Ocean. The wartime strategy of the United States in particular, and that of the Allied powers in general, was to "beat Germany first," meaning to give priority to the European theater in the overall conduct of the war against the Axis powers, and then turn to Japan and defeat it.[4]

Coming of the "Atomic Age" and the "Missile Age"

World War II ended with a decisive victory of the Allied powers by defeating Germany and Japan. The Great War came to a close with a landmark event in the history of the warfare. The United States dropped atomic weapons on Hiroshima and Nagasaki, on August 6 and August 9, 1945, respectively, resulting in the surrender of Japan, which had lost hundreds of thousands of its citizens in a matter of days.

American atomic bombs that were dropped on two major Japanese cities heralded the beginning of a new era, which would soon be characterized with a "delicate balance of terror" between the major players.[5] The coming of the "atomic age" was not in itself the only cause of the start of a whole new era in world history. Combined with the coming of the "missile age," the magnitude of the threat that was perceived by the United States from its wartime ally, but political antagonist, Soviet Union, has grown significantly.

The German V-2 rockets may not have changed the pace of the Great War for the Nazis, but they have been a powerful source of inspiration for the Americans about the pace of the developments that would take place in the postwar period. The power of scientific accumulation in a country, especially under the pressure of serious concerns about national security, generates further momentum for innovative research and discovery. Cognizant of the achievements made in the field of rocket/missile development prior to and during World War II, the United States could very well foresee the extent of the potential developments in these fields in the hands of the Soviet Union in the aftermath of the Great War.

Both the Soviets and the Americans were doing their best to get hold on to the engineers who were involved in these top secret projects of Nazi Germany. They also tried to locate the material and technical parts of the rockets, as well as the ones that had not been used during the war. These and other attempts of the United States and the Soviet Union were indeed clear indications of the arms race that would soon take place between the two.

The potential capability of the Soviet Union to develop missiles that could fly very long distances, enough to cross the oceans, carrying large warheads could very well be used to strike the heart of the United States in a future conflict. Such an eventuality would undermine the value of the oceans that hitherto served as natural barriers to protect the United States mainland against the overseas powers, this time the Soviet Union.

In the face of such probable scenarios, the wisest strategy for the United States would be to have a foothold in Western Europe so as to have a forward defense capability against the Soviet Union. As such, the United States would be close to the Soviet territory having the capability to strike, if necessary, from a shorter distance, and also to prevent attacks while they would still be at their vulnerable stages.

Hence, unlike the previous administrations, President Truman decided to stay in Europe for as long as possible. Such a decision would necessitate fulfillment of certain conditions. One such condition would be to create an institutional framework in Western Europe within which the presence of the United States could be both legal and legitimate. A second condition would be to build such an institutional framework on a solid ground that would require consolidation of the political and economic structures of the war-torn Western European states that had just come out of a long and extremely damaging war.

Emergence of NATO and the EEC

A logical outcome of these two conditions for the United States would be to boost the efforts to start the political and economic integration process among the Western European states, while at the same time supporting the initiatives to build a military framework, which would complete the picture for a coherent alliance system that would constitute the fundamentals of the transatlantic links between Western Europe and North America.

The decision of the United States to remain in Europe paved to the erection of two powerful institutional frameworks on the continent, one of which was the North Atlantic Treaty Organization (NATO) in the military domain, and the other was the European Economic Community (EEC) in the political and economic domains.

The Washington Treaty signed on April 4, 1949 has established NATO with a view to protecting the Western lifestyle, meaning democratic regimes and free market economies, against possible incursions from outside, meaning the Soviet Union. Indeed, nowhere in the text of the Washington Treaty is there the name of a country mentioned as the "enemy" of the members of the Alliance. However, the delimitation of the area of responsibility of the allies to defend and the description of the challenges posed to the members have clearly hinted at the Soviet Union as the threat, against which the Alliance was really formed.

Turkey's Entry into the Western Security Framework

Had the United States decided to return home after the fall of the Nazi Germany and to remain aloof to what would happen in Europe, as has been the case after World War I, instead of erecting a military pact against the communist threat, Turkey might have faced with a number of serious difficulties in countering the demands of the Soviet Union that Eastern European nations had. Because, with the haste of the victory gained in the Great War, the Soviet leader and the Secretary-General of the Soviet Communist Party Josef Stalin claimed exclusive rights on the administration of the Turkish Straits, namely the Bosphorus and the Dardanelles in northwestern Turkey, and the return of the northeastern provinces of Turkey such as Ardahan and Kars to the Soviet Union. The "Containment" policy of the United States, which also envisaged a proper role for Turkey on its side, helped deter possible Soviet aggression that could have resulted from such claims.

The emergence of NATO and the EEC had mostly favorable implications for Turkey in the political, economic, and military domains throughout most of the post–World War II period. Yet, each of these institutions had separate, and at times parallel, life cycle in its relations with Turkey, experiencing a number of difficulties as well as attaining a certain degree of harmony. The net effect, however, has been to forge Turkey's place in the West, especially by means of its NATO membership.

IMPACT OF NATO ON TURKEY'S FOREIGN POLICY

Turkey's entry into the Alliance was not a straightforward development. Under the pressure of the claims of the Soviet Union, Turkish decision-makers wished for an early membership in NATO. However, the British and the French had other designs in mind as far as Turkey was concerned, which envisaged some sort of a guardianship of the southeastern flank of Europe without necessarily having institutional links with the NATO members that would require their formal commitment to Turkey's security.

In other words, Western European members of NATO wished to keep Turkey outside of NATO, yet asking Turkey to help protect the European interests across the Middle Eastern region without letting Turkey to reap the benefits in return. What the Western Europeans had in mind was not acceptable from Turkey's standpoint. Hence, Turkey lobbied the United States to help advance its cause to become a full member of the Alliance.

Turkey's aspirations toward NATO membership were indeed in conformity with the grand strategic designs of the United States for the post–World War II period, which could be summarized as *Containment* policy toward the Soviet Union. With its highly strategic geographical location on the crossroads of three regions, namely the Balkans, the Caucasus, and the Middle East, controlling the highly strategic sea routes between the Black Sea and the eastern Mediterranean, namely the Straits of Bosphorus and the Dardanelles, Turkey was perfectly fitting into the geopolitical and geostrategic calculus of the United States.

Turkey's participation in the Korean War in 1950 by sending a brigade consisting of some 6,000 troops to fight against the communist threat shoulder to shoulder with the United States has clearly underscored its value as a military-strategic asset for the members of NATO in the defense of the transatlantic area. As a result of this positive image created in the eyes of the United States and the Western European states, the decision to invite Turkey to join the Alliance (together with Greece) was taken in September 1951 and realized in February 1952.

The military-strategic role that the United States had in mind for Turkey and Greece, as new members of NATO, was to use their territories both as natural barriers between the Soviet Union and the oil-rich Middle East and the eastern Mediterranean regions, and as forward defense bases against possible Soviet offensives on the Western European members of the Alliance. Turkey, having common borders with the Soviet Union, had a much more difficult and risky role to play in the contingency plans of NATO, especially after West Germany joined the Alliance in May 1955, a development that prompted the creation of the Warsaw Treaty Organization, or the *Warsaw Pact,* as a communist bloc led by the Soviet Union.

Impact of NATO Membership on the Relations with the Soviet Union

Not surprisingly, the Soviet Union considered Turkey's membership in NATO as inimical to its interests in the region and an open challenge to its security. Hence, the Soviets protested Turkey's acceptance of the invitation to membership in the Alliance by issuing a note on November 3, 1951 stating that NATO was indeed an offensive organization, rather than being a defensive organization, and the invitation extended to Turkey, being a country with no connection to the Atlantic Ocean whatsoever, by the Alliance would mean nothing but the expression of the desire of the imperial powers to use the Turkish territory to establish an aggressive front toward the Soviet Union.[6]

Turkey replied to the Soviet note on November 12, 1951 stating that the allegation of aggression was an insult to the honesty of Turkish foreign policy, and if the Soviet Russia could sincerely assess its own status and its attitude, it would acknowledge the existence of genuine reasons for Turkey to be concerned about its own security. The Turkish note also emphasized the fact that Turkey was facing claims that were threatening its national defense and territorial integrity.[7]

Turkey Ties Down the Red Army in the Caucasus

When Turkey joined NATO, the parties tacitly agreed that Turkey would help contain the Soviet Union. Should deterrence have failed, Turkey would have made its facilities available to NATO and would have distracted as many Soviet forces as possible from a campaign in Central Europe.[8] In other words, Turkey risked its own devastation and invasion as a NATO ally by sitting in the immediate neighborhood of the Soviet Union simply because the military thinking of the Alliance focused on the central front as the main area of Soviet-Warsaw Pact threat, putting an overwhelming emphasis on the contingency of a massive attack through Germany into Western Europe. NATO's strategic calculations developed around this priority, and Turkey's contribution was considered in function of such a contingency.[9]

Turkish Army, largest in NATO after the United States, tied down around 30 Warsaw Pact divisions. Without Turkish alignment, the Soviets would be able to concentrate more massively against the central front. Secondly, Turkish membership of NATO exposed vast areas in the USSR to Western monitoring. Thirdly, Turkey and the Alliance controlled the Straits and the Aegean passages. Turkey's neutralization (followed by that of Greece) would shift NATO's defensive line in the Mediterranean back to Italy and to the line from Sicily to Cape Bon, further complicating the Western defense posture in Europe. In time of war, Turkey would have to engage the Soviet-Warsaw Pact forces in two theaters, the Thrace-Straits area and Eastern Turkey where it shared a 610-kilometer common border with the Soviet Union. Only in Finnmark area of northern Norway did another NATO ally shared a frontier with the USSR. Turkey was the only NATO member facing the Warsaw Pact threat from two opposing directions.[10]

Nevertheless, thinking in terms of the paradoxical logic of strategy, the bigger the Soviet threat was perceived, the higher the contribution of the West would be expected by the Turkish political and security elite. Their overwhelming belief was that in return to the risks taken as a frontline state, Turkey would fall under the NATO's deterrent and defense umbrella, and the Alliance would provide economic and military assistance to modernize the Turkish armed forces.[11] Hence, in return for the risks taken and the contributions made to the European balance of military forces, Turkey enjoyed NATO's collective defense commitment and received military and economic assistance mainly from the United States and, to a much lesser extent, from Germany.[12]

Mutual Threat Perceptions

Due to the fact that the Soviet Red Army had to deploy a sizeable portion of its capabilities in the Georgian, Armenian, and Azerbaijani Soviet Republics neighboring Turkey's eastern provinces, its ability to launch a powerful assault on the Western European nations had diminished significantly. On the contrary, the ability of the Soviet Union to invade large segments of the Turkish territory from the east had grown considerably. Moreover, the Soviet Army across the border needed only a few days to get ready in order to launch a surprise attack on Turkey.

Hence, the Turkish-Russian relations have been greatly affected from the psyche that was created under these circumstances, and the relations between Turkey and the Soviet Union were heavily dominated by mutual threat perceptions. Turks feared a sudden incursion of the Red Army into the Turkish territory that could lead the way to the split of the country or even a regime change with the help of its collaborators inside Turkey. Therefore, Turkey stood firm against such a possibility. On the other side, the Soviets feared a U.S.-sponsored attack on its military-strategic sites as well as large population areas, many of which were at an arm's length from the NATO bases in Turkey where nuclear missiles and nuclear bomber aircraft were deployed in significant numbers.[13]

During the 1960s and 1970s, the Soviet threat was felt more explicitly both in Turkey and in the United States as the Soviet Union closed the gap with the United States in the nuclear field. The Soviets increased their military presence and capabilities both in conventional and in unconventional weaponry along Turkey's eastern frontier as well as their naval presence in the Mediterranean. The Soviet Union's growing military presence both in quantitative and in qualitative terms across the southern flank of NATO prompted the Alliance in general, and Turkey in particular, to rely extensively (though gradually) on nuclear forces.[14]

The North Atlantic Treaty did not involve any concrete undertaking on the part of member states with reference to the deployment of nuclear weapons or any other specific weapons systems. Nuclear weapons were deployed in Turkey according to the decision taken at the NATO summit in Rome in 1959. Soon after, the U.S.-origin Thor missiles and Jupiter missiles were started to be deployed in Italy and Turkey, respectively. The deployment of these American Intermediate Range Ballistic Missiles (IRBMs) on Turkish territory, which could hit a wide range of strategic targets inside the Soviet Union, caused a lot of anger on the part of the Soviets. Added to these were the serious complaints about the reconnaissance flights on the Soviet territories by the American U2 aircraft taking off from the NATO bases in Turkey.

In response to the IRBMs deployed in Turkey, the Soviet Union started to build bases in Cuba, right next door to the United States, for its nuclear missiles that would intimidate the American decision-makers. These developments led the way to the Cuban Missile Crisis, which was experienced between the United States and the Soviet Union in October 1962. The "tit-for-tat" game brought the world to the brink of a hot confrontation between two superpowers that would involve the possible use of nuclear weapons. Hopefully, the crisis was resolved, but at the expense of the missiles that were recently deployed in Turkey. The Jupiters, which would soon be returned to the United States anyway due to a decision that was taken prior to the crisis, were withdrawn from Turkey without, however, consultations with the Turks.

A New Page in Turkish-Soviet Relations after the Cuban Missile Crisis

Following the missile crisis, Turkey and the Soviet Union opened a new page in their relations placing more emphasis on augmenting economic and cultural relations. At first sight, establishing sound relations between two countries that had diametrically different economic systems and political regimes might seem a little confusing. However, with Khrushchev the Soviet Union had entered a new phase in its relations, possibly under the trauma that was recently experienced in Cuba. It was not only Turkey with which the Soviet Union tried to intensify as well as to diversify its relations at that time. Under the rule of the Iranian Shah Reza Pahlavi, who had recently launched the "White Revolution" to improve the economic and social welfare conditions of the population, Iran also engaged in economic and cultural exchange with the Soviet Union.

It is interesting to note that, at this particular junction in regional politics, both Turkey and Iran were frustrated with the manner the United States treated its allies vis-à-vis the threats they perceived from the Soviet Union.[15] The U.S. presidents were unwilling to provide sophisticated weapons to Iran in large quantities on the grounds that the Shah was exaggerating, if not miscalculating, the "external threats" perceived from the Soviet Union and its Middle Eastern neighbors, such as Egypt under Nasser. However, because of Iran's strategic importance, U.S. presidents ultimately yielded, albeit reluctantly, to the demands of the Shah Reza Pahlavi to some extent.[16]

In the case of Turkey, following the tragic events in Cyprus in December 1963 to which Turkey reacted with a limited air operation to "show flag" over the island, which was inhabited both by Turkish and by Greek Cypriots, U.S. President Lyndon Johnson sent a bitter letter to the Turkish Premier İsmet İnönü reminding bluntly that the United States would not side with Turkey in case its intervention in the Island prompted a Soviet aggression. In other words, the United States underlined the fact that NATO would not honor its Article 5 (solidarity) commitment if Turkey acted with a view to protecting its national interests in the eastern Mediterranean in a way the United States would not approve (under the pressure of the powerful Greek lobby on the Capitol Hill). In response to the unfriendly attitude of his American counterpart, İnönü made a historic statement by saying "a new world order would be established and Turkey would take its side" implying that Turkey could intensify its relations with the Soviet Union. Unsurprisingly, the Soviet Union wanted to take advantage of the degree of frustration that was experienced in the relations of the United States with its staunch allies Iran and Turkey, which were brought together as part of the Containment policy. Hence, the Soviets wished to deepen the crack in these strategic relations by extending several projects to Turkey (and to Iran), especially in the field of heavy industries by establishing iron and steel manufacturing plant, petroleum refinery, glassware factory, hydroelectric plant, and the like.

Impediments to Improving Bilateral Relations

İnönü's historic statement notwithstanding, expecting the deepening and widening of Turkey's relations with the Soviet Union would be far too fetched a scenario for basically two reasons. First, out of almost 500 years of historical relations between the Turks and the Russians, total of some 35 years or so had passed without confrontation thus leaving deep traces of animosity in the mind-sets of the people on both sides. The fear of "Russian bear" is still vivid in some circles within the Turkish society, including civil and military ruling elite as well. Except for the helpful hand that was extended to Atatürk by Lenin during the War of Liberation against the occupying powers back in the early 1920s and the short period of warmer relations in the 1960s, Turks have always been wary of the secret ambitions of the Russians. The extent of the aid provided by Lenin to Atatürk is not known for sure. But experts on the subject and military historians talk about some 200 kilograms of solid gold, arms, machine guns, and ammunition sent to the Turks. Even the military aid that was provided by Lenin was not very much appreciated because of the suspected motivations behind such a support. Most Turks believed that Lenin helped Atatürk so as to enable him to fight successfully against the Western powers with a view to keeping them away from his neighborhood, probably with a secondary consideration to control Turkey at successive stages when left one-on-one.

The second reason was the geostrategic and geopolitical value of Turkey for the United States in particular, and the West in general. Despite relative relaxation in world politics during especially the Détente period, the Cold War was going on and the Soviet long-range nuclear ballistic missiles were still targeting the United States and Western Europe. Regardless of what was going on in the bilateral relations between Turkey and the United States due to some deep divergences of opinions in regional politics, NATO had to stand firm against the threats posed by the conventional as well as unconventional military capabilities of the Warsaw

Pact countries. Hence, the spring air in the Turkish-Soviet relations could not, and did not, last very long.

That said, Turkey and the Soviet Union had quite balanced relations since then, based on the good neighborly relations principle, emanating from being linked to each other geographically both on land in the Caucasus and also by sea over the Black Sea. Even during the height of the Cold War, Turkey and the Soviet Union resolved their differences with respect to the complex maritime issues such as the delineation of the territorial waters and the exclusive economic zones in the Black Sea. If one considers the fact that being NATO allies, Turkey and Greece have not been able even to identify the nature and the scope of the problems in the Aegean Sea, the value of resolution of such thorny issues between two rivals like Turkey and the Soviet Union was highly remarkable. Nevertheless, Turkey and the Soviet Union have not been able to diversify their economic relations that would go beyond oil and natural gas supplies of the latter. That was quite normal due to the lack of technological products or goods and services that the Soviet could offer Turkey. Neither was Turkey capable of satisfying the demand of some quality products that the Soviet elite would like to consume. Hence, economic interactions remained limited. The second half of the 1970s and the 1980s witnessed dramatic deterioration of the American-Soviet relations, especially after the invasion of Afghanistan by the Soviet military in 1979. The American "Star Wars" project, on the other hand, which ostensibly aimed at erecting a Strategic Defense Initiative (SDI) capability in order to prevent the Soviet nuclear ballistic missiles from reaching the U.S. territories, caused further sharpening of the Cold War rivalry. Quite normally, the return to the rhetorical statements of the Cold War period has resulted once again in a significant increase in the degree of caution in the relations between Turkey and the Soviet Union.

Impact of NATO Membership on the Relations with Balkan Countries

Turks have ruled the Balkans for five centuries during the Ottoman Empire. However, consecutive defeats that were experienced in the Balkan Wars in 1912 and 1913 have resulted in the loss of large sums of Ottoman territories in Western Thrace (today's Macedonia, Albania, and northern Greece) and in the Aegean (Crete island in particular). With the Lausanne Treaty, which determined the borders of the modern Republic of Turkey, the Eastern Thrace, or simply Thrace, remained within the Turkish territory making frontier with Greece and Bulgaria.

Geopolitical and Geostrategic Significance of the Balkans

From Turkey's perspective, the Balkans exhibits a number of strategic features. First and foremost is the cultural link between the citizens of Turkey and the

Turkish and/or Muslim communities living in almost every country in the region. Moreover, there are millions of Turkish citizens whose ethnic origins come from the Balkans, such as the Albanians, Bosnians, and the like.

Second, the Balkans is the gateway to Western Europe, which means more than a geographical area to most Turks who have long turned their face to the West for the modernization of the Ottoman as well as the modern-day Turkish societies and the administrations.

Third, the Balkans is situated in the immediate proximity of the highly strategic waterways under the sovereign control of Turkey, namely the Boshporous and the Dardanelles, as well as the most developed region of Turkey in terms of the economic activities and population wise.

Because of these three major reasons, among others, it is essential that Turkey have good neighborly and stable and predictable relations with the Balkan states. However, this has not been an easy task to achieve at all times from Turkey's standpoint. With a view to attaining this goal, Turkey joined the "Balkan Entente," which was signed in 1934 among Turkey, Greece, Romania, and Yugoslavia in the aftermath of the Nazi Party coming to power in Germany and Italy's expansionist policies toward the eastern Mediterranean. A similar "Agreement of Cooperation and Friendship" known as the "Balkan Pact" was signed among Turkey, Greece, and Yugoslavia in 1953.

But, these initiatives have not proved successful in bringing a long-lasting peace and stability to the region due to a number of factors. One particular reason for the volatility of the region has been the multiethnic and multireligious character of the communities living in a relatively small area and in relatively densely populated neighborhoods. Small sparks of friction between multicultural communities have been more than sufficient to set the region on fire, as has been experienced very dearly both at the beginning and at the end of the twentieth century.

Another reason has been the interest of external powers in this highly strategic yet equally difficult geographical location. So long as a single great power, or a hegemon, controlled the Balkans, much of the volatility could have been subdued. But the demise of the regional hegemons paved the way to conflict and confrontation among the local actors who had postponed their ambitions to resolve their differences by resorting to force if necessary. For instance, the decline and the eventual demise of the Ottoman resulted in the Balkan Wars. Most recent example has been the disintegration of Yugoslavia, a process that was indeed anticipated by some experts when Josip Broz Tito, the founder and the leader of Yugoslavia, passed away in 1980. Then, what retarded the "inevitable" to take place in Yugoslavia for almost a decade was the impact of the Cold War rivalry that had entered its last, and maybe the most alarming, phase with the "Star Wars" rhetoric. Nevertheless, the demise of the Soviet empire lifted the heavy blanket that helped suppress the local conflicts for ages, which were soon to erupt like a volcano.

Military-Strategic Significance of the Balkans

The military-strategic significance of the Balkans for Turkey emanated from the tangential dispositions of two rival blocs of heavily armed countries in a relatively small geographical area. Because its immediate neighbors Bulgaria and Romania were members of the "Iron Curtain," Turkey—being a member of the North Atlantic Alliance—had to maintain a sizeable military capability in the Thrace region in order to promptly and adequately counter any concerted attack that could come from the Warsaw Pact countries in the west, which would be engineered by the Soviet Union in the east. Hence, fully aware of the over-whelming superiority of the Warsaw Pact countries in conventional weapons systems, Turkey relied heavily on the presence of nuclear weapons on its territory for national security. The Turkish political and security elite considered these weapons systems to be a credible (albeit limited) deterrent against the Warsaw Pact countries in general, and the huge military might of the Soviet Union in particular. As the deployment of the U.S. intermediate range nuclear (Jupiter) missiles to Turkey was seen on the horizon, the Soviet Union initiated counter-measures at the international level. A proposal for establishing a Nuclear-Weapons-Free Zone (NWFZ) in the Balkans was then put forward by the Soviet Union on June 25, 1959. In line with their proposal the Soviets "recommended" to Turkey not to accept nuclear weapons on its soil, which could hit targets in the Soviet Union and would therefore be targeted by Soviet nuclear missiles. However, Turkey did not give in to the Soviet's threatening statements and opposed a nuclear-weapons-free Balkans.[17]

The proposal was reiterated in the early 1980s by the Balkan members of the Warsaw Pact. It was believed that the non-deployment or removal of nuclear weapons from the territory of Turkey would expose the country to a very difficult military situation. For Turkey, the existence of nuclear weapons on its soil meant the active presence and full backing of NATO in general, and the United States in particular, in contingency plans involving the Warsaw Pact countries. Hence, Turkey did not opt for a nuclear-weapons-free Balkans once again even though such a proposal might have had political advantages for some countries and politicians in the region in terms of the opportunities it presented to conduct "high politics" with the help of disarmament rhetoric. For instance, Greece, despite the fact that it was a NATO ally, not only welcomed the idea of a Balkan NWFZ but also became a cosponsor of subsequent proposals tabled by Bulgaria, which was a member of the Warsaw Pact.[18]

In the political domain, Turkey's relations with the Balkan states have varied depending on the attitude of individual nations. Whereas the relations with Romania have been significantly improving under the Nicolae Ceausescu regime, so long as the conjunctural factors were permissive, relations with Bulgaria wors-ened dramatically due to the malicious treatment of the Turkish and Muslim minorities by the Todor Jivkov regime, until both of them were toppled in late 1989 following the fall of the communist bloc.

Impact of NATO Membership on the Relations with Middle East States

After taking over the control of the Balkans as early as the fifteenth century, the Ottoman Empire expanded its rule to much of the Middle East and North Africa, a region stretching from the Strait of Gibraltar in the west to the Persian Gulf in the east, starting from the sixteenth century. These territories, however, were lost to the British and the French in the nineteenth century partly due to the collaboration of the local communities with the external powers. The pain of the loss of the long-ruled territories aside, the impact of the way they were lost—because of the "betrayal" of the Arabs—has been tremendous and left deep traces in the minds of most Turks. The Middle East was since seen by Turkish political and security elite as a zone of intricacies that must be stayed away from interfering with local political and military affairs. This has been one of the unwritten rules of Turkish foreign policy for most of the twentieth century. Turkey's membership in NATO has further consolidated the policy of staying aloof from Middle Eastern politics. The impact of NATO was mainly due to the limitations in its primary area of responsibility, which had originally excluded the Middle East. Article 6 of the Washington Treaty that established NATO in April 1949 stipulates that:

> For the purpose of Article 5, an armed attack on one or more of the Parties is deemed to include an armed attack:
>
> . . . on the territory of any of the Parties in Europe or North America, on the Algerian Departments of France, on the territory of or on the Islands under the jurisdiction of any of the Parties in the North Atlantic area north of the Tropic of Cancer;
>
> . . . on the forces, vessels, or aircraft of any of the Parties, when in or over these territories or any other area in Europe in which occupation forces of any of the Parties were stationed on the date when the Treaty entered into force or the Mediterranean Sea or the North Atlantic area north of the Tropic of Cancer.

Turkey's membership did require the inclusion of the entire Turkish territory in the contingency plans concerning the area to be defended against armed attacks from outside as stipulated in Article 5 of the North Atlantic Treaty.

Middle East Being the "Out-of-Area"

Nevertheless, in the eyes of the most Western European members of NATO, the Middle East has long been considered to be out of the area of their responsibility to defend against the Soviet encroachment, with the exception of some limited planning covering the oil-rich Gulf region. Hence, Middle East was since seen simply as "out-of-area." There were a number of reasons for considering the Middle East as "out-of-area." First and foremost, even if it was not explicitly stated in the text of the Treaty, the North Atlantic Alliance was formed, in the first place, against the threats posed by the Soviet Union to the Western European nations. Hence, anything that would increase the threat level perceived from the Soviet Union and the Warsaw Pact would be unacceptable to especially the Western European members of NATO. In this respect, Turkey's relations with its Middle Eastern neighbors, particularly Syria and Iraq, both of which were close friends of the Soviet Union, would carry the risk of involvement of the Soviets in any conflict between them and Turkey.

Turkey's relations with Syria and Iraq were not good because of the deep divergences of opinions regarding, for instance, the ways and means of using of the waters of the Euphrates and the Tigris rivers that are originating from Turkey and flowing through the Syrian and Iraqi territories all the way down to the Gulf. In addition to the conflict over the waters, Turkey and Syria have also disagreed over the status of Hatay district of Turkey, which was annexed to Turkey in 1939 after a period of French occupation when Syria was governed under the French mandate. Hatay is still depicted within the Syrian borders in official maps used by the Syrians. Moreover, the support of Syria to terrorist organizations such as Armenian Secret Army for the Liberation of Armenia (ASALA) and the *Partiya Karkerên Kurdistan* (PKK) strained the relations even further. Hence, if Turkey entered in a conflict with Syria and/or Iraq because of such contentious issues, and if NATO had to honor its Article 5 commitment and involved in the conflict on the side of Turkey, the Soviet Union would most likely side with its Middle Eastern allies Syria and Iraq. Such eventualities would run the risk of escalation of a bilateral local conflict to one between NATO and the Warsaw Pact, and also possibly to a superpower confrontation that might even lead to a nuclear exchange. No members of NATO would, therefore, like a conflict between Turkey and Syria or Iraq to break out that could pave the way to an East-West confrontation. With these in mind, Turkey was advised (informally, though) by its NATO allies not to act in such a way that would cause a confrontation with Middle Eastern neighbors and to keep the profile of its relations low with the regional states.

Apart from such military-strategic considerations, as a second reason, one must bear in mind that, following World War I, Syria and Iraq were under the French and British mandates, respectively. Even after Syria and Iraq gained their independence, economic and cultural relations with France and Britain were maintained at certain levels. Thus, neither Britain nor France would like to side with Turkey against Iraq or Syria even if there would be no fear of escalation of the conflict to a superpower rivalry.

A third reason why Turkey's membership on NATO has further consolidated Turkish policy to remain aloof from the region was Turkey's force posture, which heavily depended on the threat perceived from the Soviet Union on the northeastern frontier and Bulgaria on the northwestern frontier. The bulk of Turkey's military capabilities were allocated to the contingencies involving a Soviet offensive on Turkey's eastern provinces, possibly with a concomitant attack of Bulgaria from the Thrace region. As such, Turkey was left with hardly any meaningful military capability, especially the land forces that could be deployed along its southern and southeastern frontiers neighboring Syria, Iraq, and Iran. Considering the role of the military power in backing political decisions, Turkey's ability to deter its neighbors from advancing their policies such as supporting terrorism that were damaging the Turkish national interests was limited because of the limited military capabilities, which could be allocated to contingencies that would involve its Middle Eastern neighbors.

The "Out-of-Area" and the Relations with Israel

While the Turkish security elite worried about the possibility of being left high and dry by their European allies, Turkey actually opposed the inclusion of "out-of-area" intervention in NATO plans. Turkey did not fear aggression from the Middle East as much as it feared being dragged into the Middle East's own internal conflicts, especially between Israel and the Arab states. The Turkish concern derived from the depth of the American commitment to Israel—a commitment demonstrated in the midst of the Arab-Israeli war of 1973, when the United States went to the brink of war with the Soviet Union in defense of Israel. For a host of reasons, it had been a cardinal principle of Turkish foreign policy to avoid taking sides in the Arab-Israeli dispute. The Turkish military did not want to be placed in a situation where it might be expected to assist in U.S. operations specifically designed to back up Israel in its conflict with neighboring Arab states—a conflict which, until the late 1970s, showed no signs of abating.[19] The Arab-Israeli wars of the 1960s and 1970s, Turkey's dependency on Arab oil after the 1970s, and the Palestinian *Intifada* movement in the 1980s have all created major obstacles to attempts from both sides to widen the scope of bilateral relations.[20]

Turkey was only slightly less ambivalent about Western efforts to institutionalize cooperation among the states of the "northern tier": Turkey, Iran, Afghanistan, and Pakistan. The so-called Baghdad Pact of 1955, the Central Treaty Organization of 1959, and the Regional Cooperation for Development (RCD), established in 1964, were all intended to counter Soviet penetration. All of them were flawed, weak, and ineffectual—and all of them were further reminders to the Turks of the primacy of their ties to Europe. Turkey was not oblivious to potential threats emanating from the Middle East but believed it could deal with its adversaries on its own, and it wanted to decide for itself how and when to defend its interests in the region, without having to answer either to Europe or to the United States.[21]

Impact of NATO Membership on the Relations with Greece

Inclusion of Greece and Turkey into the North Atlantic Alliance would clearly run the risk of naturalization of the deeply rooted problems of the two allies. But, on the other hand, bringing the two rivals under the roof of a powerful military organization, which would have far-reaching military and political capabilities to enforce peace between them, could also be seen as a golden opportunity. Nevertheless, Turkey's and Greece's memberships have neither caused serious cracks on the military bloc nor paved the way to a fair and lasting peace between the two nations. The Alliance has developed political and military mechanisms and channels that helped contain the possibility of any confrontation between Greece and Turkey causing a deficiency in NATO's capabilities to deter the Soviet Union and the Warsaw Pact countries.

The rules of the game in containing the possible spillover effects of a Turkish-Greek confrontation were indeed clear and simple: No such confrontation would be acceptable for the other members of the Alliance; therefore, it must not be allowed to break out (primarily through diplomatic initiatives with the mediation of other allies, the United States being at the forefront). But, if the Alliance failed to prevent such an occurrence, the confrontation must be halted in its earliest phase possible, even by resorting to military enforcement measures, if necessary, regardless of their consequences for the two conflicting states, for the sake of preserving the supreme interests of the Alliance. No official documents or political statements can be found in regard of the mechanism depicted above because these were unwritten rules developed over the years and communicated to the parties concerned through informal but effective channels. This was simply because of the fact that it would be totally inconceivable for a military alliance to formally acknowledge the possibility of a hot confrontation between two or more of its members and to officially draw up contingency plans accordingly. Against this background, it would not be unfounded to argue that the impact of Turkey's membership in NATO on its relations with Greece has been, on the overall, positive and constructive, with of course some reservations, such as the "Johnson letter" incident.

NOTES

1. Ali L. Karaosmanoğlu, "The Evolution of the National Security Culture and the Military in Turkey," *Journal of International Affairs,* 54, no. 1 (2000): 199–217.

2. Stanford Jay Shaw and Ezel Kural Shaw, *History of the Ottoman Empire and Modern Turkey* (Cambridge: Cambridge University Press, 1977).

3. Central powers were consisting of primarily the German Empire, the Austria-Hungarian Empire, Bulgaria, and the Ottoman Empire. Entente powers were consisting of France, Great Britain, Russia, Italy, and the United States which joined the war at a later stage.

4. Allied powers were consisting of literally the same countries as in World War I, namely the Great Britain, France, the Soviet Union, and the United States. Other countries such as Australia, New Zealand, Canada, China, South Africa, Bolivia, Mexico, and Brazil from overseas, as well as Norway, the Netherlands, Belgium, Poland, Denmark, Greece, and Yugoslavia from Europe. The Axis powers were consisting of Germany, Italy, and Japan as the main actors, which were joined by Bulgaria, Romania, and Hungary.

5. Albert Wohlstetter, "The Delicate Balance of Terror," in *US Nuclear Strategy: A Reader*, ed. Philip Bobbitt, Lawrence Freedman, and Gregory F. Treverton (London: The Macmillan Press, 1989), 143–67.

6. Ergun Hiçyılmaz, "Tarihte 'Gel Kore'ye Gir NATO'ya' Süreci" [The "Come to Korea, Enter NATO" Process in History], *Sabah*, http://arsiv.sabah.com.tr/2004/07/04/cp/hob114-20040627-102.html.

7. Ibid.

8. Bruce R. Kuniholm, "Turkey and the West," *Foreign Affairs* 70, no. 2 (1991): 41.

9. Ali L. Karaosmanoğlu, "Europe's Geopolitical Parameters," in *Turkey, Central and Eastern European Countries in Transition*, ed. Subidey Togan and V.N. Balasubramanyam (New York: Palgrave Press, 2001), 271–89.

10. Ibid.

11. Mustafa Kibaroğlu, "Turkey," in *Europe and Nuclear Disarmament*, ed. Harald Müller (Brussels: European Interuniversity Press, 1998), 161–93.

12. Karaosmanoğlu, "Europe's Geopolitical Parameters."

13. Hans M. Kristensen, *US Nuclear Weapons in Europe: A Review of Post-Cold War Policy, Force Levels, and War Planning* (Washington, D.C.: Natural Resources Defense Council, February 2005), 9.

14. Kibaroğlu, "Turkey."

15. Kenneth M. Pollack, *The Persian Puzzle: The Conflict between Iran and America* (New York: Random House, 2004).

16. Mustafa Kibaroğlu, "Iran's Nuclear Ambitions from a Historical Perspective," *Middle Eastern Studies* 43, no. 2 (March 2007): 223–45.

17. Kibaroğlu, "Turkey."

18. Ibid.

19. Mustafa Kibaroğlu, "Turkey and Israel Strategize," *Middle East Quarterly* 9, no. 1 (Winter 2002): 61–65.

20. Mustafa Kibaroğlu, "New Tests for Turkey's Evolving Security Relationship with Israel," *Terrorism Focus* 5, no. 7 (February 20, 2008), www.jamestown.org/terrorism/news.

21. Ibid.

CHAPTER 4

Turkey's Foreign and Security Policies in the Post–Cold War Period: *The Neighborhood*

With the end of the Cold War period, the Balkans, the Caucasus, and the Middle East, which constitute Turkey's immediate neighborhood, have become the centers of attention in world politics. The war in the Gulf provoked by Iraq's invasion of Kuwait, ethnic conflicts in the Caucasus flared up with the collapse of the Soviet Union, and atrocities in Yugoslavia erupted by the secessionist demands of Slovenia, Croatia, and Bosnia-Herzegovina have long constituted the top priority items on the world political agenda. The political geography of all three regions have undergone significant developments paving the way to the emergence of new independent states and radical changes in the regimes of the existing states. Unlike the Cold War era during which the states had limited room to maneuver in their relations with neighboring states because of the fear of disrupting the stability in the bipolar international system, the new era is characterized with uncertainty and instability.

In the Balkans, much of the instability is eventually settled with the involvement of the United States in the equation with its military might and heavyweight diplomacy enforcing peace agreements between the fighting parties, and the European Union (EU) using its "soft-power" to heal the wounds of past atrocities. There are still contentious issues such as Kosovo's proclamation of independence from Serbia, which is likely to remain a major foreign and security policy issue for many countries in the greater region. The expansion of the EU toward the Southeastern Europe by admitting Bulgaria and Romania as full members and by giving membership perspectives to Croatia and Serbia raises hopes that the conflict might be contained and resolved eventually.

In the Caucasus, the level of tension has been at times up or down depending on a number of factors. For instance, attempts of the United States to penetrate into the region under the pretext of its "global war on terror" strategy cause strong reactions of Russia, which in turn pursues controversial policies toward the regional actors with a view to restoring its supremacy in regional politics. Russia's ability to influence the management of the intrastate conflicts is the prime underlying factor in the current state of affairs in regional politics, which is still far from being stable due to the presence of so-called "frozen conflicts" across the region as identified by the Organization for Security and Co-operation in Europe (OSCE).

The Middle East has gone through a series of traumatic developments, which had serious implications extending beyond the region's boundaries. The "Gulf Wars" in 1991 and 2003 resulting from the ambitions of Iraq to become a regional hegemonic power as well as the desire of the United States to transform the entire region from radical autocratic and totalitarian regimes into moderate democracies have shaken the foundations of the long-established sets of relations among the regional actors. Similarly, the pace of developments in the American-Iranian relations due to the ambitious nuclear program of the latter added more strain to the already strenuous relations across the region. Controversies arising from the mere presence of the State of Israel whose right to exist is not recognized by most states in the region have been no less significant for the lack of stability in the greater Middle East.

Turkey, being at the epicenter of these three regions, found itself surrounded with arcs of instability on almost every direction. Due to the high degree of uncertainty in the international system, the task of the Turkish decision-makers to formulate adequate foreign and security policy options that would best serve Turkey's national interests has become increasingly difficult. Anticipation of the dramatic shifts in the power structures at global and regional levels has been very crucial for determining Turkey's foreign policy orientations and security strategies in such a chaotic neighborhood.

REDEFINITION OF EXTERNAL AND INTERNAL THREATS

The end of the Cold War had a powerful impact on the security of Turkey in many respects. Since 1952 and throughout the Cold War years, Turkey had enjoyed the rather privileged status of being a NATO member. With its geostrategic location as a flank country and the second largest standing army in the Alliance after the United States, Turkey became an indispensable ingredient of the security of the Western world. Hence, not much room was left for the Turkish political elite to worry about national security who counted, to a considerable extent, on the United States in the first place, and on NATO in general, as far as the Soviet threat was concerned.

Implications of the Collapse of the Soviet Union

The end of the Cold War, which literally meant the disappearance of the threat perceived from the Soviet Union, caused drastic changes in Turkey's security environment. Not all of these changes were unfavorable, though. Former Soviet republics in the Caucasus such as Georgia, Armenia, and Azerbaijan have emerged as independent states. One of the most striking outcomes of this development was that, for the first time in the four-century-old history of Turkish-Russian relations, the two nations have been geographically separated, if one excludes the neighborhood across the Black Sea. From a military-strategic point of view, the dissolution of the common borders with the Soviet Union has contributed greatly to the security of Turkey.

Impact of the Collapse of the Soviet Union on the Russian Military Thinking

The impact of the collapse of the Soviet Union has been devastating on the Red Army just like many other former Soviet institutions and organizations. There was a chaos in the administration of the military units, and central authority and discipline were lost especially in the flank zones, such as the Caucasus. Many Russian officers who were deployed in the former Soviet republics have either quit or deserted their positions to return home so as to earn a new life. Those who remained were asked by the governing authorities of the newly emerged independent states such as Georgia and Azerbaijan to evacuate their bases at an early date. Hence, the Soviet Red Army was decimated both in numbers and in its composition in the Caucasus region where its troop concentration level was used to be around 400,000 strong during the height of the Cold War. As such, the minimum time that was then required for Turkey's colossal ex-neighbor to launch a surprise attack was estimated to have increased to approximately a year, from a figure that used to be expressed in weeks, if not days.[1] This has been a great relief for Turkey who had focused its attention on its northeastern borders for decades.

The deterioration of the military capacity of the Russian Armed Forces in the immediate aftermath of the demise of the Soviet Union required a quick fix so as not to pave the way to further disintegration and more chaos in and around the Russian Federation. With two dozen autonomous republics and the multiethnic and multireligious societal structure spread over a large territory, the Russian Federation is almost a replica of the Soviet Union. Russian security elite who feared a new round of disintegration have started to make references in their political statements and public discourse to the nuclear weapons capability of Russia, which was least affected from the trauma of disintegration and still intact. The statements of Russian political and military elite underlined the fact that any attempt of outside powers to interfere with the politics of the former Soviet landscape, which was identified by them as "near abroad," would be confronted with a powerful military response, if necessary, including the possibility of resorting to nuclear weapons as well. In other words, due to the fear of presence of states that might want to exploit Russia's much weakened political, economic, and military situation, the Russian elite hinted at the possibility of resorting to their nuclear capacity, even in the early phases of any conflict. By doing so, they wanted to deter both the external powers and the Newly Independent States (NIS) from engaging in any collaborative political designs that could harm Russia's supreme national interests. Accordingly, the new Russian military strategy was pronounced in October 1993 in accordance with the requirements of the "near abroad" doctrine.

Origins of Russian "Near Abroad" Doctrine

The "near abroad" doctrine and the respective military strategy of the Russian Federation, which was formulated in the early 1990s, exhibited a number of important features and significant differences from the one that was adopted by the Soviet Union. Whereas the "near abroad" doctrine made explicit references to the possibility of resorting to nuclear weapons in the 1990s, the military doctrine of the Soviet Union was based on the "no-first-use" strategy in the 1980s. Confident with the military superiority of the Warsaw Pact countries in the field of conventional weapons, in 1982 the Soviet leadership had launched a "peace offensive" and declared that the Soviet Union and the Warsaw Pact countries would not be the first to resort to nuclear weapons in any conflict, provided that the other side, meaning the NATO countries, did not use nuclear weapons either. In addition to the expression of self-restraint in using nuclear weapons, the Soviet leadership proposed to the NATO members to adopt a similar no-first-use policy as well. But, NATO's response was not affirmative because, throughout the Cold War, the strategic concepts of NATO asserted the right of the Alliance to resort to nuclear weapons at any stage of an aggression. In other words, NATO strategies have always been a "first-use" strategy. NATO's first-use strategy did by no means imply a preemptive use, which means the use of nuclear weapons before any aggression occurs. Rather, the first-use strategy implied that NATO would be the first to use nuclear weapons, during an aggression, in regard of the fact that no other option might be a better response for defending the NATO territory against the aggressor. NATO countries had to rely on their nuclear capabilities in order to offset the superiority of the Warsaw Pact countries in conventional weaponry because it was envisaged that NATO might not win a war without resorting to nuclear weapons, whereas the Warsaw Pact might, with its conventional superiority. Although a clear-cut comparison between the conventional weapons arsenals of the NATO and Warsaw Pact countries is hardly possible, it was generally estimated that the Warsaw Pact had a "1.5 to 1" superiority over NATO.

The tide has turned with the dissolution of the Warsaw Pact and the disintegration of the Soviet Union. The disproportionate situation between the conventional weapons arsenals of the former rivals was also reversed. As NATO survived and enlarged toward the east, with eventual memberships of the former Warsaw Pact countries such as Poland, the Czech Republic, Slovakia, Bulgaria, and Romania, Russia has undergone dramatic changes and economic hardship. The imbalance in the conventional weapons systems then turned out to be in favor of NATO much more than it was the case for the Warsaw Pact during the Cold War. Therefore, the Russian military elite felt compelled to revise their decade-old "no-first-use" strategy and to declare instead that Russia would again reserve its legitimate right to resort to nuclear weapons, in case an aggression occurred by a nuclear weapons state or an ally of a nuclear weapons state, regardless of the weapons used by the aggressor.

Emergence of the "Turkic World" in the Former Soviet Landscape

One of the results of the collapse of the Soviet Union was the emergence of the NIS. This dramatic development brought with it new hopes and opportunities as well as worries and dilemmas for Turkey. One practical result of this development was that the number of Turkey's geographical neighbors increased overnight. Among the new states that gained their independence from the Soviet Union were Azerbaijan, Turkmenistan, Uzbekistan, Kyrgyzstan, and Kazakhstan with which Turkey had deep historical and cultural ties. Similarly, Iran was also a regional country that shared many aspects of its history, culture, religion, and language with the new independent states in the Caucasus and Central Asia.

Hence, the possibility that Iran would establish comprehensive relations with these states caused alarm in Western capitals. The fundamentalist Iranian regime and its attitude toward the West that was generally perceived as "hostile" were the main sources of this concern. One major objective of the Western countries was to contain Iran's expansionist ambitions by not allowing it to export its fundamentalist regime to the NIS. Turkey, with its secular democracy and market economy, was considered in Western capitals to be a feasible alternative to Iran. Turkey was also thought to be well equipped to act as a role model for the NIS and to help the new states survive the painful and dangerous period of transition after the collapse of the Soviet system. Even in the absence of the genuine support extended by the West to Turkey, due to its historical and cultural ties, Turkish political and security elite would have felt compelled to offer solutions to the problems of the "Turkic world." Nevertheless, clashes between Turkic and non-Turkic identities in that region increased as the Soviet system disintegrated. Hence, the conflict between Armenia and Azerbaijan arising from the dispute over the status of the Nagorno-Karabakh region has become a test case for Turkey with regard to its capabilities and its ability to properly "lead" the newly independent states of Turkic identity.

The dispute over the mountainous Karabakh region has its roots deep in history. There have always been clashes between the Azeri Turks and the Armenians over this strategically very important piece of land. The Soviet rule put a halt to the hostilities for a long period. In the late 1980s, however, the Soviet Union was weakening under the *Perestroika* and *Glasnost* meaning "restructuring" and "openness," respectively, initiated by the last Secretary-General of the Soviet Communist Party Mikhail Gorbachev. Even though these two major initiatives were taken by the Soviet leadership with a view to gaining a new momentum to the ailing Soviet economic and political system, serious difficulties have started to be experienced in keeping the Union together in the face of the secessionist claims coming first from the Baltic states and spreading throughout the other republics in the Caucasus and Central Asia. Hence, the genie was out of the bottle, and the process of disintegration had started and could not be reversed. Concomitantly, hostilities and clashes between Armenia and Azerbaijan resumed in 1988 and reached its peak in early 1992, weeks after the formal disintegration of the Soviet Union in December 1991. Skirmishes came to an end with the cease-fire agreement of May 12, 1994, leaving behind some 5,000 deaths, 50,000 wounded, and approximately one million people dislocated because of the Armenian occupation of the Nagorno-Karabakh region of Azerbaijan, which constitutes some 20 percent of its territory.

One of the most dramatic events of the war between Armenia and Azerbaijan was the massacre of Hocalı on the night of February 25–26, 1992 where more than 600 civilians were killed by Armenian military. With the support of 366th Russian regiment deployed in the region, the Armenians carried out a schemed and systematic massacre on the night of February 25, 1992 by cutting all entry and exit routes of Azerbaijan's Hocalı village which holds 7,000 residents. Civilian and unarmed Turks were massacred by the Armenians who did not spare targets, killing infants, women, the elderly and young ones. According to official reports, 613 people were brutally murdered that night. The fatalities included 83 children and 106 women, who were subject to cruel tortures, while 487 were severely wounded and 1,275 were taken hostage. The remaining civilians were able to survive only after outstanding efforts. Twenty-six children lost their mothers and 130 were left without a father. The March 1, 1992 issue of the *Sunday Times* covered the Hocalı events as "Armenian soldiers wiped out thousands of families." Furthermore, in the March 13, 1992 issue of Russian newspaper *Izvestia,* Captain Leonid Kravets, who was involved in the incidents, said he saw hundreds of dead bodies on a hill nearby Hocalı, most of which were killed with special torture methods.[2]

The most Turkey could achieve in this regard was to participate in the Minsk Group established under the auspices of the Conference on Security and Cooperation in Europe (CSCE), which was later grown into the Organization for Cooperation and Security in Europe.[3] Armenia, Azerbaijan, Belarus, the Czech Republic, Slovakia, France, Germany, Italy, Russia, Sweden, Turkey, and the United States participated in the negotiations that took place within the framework of the Minsk Group. The function of the Group was to define the emergency measures required to ensure a cessation of hostilities. Later, the Minsk Group served to monitor the cease-fire imposed by United Nations Security Council Resolution 882, of which Turkey was a cosponsor together with Russia and the United States. This dispute remains largely unresolved in spite of the efforts of Turkey and other members of the Group.[4]

Turkey's Changing Military Force Posture

The force posture of the Turkish military during the Cold War years was heavily determined with the threat perception of the authorities who had assigned considerably more emphasis to the northeastern part of the country bordering the Soviet Union as well as the northwestern part bordering the Warsaw Pact member Bulgaria. However, a series of developments have either compelled or enabled Turkey to make drastic changes in its force posture and the deployment of its military capabilities inside the country.

Implications of Iraqi Invasion of Kuwait

First of these developments was Iraq's invasion of Kuwait on August 2, 1990, which forced the Turkish military and security elite to be seriously concerned with the possible consequences of the ensuing events thereof. Even though Turkey and Iraq had a number of contentious issues on their agenda, such as the allocation of the waters of the Tigris and the Euphrates rivers, both of them originating from Turkey and flowing through Syria (Euphrates) and Iraq (Tigris), their bilateral relations were, on the average, good. During the war between Iraq and Iran from 1980 to 1988, Turkey did not take sides, and rather pursued an "active impartiality" policy. In this context, Turkey did its best to be a facilitator of efforts to cut a peace deal between the two countries by meeting with the representatives of both sides and also helped keep open the communication channels as well as the trade routes of Iraq and Iran with the outside world. In return for the constructive role that Turkey played in the difficult times of Iraq, the Iraqi leader Saddam Hussein granted Turkey the right to "hot pursuit" of PKK terrorists who used to find refuge in the Syrian territory as well as the Kurdish-dominated northern part of Iraq.

In the period leading up to the invasion of Kuwait by Iraq, dramatic changes were taking place in the Eastern Bloc paving the way to the fall of the Berlin Wall and the collapse of the Warsaw Pact. Similar developments were also expected to take place in the Western Bloc, suggesting the coming of the end of the North Atlantic Alliance. During an official visit of Turkish Premier Yıldırım Akbulut to Iraq, Saddam Hussein was observed to be sarcastic in his comments as well as suggestions as to how Turkey should behave once NATO collapsed. Added to these, rumors about the weapons of mass destruction (WMD) programs of Iraq, and its effort to build the "mother of all weapons," which was halted with the seizure of some of its parts in İstanbul during an antismuggling operation, raised the level of threat perception of Turkish authorities from Iraq and its dictator Saddam Hussein. Thus, when Iraq invaded Kuwait, Turkey was quick to take political, military, and economic countermeasures both unilaterally and along with the international community in conformity with the United Nations Security Council (UNSC) Resolutions.

The rather quick pace of Turkish response to Iraq's invasion of Kuwait was unprecedented in the history of the foreign policy behavior of Turkey. That was due to a number of reasons, one of which was the sequence of quick developments taking place in world politics that had elevated the threat perceptions in the eyes of Turkish authorities. The other, however, was the personality of then Turkish President Turgut Özal who had served also as Prime Minister from 1983 to 1989. Turgut Özal, formerly a top bureaucrat, and then State Minister in charge of improving the economic situation, which had undergone turbulent years in the second half of the 1970s, was known for his pragmatic approach to solving complex problems, thus improving the living conditions of millions of Turkish citizens with the economic and political decisions he had suggested to the Military Council, which governed the country with its supreme authority following the military coup d'état of September 12, 1980 staged by the then Chief of General Staff General Kenan Evren and the Force Commanders in response to the deteriorating anarchic situation in the country. With the decision of the Military Council to restore democratic regime in the country, Özal established the *Anavatan* (Motherland) Party and participated in the first general elections in November 1983 where he received 45 percent of the votes and formed his single party government. During his tenure as Prime Minister, Turgut Özal acted as the most powerful man in domestic politics and also took many foreign policy decisions without necessarily consulting with the relevant institutions in the country, such as the Ministry of Foreign Affairs or the General Staff.

Hence, when Iraq invaded Kuwait, many of the foreign policy decisions of Turkey were taken by President Özal through his telephone diplomacy with the world leaders such as the American President George Bush and the British Prime Minister Margaret Thatcher. For instance, the decision to shut down the oil pipeline between the northern Iraqi city Kirkuk and the eastern Mediterranean port of Turkey in Iskenderun was taken under the leadership of Özal, who used his Presidential right to preside over the Council of Ministers of the Akbulut government. It is interesting to note that the decision to shut down the Kirkuk-Iskenderun pipeline was taken on the day the UNSC adopted the Resolution 661 on August 6, 1990, which decided to impose sanctions on Iraq by asking all states to prevent "the import into their territories of all commodities and products originating in Iraq."

On the military front, President Özal met with then U.S. Secretary of State James Baker during his visit to Ankara. Özal and Baker agreed on the necessity to take military measures against Iraq in close collaboration between the two long-standing allies. The United States asked Turkey to increase the level of its troop concentration along the Iraqi border in order to increase pressure on the Iraqi leader Saddam Hussein who was then seemingly not very much affected from the reactions to his invasion of Kuwait coming from various parts of the world. Both as a preliminary measure against the threats posed by the attitude of the Iraqi leader toward Turkey and to satisfy the expectations of the United States, Turkey decided to increase the level of troop deployment in its southeast. The recent collapse of the Warsaw Pact had eased the degree of the threat perceived from Bulgaria. Thus, approximately 100,000 mechanized troops were transferred from the Bulgarian border to the southeastern part of Turkey, and they were deployed mainly along the Iraqi border.

Implications of the Abolishing of the Soviet Threat

The second development that enabled Turkey to go toward making drastic changes in its force posture was the disintegration of the Soviet Union in December 1991 and the emergence of independent states across Turkey's northeastern border. These historic developments enabled the Turkish security elite to reassess the threats perceived from the region. The elimination of the possibility of a large-scale surprise attack of the Red Army made it unnecessary to allocate the bulk of the Turkish military capabilities toward Soviet Union any more. Maintaining a large army on the northeastern part of Turkey caused a number of difficulties for the Turkish military. The region was mountainous and extremely cold during the long winter seasons with temperatures falling well below the freezing levels such as −50 or even lower. Conducting military maneuvers and the training of hundreds of thousands of Turkish soldiers were not only formidable tasks to achieve but also very costly to finance putting a lot of pressure on the already weak Turkish economy for decades. Hence, the possibility of shifting the military units away from the northeastern frontier was much welcomed both by the political and by the security circles in Turkey.

Implications of Conventional Arms Limitations

The third development that enabled Turkey to divert its military capabilities from the Soviet and Bulgarian borders toward the Iraqi and Syrian borders stems from the implementation of the Conventional Forces in Europe (CFE) Treaty, which entered into force in 1990. The CFE Treaty was negotiated between NATO and the Warsaw Pact countries starting with the Helsinki Process in 1975 and all through the 1980s. The Treaty envisaged drastic cuts in the five categories of conventional force levels of the militaries on both sides of the *Iron*

Curtain.[5] These five categories were main battle tanks, armored personnel vehicles, artilleries, attack helicopters, and combat aircraft. All five categories of these weapons systems, which are highly mobile with high fire power capacity, are essential to launch *blitzkrieg*-type saturation bombing operations. Hence, cutting the numbers of these military capabilities down to lower levels would greatly diminish the possibility of a surprise attack. As such, the "delicate balance of terror" that was achieved between NATO and the Warsaw Pact, thanks to the presence of huge numbers of nuclear weapons in the military arsenals of both sides, would be further enhanced with the elimination of the fear of the possibility of a large-scale surprise attack by either side.

As a consequence of these developments, the military planners in Ankara shifted their attention from Turkey's northern neighbors Bulgaria and the Soviet Union to southern and eastern neighbors Syria, Iraq, and Iran, and redeployed the military units accordingly. In less than a decade, Turkey's troop deployments in the region increased almost fivefold from a figure like 60,000 infantry and gendarmerie troops in the early 1990s and reached a figure like 300,000 in 1998, when a crisis erupted with Syria. Beside the numerical increase, the quality of the troops, including Special Forces, also improved. New equipment such as light and heavy artillery, armored vehicles, and attack helicopters were sent to the region, enabling the military to wage cross-border operations in northern Iraq. These deployments have been possible thanks to an exceptional arrangement in the CFE Treaty that increased Ankara's freedom of action in the region.[6] In the context of the CFE Treaty, most part of Turkey's southeast was left outside of the treaty limitations. This would mean that Turkey would not have to lower dramatically the number of its military assets in the five categories of weapons systems. Moreover, Turkey would also be able to receive some of the excess weaponry from its NATO allies that would have to be dismantled because of the treaty obligations of these countries. Germany, for instance, sent some of its heavy armory to Turkey instead of dismantling them.

New Stance toward Iran and Syria

The increase both in quantity and in quality of Turkish military capabilities in its southeast, neighboring Syria, Iraq, and Iran, enabled Turkey to develop a new stance toward these countries, each of which have been a source of serious concerns with their military capabilities and political intentions.

In the first half of the 1990s, Iran and Turkey have found themselves in a rivalry over the question of who would lead the post-Soviet states that emerged in the Caucasus and Central Asia. Moreover, with the end of the eight-year war with Iraq in 1988, Iranian Mullahs have started to turn their attention to Turkey whose secular democratic regime was perceived as a threat to the Islamic fundamentalist regime in Iran. Turkey's secular elite blamed Iran for supporting religious extremist groups in Turkey. They also held Iran responsible for a series of assassinations that claimed the lives of a number of prominent secular intellectuals who, in their writings and speeches, had pointed out the dangers of the Iranian fundamentalist Mullahs' designs over Turkey. Moreover, Turkish security officials have, on a number of occasions, provided evidence about Iran's logistical support to the PKK terrorists who found refuge on the Iranian side of the border. Turkey and Iran did not have any serious claims over the territory of each other since the Kasr-i Shirin Treaty of 1639 between the Ottomans and the Safavids, nor have they fought each other. But the military capabilities of Iran that comprised chemical and possibly biological weapons stockpiles, serious attempts to acquire advanced and comprehensive nuclear capabilities primarily from Russia and China, and ballistic missile capabilities with ranges over a 1,000 kilometers acquired through intensive collaboration with North Korea have all become major sources of worry for Turkish security elite.

On the other hand, relations with Syria were not very much promising either, primarily due to their documented support to the PKK terrorist organization. The head of the PKK, namely Abdullah Öcalan, was able to run his terror organization from his apartment in Damascus, Syria's capital city. Moreover, Syria had historical claims on Turkey's Hatay province, which was annexed to Turkey in 1939 as a result of the agreement between Turkey and France which was the mandatory power in Syria following the end of World War I. Hatay is still depicted in the official maps of Syria as a Syrian city.[7] In addition to such historical claims, Syria also had claims on the waters of the Euphrates and Tigris rivers originating from Turkey and crossing the Syrian territory in midcourse in its flow down to the Gulf through Iraq. Syria used its privileged position in the Arab League to accuse Turkey of "using water as a weapon" especially in the year 1990 when the flow of the Euphrates had to be cut off for about a month in order to complete the construction of the Atatürk Dam, one of the biggest dams in the world. Even though Turkey warned Syria well in advance to take necessary precautions so as to collect enough water in its reservoirs and also allowed excessive amounts of water prior to the temporary cutoff, Syria preferred to use an inflammatory rhetoric to put pressure on Turkey in the international arena.

Syria, with which Turkey was at odds in the political arena, became a serious case for concern, just like Iraq and Iran, also due to its WMD capability and ballistic missiles as their delivery vehicles. Because Turkey is within the range of ballistic missiles deployed in those neighboring countries, one might expect that in the face of such a threat, Turkey would soon embark on a crash program to develop its own WMD capability. On the contrary, relying on nuclear, biological, or chemical (NBC) weapons development as an effective deterrent or a countermeasure was out of question for Turkey. Rather, Turkey has persistently pursued a policy to become a state party to international nonproliferation agreements that sought to curb the spread of mass destruction weapons and their delivery vehicles.[8]

One particular reason for Turkey to give its utmost support to international efforts spent for strengthening the existing international nonproliferation regimes has been the widespread belief among the Turkish security elite that effective verification mechanisms of NBC nonproliferation treaties might create serious impediments to aspiring states in their engagements with WMD development and thus might provide strong assurances to Turkey in its relations with its neighbors. Thus, in order to counter the threat posed by its Middle Eastern neighbors, Turkey believed that it had a number of advantages. First, Turkey has long relied on the positive security assurances provided by the Atlantic Alliance. NATO's deterrent was considered by Turkey to be effective with respect to the threat posed by NBC-capable states in its immediate neighborhood. Second, Turkey relied on a forward defense strategy (the "land-air doctrine") that was believed to provide enough credibility to deter even unconventional armed attacks from its neighbors.

In the second half of 1990s, the Turkish military has become capable of launching a comprehensive ground operation, on a short notice, with the involvement of tens of thousands of troops fully equipped and mechanized. Added to this, the air power capability can provide the troops on the ground with close air support through F-16 combat aircraft, and Sikorsky and Super Cobra attack helicopters. Early warning aircraft (AWACS—Airborne Warning and Control System) as well as refueling aircraft that entered the inventory of the Turkish Air Force increased both the range and the operational capability of the combat aircraft involved in operations. Hence, the overall operational capability of the ground forces in combination with the air units is considered to give Turkey the capability to conduct large-scale military operation in the territory of the enemy, if need be, in a considerably short time.

Turkey's capability to retaliate was believed to constitute a credible deterrent against its southern neighbors. The impact of the increased troop deployment along southeastern borders of Turkey was clearly felt by the Syrian leadership during the short-lived crisis between the two countries in October 1998. Syria was long being accused by Turkey of giving logistical support to the Armenian terrorist organization ASALA which assassinated many Turkish diplomats and citizens all over the world in the 1970s and early 1980s. ASALA claimed to take the revenge of the so-called "Armenian genocide" allegedly committed by the Ottoman Empire in 1915. ASALA was using the Syrian territory as well as the Lebanese territory under the Syrian control for training and all sorts of other activities, including smuggling of arms and explosives. Syrian authorities have not only denied Turkey's claims on this matter but also refused to cooperate.

Starting from the mid-1980s, in addition to ASALA, Syria has both organized and supported the PKK terrorist organization that waged a separatist movement in Turkey. PKK attacked the villages and killed civilians, including women and children, in mostly the southeastern part of Turkey, which was socioeconomically the least developed province of the country and inhabited heavily by the Kurdish citizens of Turkey. Despite its Kurdish separatist rhetoric, the PKK specifically targeted Kurdish villagers who have not supported their separatist claims. At the beginning, Turkey was caught unprepared to effectively counter such attacks. The security forces had to be reorganized, restructured, and redeployed so as to develop a military capability commensurate with the dimensions of the threat posed by PKK to the security of the citizens and the unity of the nation. Bearing in mind the fact that the primary concern of the military back in the 1980s was the threat perceived from the Soviet Union, the task of conducting counterterrorist operations was left to the Gendarmerie and the Police until after the collapse of the Soviet Union. The attacks of the PKK on the villages and the fighting between the security units and the PKK claimed the lives of tens of thousands of people on both sides over a decade until mid-1990s. The Turkish General Staff took over the responsibility to conduct the counterterrorism campaign since then and brought to an end, albeit temporarily, with the capture of Öcalan, the head of PKK, in February 1999. Getting this result, however, was not easy and brought Turkey and Syria to the brink of war.

Turkey had warned Syria, time and again, on its support to the PKK (and to ASALA previously). Nevertheless, none of Turkey's warnings have been taken seriously by the Syrian authorities throughout the 1980s and 1990s. Whenever a Turkish Prime Minister or a President sent a formal letter to the Syrian leadership requesting to stop its support to the PKK, Hafez Al Assad, then President of Syria, looked at the troop concentration level of the Turkish Army across the border and saw literally nothing that would make him scared of the possibility of a Turkish incursion. Turkey was not able to push the Syrian leadership toward cooperation any further partly because of the lack of enough military capability along the Syrian border that could be put behind the political stance toward Syria and also partly due to the warnings of especially the European members of NATO advising Turkey to stay away from getting involved in any conflict with its Middle Eastern neighbors, due to their fear of escalation to a conflict between NATO and the Warsaw Pact because of the close links of the Soviet Union and Syria.

However, due to the dramatic changes that have occurred with the end of the Cold War period, Turkey's troop concentration and the state of readiness and the level of training of its military were increased considerably. Confident with the ability to put enough military power behind its political claims, Turkey gave a precise ultimatum to Syria in October 1998. The official position of Turkey was publicly announced by the then President Süleyman Demirel during his speech on the opening day of the TGNA on October 1, 1998. Prior to that, General Atilla Ateş, then Commander of the Land Forces, had made statements to that effect in front of the journalists right on the Turkish-Syrian border stressing the fact that Syria's incessant support to the PKK could no more be tolerated. The message from the military and political wings of Turkey was clear: Syria should stop supporting the PKK and should expel Öcalan out of Syria. Close coordination between the top politicians and the Turkish General Staff as well as the proper use of the public diplomacy made it clear that this time Turkey was both ready and capable of coercing Syria to act along the lines of its, indeed decades-old, request.

The severity of the situation was acknowledged both by Syria and by the Arab League. Egyptian President Hosni Mubarak visited both capitals and tried to prevent a war between Turkey and Syria. Hafez Al Assad was a very clever and pragmatic leader. He was aware of the possible consequences of Syria's continuing support to the PKK. Not only was Turkey powerful militarily, but also Syria had lost the support of the Soviet Union. The Russian Federation was neither willing nor capable of taking strong measures against Turkey, with the exception of its nuclear capability. But, it would be a risky and also a far-fetched scenario to expect Russia to threaten Turkey with the use of nuclear forces because of its righteous stance toward Syria.

Considering all these, Syria took a rational decision as expected and expelled Öcalan out of Syria. Öcalan's journey, which had stopovers in Moscow, Rome, and the Greek Embassy in Nairobi, Kenya, ended in a prison in Turkey. Öcalan was given a fair trial and sentenced to life for treason and committing various crimes, including terrorism. Syria signed the "Adana Protocol" later in 1998 with Turkey committing itself not to give any more support to any groups that would damage the national interests of Turkey. Since then, Turkish-Syrian relations have developed considerably in the political domain. Nevertheless, major issues, which have been serious bones of contention between the two states, such as the waters of the Euphrates and the Tigris rivers and the Hatay issue, remain unresolved. Beshar Al Assad assumed the Presidency after the passing of his father Hafez Al Assad and paid a couple of visits to Turkey. When asked, during his official visits, as to how and when the major problems between Turkey and Syria would be solved, Beshar Assad told the journalists "time will solve the problems."

New Era in the Relations with Israel

The desired result from the coercive diplomacy toward Syria was achieved thanks to the timely combination of a number of factors, which were, among others, the careful planning and execution of the steps in the crisis management by the Turkish political and security elite. In addition to the deterrent capability of the Turkish Army and the high degree of cohesion and coordination within the state mechanism, the relations with Israel that had reached its peak around that time had also a significant role to play prior to and during the crisis.

Turkey was among the first states to recognize the State of Israel and to establish diplomatic relations in 1949. Indeed, the relations between the Turks and

Jews go back half a millennium to a time when the Ottoman sultan embraced Jews who were being persecuted and forced to flee Spain in 1492. Jews soon filled the elite ranks of the Ottoman administration and were always loyal to the Sultans. Ottoman Jews also supported the Turkish War of Liberation in the aftermath of World War I. Despite the early establishment of diplomatic relations, Turkey and Israel have not been able to gain much momentum to their bilateral relations due to a number of reasons. The conservative policies and Islamic overtones of the speeches of Prime Minister Adnan Menderes who governed Turkey from 1950 to 1960 did not facilitate the efforts of his Israeli counterpart David Ben Gurion to launch comprehensive relations with Turkey. The Arab-Israeli wars in the 1960s and 1970s, the Organization of the Petroleum Exporting Countries (OPEC) crisis and Turkey's dependency on Arab oil, the Jerusalem Law declaring the Jerusalem to be the capital of Israel, and the Palestinian *Intifada* movement in the 1980s have added further strains on the efforts to advance the relations to a desirable level.

Turkey had to take into consideration the possibility of a boycott by Arab nations in their oil supplies to Turkey, as was the case against the United States because of its intervention in the 1973 "Yom Kippur" war on the side of Israel. It is worth noting at this point that, had Libya not supplied Turkey with fuel oil for the naval vessels and jet fuel for combat aircraft, Turkish Armed Forces (TAF) would have not been able to launch its amphibious "Peace Operation" on Cyprus in July 1974, as a response to a Greek Junta-sponsored coup on the island by the Greek Cypriots.

Similarly, when the Turkish generals staged a military coup d'état on September 12, 1980, as a reaction of the deteriorating situation in domestic politics, which was in steady chaos in the second half of the 1970s, and the high inflation rates in the economy, Turkey faced serious difficulties in injecting financial resources to its economic program from the European capitals who severely criticized the rule of the Military Council in Turkey. The only plausible source to fund the Turkish economy, which was undergoing comprehensive restructuring under the conduct of Özal, was the Arab capital.

Moreover, the high degree of sympathy with the Palestinian cause among the Turkish public, which was increased with the first *Intifada* movement that was launched in 1987, also created serious obstacles in front of the attempts to augment the level, and to enrich the content, of Turkish-Israeli relations during most of the Cold War period.

However, the first Gulf War following the invasion of Kuwait by Iraq, which led to a decisive defeat of the latter, and the "Peace Process" that started between the Arab nations and Israel in its aftermath, both in Madrid and in Oslo, lifted many of the tacit embargoes on the attitude of Turkey toward Israel. There was no reason to be concerned with the possible reactions of the Arab nations to Turkey's intensified relations with Israel while they were meeting with Israel both in the open in Madrid and behind the closed doors in Oslo. Hence, one of the first steps that were taken by Turkey was to elevate the level of representation in Israel to Ambassadorial level, which was lowered to the level of Chargé d'Affairs as a reaction to the "Jerusalem Law" passed in the *Knesset,* the Israeli Parliament, in 1980. Then, a series of reciprocal high-level visits of ministers, prime ministers, and presidents as well as high-ranking military officers of both nations have warmed up the relations considerably.

As a result of the intensified visits of the politicians and the military personnel, Israel and Turkey signed an agreement for military cooperation in 1996. Accordingly, Israel agreed, among others, to upgrade 54 Turkish F-4 class military aircraft and to provide the Turkish Air Force with electronic warfare equipment. The significance of the military cooperation agreement between Turkey and Israel went beyond these usual transactions and reflected a new element of power politics in the Middle East both at operational and at strategic levels. At the operational level, military cooperation with Israel has provided a lot of advantages to Turkey, especially in its fight against PKK terrorism. When in 1991 the United States declared "no-fly-zones" in the northern and the southern parts of Iraq, the PKK started to use the northern Iraqi territory as a safe haven whereby it intensified its attacks on Turkish security forces and the population. Turkey felt the need both to reorganize and to restructure its security forces and also special arms and technological products such as remote sensors, night vision cameras, and the like to properly fight the terrorist organization.

The early 1990s were also the years of great transformations in Europe where concepts like human rights, cultural rights, and ethnic diversity have started to gain supremacy in the political discourse across the continent. The Paris Act of 1990, which was a fundamental document making powerful references to these concepts, was also started to be adopted by all nations in Eastern as well as Western Europe. Similarly, in the United States, Democrat Party came to power with the November 1992 elections. The Clinton administration, like its European counterparts, also paid a lot of attention to the democratic norms and values in its relations with other nations, including Turkey. Some of Turkey's request for military sales were either denied or delayed by the Congress on the ground of the criticisms of especially the Democrat Senators.

Hence, Turkey had encountered serious difficulties in getting support of the European nations, and of the United States, to a lesser degree, in its fight against the PKK. Most Europeans tended to see the PKK terrorism more as a result of "a lack of democratic norms and values in Turkey." Therefore, especially the political interest groups and nongovernmental organizations as well as some political parties such as the "Greens" have started to put pressure on the European governments to put a ban on the arms sales to Turkey. They were concerned with the possibility of use of these arms, if sold to Turkey, against the "Kurdish freedom fighters." Some of these allegations have gone as far away as to assert that if

Norway sold the Penguin missiles to Turkey, the Turkish Army could use them against the Kurds.[9] Beside the irrationality of any such allegations, one has to bear in mind that the Penguin missiles were antiship missiles and they could only be found in the inventory of the navies. Penguin missiles would have no use, if at all, in any counterterrorist operations.

In such an international atmosphere where most of Turkey's allies in NATO have denied critical arms supplies, Israel emerged as a country that could provide all such arms and technical devices that Turkey would need in its fight against the PKK. In addition to arms supplies, Israel also provided Turkey with critical and sound actionable intelligence about the movements and the logistical capabilities of the PKK terrorists. As such, the value of military cooperation with Israel at the operational level has been tremendous and helped Turkey gain the upper hand in the fight against the PKK.

At the strategic level, Turkey and Israel, with the inclusion of the United States, searched for ways to cooperate against the proliferation of WMD in the Middle East. In the late 1990s, the American proposal to establish a "missile shield" in the eastern districts of Turkey at the bilateral level or in the NATO framework or at trilateral level with the inclusion of Israel was seen as indicators of an emerging defense bloc among the three countries. Turkey, Israel, and the United States were expected to join their forces to counter the threat of ballistic missiles that may be tipped with WMD warheads. The military exercises called the "Anatolian Eagle" that took place in central Anatolia in early July 2001 with the participation of air force units of Turkey, Israel, and the United States and the air defense systems of these countries simulated defense as well as combat operations against a comprehensive attack from the air.[10] Such trilateral military exercises have put in place a mechanism for advanced military coordination among Turkey, the United States, and Israel. They contradicted Turkey's previous Cold War policy, which was predicated on noninvolvement in American plans designed specifically to back up Israel. But the threat of WMD and ballistic missiles has made for a fundamental change in the Turkish perspective.

Turkey's efforts to build up its deterrent posture in the Middle East through cooperation with Israel actually constituted a prudent measure and the surest way to reduce risks that might develop along Turkey's southern frontiers. The military cooperation with Israel was not simply a matter of technology transfer for Turkey. There was a mutual interest in the technological side, but Israel had its own peculiar security needs, and Turkey would have to seek to accommodate them, if it wished to derive maximum benefit from the relationship. While Turkey needed technology, Israel needed space. Israel has nuclear capabilities and also developed a missile shield based on the Arrow. But the deployment of Israel's nuclear arsenal turned out to be problematic, and a large-scale ballistic missile attack can penetrate Israel's shield and cause thousands of casualties. Because of Israel's small size, the density of its population, and the concentration of its military facilities, the penetration of its air defenses by even a single missile tipped with a chemical, biological, or nuclear warhead could wreak immense damage. As a result, Israel sought the capacity to destroy enemy missiles before their launch or soon thereafter. But Israel faced geographic limitations in taking timely and effective action against missiles launched far away or launched at very high velocity. The task would be far more difficult without a forward defense capability. This was precisely what Israel sought from Turkey in the 1990s.

Turkish airspace borders that of Iran, Iraq, and Syria. Were any of these countries preparing to launch missiles against Israel, then Israel could come to Turkey with a request to fly through Turkish airspace to deliver preemptive or preventive strikes against ballistic missile launching sites. In the late 1990s, Israel's capabilities were fighter-based, but it was procuring long-range bombers that could do the job from high altitudes.[11] Israel could call on Turkish space for another purpose. Because Israel is so small, it needs offshore strategic depth to sustain a credible and secure second-strike capability. In the event of a crisis, it would need foreign safe havens for its submarines and surface ships, and Turkey was perfectly positioned to provide them. The basis for this kind of cooperation had already been laid. According to the 1996 agreement of military cooperation, each country could deploy or temporarily station their land, air, and naval force units in the other country's territory. For that purpose, they could use one another's airspace, airports, and naval ports. As such, while Turkey looked to Israel to bolster its strategic deterrent, it expected Israel to seek a "virtual strategic depth" in return.

TURKEY AND THE TURKIC WORLD: HOPE AND DESPAIR

The collapse of the Eastern Bloc and the disintegration of the Soviet Union in the early 1990s paved the way to the emergence of a "Turkic world" composed of newly independent states, which were hitherto known as Soviet republics, namely Azerbaijan, Turkmenistan, Uzbekistan, Kyrgyzstan, and Kazakhstan, as well as the former Yugoslav republics such as Bosnia-Herzegovina and Macedonia. The historical, cultural, and religious common denominators between these newly independent states and Turkey brought about a new type of political discourse among the Turkish politicians, statesmen, and the public alike. Statements referring to a Turkic world "from the Adriatic to the Chinese Wall" have started to be heard here and there, not necessarily with a clear-cut definition as to what exactly was meant with such a discourse. There was, however, logic to such a geographical connotation used because Albania and Bosnia-Herzegovina, where Turkish minorities and Muslim populations are living, are on the Adriatic Sea, and Kazakhstan and Kyrgyzstan are neighboring China. Nevertheless, the meaning of such a discourse went beyond simply identifying places where Turks or populations of Turkish or Muslim origins were living. What was implied with this statement was rather a zone of influence, or a hinterland, of Turkey. Probably with the confidence of having ruled much of these territories in the past and also due to the disappearance of the powerful authorities of the oppressive regimes like Yugoslavia and the Soviet Union, many Turks thought Turkey could reassert its influence on these territories. However, there were a number of difficulties associated with reestablishing relations with the Turkic world.

Problems Encountered in the Relations with the Turkic World

One of the problems that Turkey encountered in its relations with the Turkic world was the powerful impact of the Socialist regimes in the Soviet Union and Yugoslavia had on the cultures, identities, and the belief systems of the populations that they governed for many decades. Particularly in the Soviet Union, starting from the 1920s, transformation of the non-Russian societies in the Caucasus and Central Asia has been one of the principal applications of the Soviet Union. All sorts of measures have been taken especially during the 30-year dictatorship of Josef Stalin as the Secretary-General of the Soviet Communist Party. Religion was banned, social and cultural peculiarities of the communities forming the Soviet Union society were disregarded, several ethnic groups such as the Tartars of Crimea were dislocated or forced to get mixed with other ethnic groups. The list of negative social engineering applications in the former Soviet Union can be further extended. Because of decades of alienation to their own cultures and identities as well as imposition of a value-free socialist culture that aimed at eradicating various religious beliefs had a devastating impact on the social and cultural fabric of these Caucasian and Central Asian populations. It would, therefore, be unrealistic to expect from these people to realize all of a sudden that they were emancipated from the scourge of the oppressive Soviet regime and that it was now the time to go back to their cultural and religious roots. Turks had to understand that it would take much more time than they had anticipated reestablishing the ties between the Turks of Turkey and the citizens of the newly independent states of Turkic and Muslim origin. Moreover, during the Soviet rule, many Russians were sent either to the Soviet republics to live there in order to strike a balance between the Russian and local populations or to fill in the ranks of governmental agencies of the non-Russian Soviet republics. For instance, the percentage of Russian-origin citizens of Kazakhstan was either equal or more than the Kazakh-origin citizens. Hence, the Turkic character of the republics was further diluted.

A second problem that Turkey encountered in its approach to the Turkic world was the frustration of the non-Russian populations with the seven-decade-old Soviet rule interfering with almost all aspects of their cultures. Once earned their independence from the Soviet Union, the newly established sovereign states were not very much enthusiastic or even ready to enter under the influence of another power regardless of its identity or intentions. Hence, Turkey's desire to "lead" the

Turkic world as a "big brother" was indeed not very much welcome among these states. It took a while for Turkish authorities to figure this out and to leave the rhetoric of "big brother."

A third issue that had to be dealt with in the relations with the Turkic world was the lack of a culture of free market economy in the former Soviet Socialist republics with which Turkey wanted to establish strong economic ties. There was an influx of Turkish businessmen who rushed to these countries, which were said to be very rich in natural resources and therefore perceived as promising markets for Turkish goods and services. However, due to the lack of a cadre of educated and skilled personnel from the regional states who would be qualified to get involved in matters like business administration, marketing, and the like, many of the hasty attempts to properly exploit the economic opportunities that emerged in the region have failed to achieve their goals and even went bankrupt. Corruption and abuse were also among the by-products of several years of experience of doing business with the region. Only the big Turkish holdings or multinational corporations that had offices in Turkey have been patient enough to enter these new markets rather slowly with a long-term plan first by preparing the ground and building a cadre of professionals both drawn from the local populations and sent from Turkey to the region and have been successful in achieving their business objectives.

A fourth major problem that Turkey faced in its relations with the Turkic world was the limit of its financial resources and capabilities in terms of meeting the economic as well as political expectations of the Turkic world. One of the primary desires of the people of the Caucasian and the Central Asian states was to improve their economic situation, which was in shambles right after the disintegration of the Soviet Union. They needed new goods and services as well as fresh financial resources that would enable them to sustain a decent life. However, the economic and financial capabilities that Turkey had in the early 1990s were limited. Moreover, in the same period, Turkey's fight against the PKK entered a new phase and intensified due to the safe havens that the PKK terrorists had found in northern Iraq by means of the "no-fly-zones" enforced by the United States against Saddam Hussein's military. The cost of PKK terrorism to Turkey, especially in the 1990s, is difficult to calculate. In addition to the loss of thousands of lives, there are estimates suggesting that terrorism cost Turkey at least a hundred billion dollars over a decade until the capture of the head of PKK Abdullah Öcalan on February 15, 1999. While on the one hand Turkey had to sacrifice the lives of its citizens and security forces as well as billions of dollars every year in its fight against terrorism, it would be far too ambitious a scenario for Turkey to be able to sponsor many of the economic activities of the newly independent Turkic states. Hence, many of the promises made by the Turkish politicians, businessmen, and others who have visited the region could not be kept primarily because of the economic difficulties that Turkey has undergone. Added to these was the disappointment with the slow progress that the newly independent states made especially in the area of exploitation of their mineral resources. Moreover, it was eventually understood that some of the forecasts about the magnitude of the resources or the reserves available were either exaggerated or it would be more costly and less feasible to invest than what was anticipated beforehand.

Similar problems have been experienced in the relations with the former Yugoslav republics that earned their independence at a much higher price. Atrocities of the Serbian military against the Muslim communities who used to live in peace and harmony during the presidency of Josif Tito have later on been subject to massacres in the hands of the Serbian military. In the face of the tragedy suffered by the Turkish and Muslim minorities in Bosnia and Kosovo, Turkey's ability to stop the atrocities was very limited. The most Turkey could do was to mobilize as much international support as possible to its efforts to bring the issue before the United Nations as well as NATO and to push for preventive measures to be put in place. However, the international community did not display a similar degree of genuine interest in the tragedy in the Balkans (or the massacres in Rwanda) as they did in the invasion of Kuwait. It was obvious that the Balkans could not offer much precious resources just like Kuwait in return for external intervention to save the lives of thousands of people who would be killed by the aggressor. Whereas it took only a few days to identify the "aggressor," as spelled out in Article 39 of the United Nations Charter, when Iraq invaded Kuwait, the world community, especially the West, was reluctant to determine the aggression of Serbia, which would be a prelude to any military action that would be authorized by the UNSC. The West rather preferred to see the fighting that was going on in the former Yugoslavia as a normal outcome of a "civil war." Thus, the West sought no reason to interfere with the "domestic affairs" of Yugoslavia.

The attitude of the West has changed and the Western powers enforced a peaceful resolution only after the pace of events went beyond the morally acceptable boundaries. A peace treaty that was brokered by the U.S. diplomat Richard Holbrooke after lengthy negotiations was signed in Dayton, Ohio in the United States on December 14, 1995 by Bosnian leader Izetbegovic, Serbian leader Milosevic, and the Croat leader Tudjman. Following the Dayton Peace Treaty, NATO forces were deployed in Bosnia so as to keep peace in the region. Turkey undertook significant role in the peacekeeping operations with the participation of significant number of troops. A similar process was experienced later in the 1990s when Serbs have turned their attention to the Kosovars who sought independence from Serbia. When Serbs resumed fire this time against the ethnic Albanians, constituting approximately 90 percent of the population in Kosovo, and the peace negotiations failed, NATO interfered with a military operation on March 24, 1999. Turkey participated in the air operations with a squadron of military aircraft which undertook a number of missions, such as reconnaissance and escorting, other than bombing Serbian targets. The reason why Turkish military aircraft did not participate in the bombing operations actively was because of the considerations given to the possible negative impact that such an act might have on the future pace of the relations between Turkey and Serbia once this tragic incident would be left behind eventually.

Against this background, it becomes obvious that Turkey would unavoidably encounter problems in its dealings with the Turkic world extending "from the Adriatic to the Chinese Wall," a huge region encompassing a lot many problems, each of which would hardly be managed by a single country no matter whom. Even if Turkey did not approach the developments taking place in these regions from an emotional perspective, it would have to be concerned with them by any means because the population of Turkey is a mixture of many descendants of the members of the Ottoman society who lived on these lands for centuries. It was, therefore, virtually impossible for Turkey to remain aloof from what was going on in the Balkans, in the Caucasus, or in the Middle East. What was needed, however, was a well-thought and well-planned long-term policy that would have to be drawn up with the contributions coming from all of the concerned parties and the institutions in the country whose inputs would lead to a consensus document and one that would serve as a guideline for all those who would be interested in intensifying relations with the Turkic world.

Importance of the Strong Ties with the Turkic World

Despite the failure to create as much powerful impact as it was hoped at the beginning of the 1990s on the Turkic world, Turkey can still be said to have achieved a non-negligible progress in advancing the level of its political, economic, and cultural relations with the newly established states in the Balkans, the Caucasus, and Central Asia. Had Turkey set its expectations at a more reasonable level at the beginning, the pace of its relations since then may have been considered even more than satisfactory. Against all the odds, all through these years, Turkey pursued several objectives in its relations with especially the former Soviet republics.

The first of these objectives was to help the newly independent states consolidate their regimes that would enable them to stand on their own feet. As such, they would be able to resist the potential claims of Russia in the future to revive the former Union in a different format. Besides being a powerful trauma for the Russians to lose their "empire" almost overnight, the extent of the economic integration of the Soviet republics required a certain degree of cooperation and coordination even after the demise of the Union. For instance, agricultural products grown in one of the Soviet republics were processed in another republic. Similarly, the raw materials of some industrial products were found in one republic whereas processed and produced in another republic. There was also a high degree of permeation within the societies of the Soviet republics in terms of national, cultural, or ethnic backgrounds. After all they were all "Soviet" citizens, but spread all over the 15 republics of the Soviet Union. Therefore, it was literally impossible to break up with one another all of a sudden. Moreover, the Russian Federation, which inherited the privileges of the Soviet Union, such as the Permanent Member seat in the UNSC and the Nuclear Weapons State status stemming from the Nuclear Nonproliferation Treaty (NPT) of 1968, was militarily the most powerful one among the new independent states. Hence, Russia used its leverages in order to keep a loose confederation of states that would enable it to sustain the required level of political and economic interactions among the former Soviet republics. Attempts to establish a Commonwealth of Independent States (CIS) or declare the "near-abroad" doctrine were all manifestations of this kind of thinking. Nearly two decades after the collapse of the Soviet Union, neither the Soviet republics have been successful in achieving their goal to stand on their own feet, which was adamantly supported by Turkey as well, nor has Russia been able to set the rules of the game in regional politics all by itself. The coming of the United States to the region, especially after the terrorist attacks of September 11, 2001 on the World Trade Center in New York and the Pentagon in Washington, D.C., made it difficult for Russia to realize some of its political objectives. The current state of affairs in the region, from Turkey's perspective, can be categorized as good enough, with few exceptions like the Armenian occupation of 20 percent of the Azerbaijani territory in Nagorno-Karabakh, the Russian proxy involvement in Georgia's domestic affairs, and again the Russian influence of the ultimate decisions taken with respect to the oil and natural gas deliveries out of the region.

The second objective pursued by Turkey in its relations with the newly independent states in Caucasia and Central Asia has been to secure its energy requirements. Azerbaijan, Turkmenistan, and Kazakhstan are known for their huge amounts of oil and natural gas reserves. Turkey wanted to exploit its close ties with these states in finalizing profitable deals in the area of establishing pipelines through its territory that would end up in Turkey or continue toward Europe. As such, Turkey hoped to become an energy hub by installing the necessary terminals where the Kazakh or Azerbaijani oil or the Turkmen gas would be sold to the European and other customers. Turkey also wished to use the strategic value of such undertakings for elevating its position in the eyes of the members of the EU with which negotiations for full membership continue. Some achievements have been recorded such as the construction of the Baku-Tbilisi-Ceyhan (BTC) oil pipeline which crosses the territory of Azerbaijan, Georgia, and Turkey. The pipeline, which is also called the "Silk Road of the 21st Century," started to operate on July 13, 2006, nearly 15 years after the first blueprints were drawn. The strategic significance of this much delayed project stems not from its economic value but more from being a catalyst in further enhancing and consolidating the relations between all three nations. The economic value of the project may become significant only if, and when, the Kazakh oil is also connected to the pipeline. Just like the natural gas pipeline project, which has not gone beyond making promises by the Turkmen leaders to their Turkish counterparts that "the project will be realized soon," the possibility of connecting the Kazakh oil to the BTC in a foreseeable future is not very likely due to the strategies pursued by the Russian leadership. Russia wants to become and remain the major oil and gas supplier at the global scale. Therefore, Russian authorities do not spare a chance to use their influence of all sorts on the Central Asian states to cut the ultimate deal with Russia, regardless of the promises they may have made to others, including Turkey. As such, Turkey's dependency on the Russian-supplied oil and gas (possibly originally bought from Turkmenistan and Kazakhstan at much lower prices) will grow considerably. This is, of course, not the desired solution to Turkey's energy problems.

The third fundamental objective of Turkey in intensifying its relations with the Turkic world, both in the former Soviet landscape and in the Balkans, is to get as much support to Turkey's foreign and security policy issues in the international arena as possible. Lobbying and image making are not necessarily the types of businesses that Turks are said to be very successful at. Except for sporadic improvements, on the average Turkey is among the countries whose image is not very promising in the West and in the Middle East. There are, of course, some explanations for such a situation. The Ottoman Empire had ruled dozens of different ethnic and religious communities on three continents for hundreds of years. There are some 40 independent states at present that emerged from the territories of the Ottoman Empire. It would be a bit optimistic to expect the descendants of the communities formerly ruled by an empire to have very positive images of the ruler (i.e., the Ottomans) and/or its successor state (i.e., Turkey) either. In addition to the memories of the past, recent rivalries of Turkey with some of its neighbors such as Greece and Armenia, on the one hand, who have very powerful lobbies in the Western capitals, and Syria and Iraq, on the other, who have long been able to influence the Arab League nations, also have negatively contributed to the perception of Turkey as a country which was constantly bullying its neighbors. On top of all these, a number of political developments such as the interventions of the military in domestic politics in almost a steady 10-year intervals, starting with 1960 coup d'état resulting in the execution of the then Prime Minister Adnan Menderes together with the Foreign Minister Fatin Rüştü Zorlu and Minister of Finance Hasan Polatkan in the Menderes Cabinet. The military intervened also in 1971, 1980, and 1997. These interventions, regardless of their rationale behind, such as "preserving the unitary and secular character of the Republic," have cast serious doubts on the level of democracy in Turkey in the eyes of most of its Western allies.

Similarly, in many Western capitals, Turkey's fight against the PKK terrorism is usually considered to be a result of a lack of enough democratic practice in the country. Most Europeans and also many Americans tend to believe that "had Turkey granted its Kurdish citizens the right to enjoy their ethnic and cultural differences, Kurds would not have started an armed struggle against the central authority." This kind of an approach presupposes that the Kurds living in Turkey are a minority group in the Turkish society. This is not at all the case. The minority status is defined in the Lausanne Treaty, the founding documents of the Republic of Turkey. Accordingly, the non-Muslim citizens of Turkey, namely the Armenian Christian, Greek-Roman Orthodox, and the Jewish citizens, are granted the minority status as well as rights and privileges. The rest of Turkish citizens have equal Constitutional rights and liabilities, and they are treated equally before law. Kurds, or other citizens of Turkey from diverse ethnic origins, have not been subject to discrimination in entertaining their rights and opportunities. There is indeed no tradition in Turkey to ask one's ethnic origin for any purpose such as recruiting employees or appointing bureaucrats or else. Therefore, it is not possible to know for sure as to who is from which ethnic background specifically. Considering that there have been many mixed marriages among the populations who lived in the Ottoman lands for many centuries and in Turkey later on, it is virtually impossible to trace one's ethnic affiliations for more than a few generations back and to find people coming purely from one ethnic race. That would be a futile exercise. Yet, there is some common knowledge about some of the prominent personalities in Turkish politics such as the former Presidents Cemal Gürsel and Turgut Özal and the former Speaker of the TGNA Hikmet Çetin are known for being of Kurdish origin. Ministers, high-ranking bureaucrats, generals, community leaders, artists, scholars, and intellectuals who have had foremost positions in the Turkish society are of various ethnic backgrounds, including Kurdish. But, they are seen by the entire population as a richness of the Turkish society. Hence, associating a group of terrorists, only a fraction of whom are from Turkey and of Kurdish origin, with honorable Kurdish citizens of Turkey is very much simplification of a very complex issue like the PKK terrorism that has its roots both in history and outside of Turkey as much as inside.

Turkey needs to approach the issue of improving its image and also explaining properly its position vis-à-vis the international political developments very seriously in order to be able to attain its political and diplomatic goals in the international arena. Emergence of a Turkic world can be seen as an opportunity to mobilize support to Turkey's foreign policy issues and also to promote projects that may help improve regional peace, security, and stability. There are remarkable examples in this regard. For instance, the Black Sea Economic Cooperation (BSEC) Organization, which was initiated by Turkey in the beginning of the 1990s, has managed over the years to achieve the goal, among others, to become a platform where most difficult regional political, economic, and military issues between the rivals could be discussed around a table with high-level participation of representatives from the Balkans to the Central Asia. Turkey also played a very constructive role in making the newly independent states full or associate members of international organizations such as the Council of Europe and NATO.

There are, of course, limits to what Turkey can accomplish in mobilizing the support of the Turkic world. The new sovereign nations are also subject to international law and international regimes that may have constraining effects on their foreign policy decisions. For instance, the UNSC Resolutions concerning the Cyprus issue is one such factor that prohibits the realization of some of the collaborative projects between these nations and the self-proclaimed Turkish Republic of Northern Cyprus, which is recognized only by Turkey. Such limitations notwithstanding, at least the value of the moral support that Turkey receives from a wide geographical region extending "from the Adriatic to the Chinese Wall" cannot be underestimated, and it may be a reminder of what Turkey should do in order to realize some of its ideals that might contribute more to the maintenance of peace and security in its region as well as in the rest of the world.

NOTES

1. Authors' conversations with Turkish military experts in 1996.

2. "Hocali Massacre," *L'Actuel: Online Newspaper,* http://www.lactuel.be/detail.php?id=3103.

3. Mustafa Kibaroğlu, "Impact of the Northern Tier on the Middle East: A Rejoinder," *Security Dialogue* 27, no. 3 (September 1996): 319–24.

4. Mustafa Kibaroğlu, "Turkey," in *Europe and Nuclear Disarmament,* ed. Harald Müller (Brussels: European Interuniversity Press, 1998), 161–93.

5. Richard A. Falkenrath, "The CFE Flank Dispute: Waiting in the Wings," *International Security* 19, no. 4 (1995): 118–44.

6. Ali L. Karaosmanoğlu and Mustafa Kibaroğlu, "Defense Reform in Turkey," in *Post-Cold War Defense Reforms: Lessons Learned in Europe and the United States,* ed. Istvan Gyarmati and Theodor Winkler (New York: East West Institute, Brassey's, 2003), 135–64.

7. See http://www.syriatourism.org.

8. Turkey is a state party to international treaties like the NPT, the Chemical Weapons Convention (CWC), the Biological and Toxin Weapons Convention (BTWC), and the Comprehensive Test Ban Treaty (CTBT). See Kibaroğlu, "Turkey," 161–93. Also see Duygu B. Sezer, "Turkey's New Security Environment, Nuclear Weapons and Proliferation," *Comparative Strategy* 14, no. 2 (1995): 149–73.

9. Conversations with high-ranking Turkish military officers in 1998.

10. Ed Blanche, "Israel and Turkey Look to Extend Their Influence into Central Asia," *Janes Intelligence Review,* August 2001, 34.

11. Conversations with Efraim Inbar, Director of Begin-Sadat Center for Strategic Studies, Bar-Ilan University, Ankara, June 2001.

CHAPTER 5

Turkey's Foreign and Security Policies in the Post–Cold War Period: *The Alliances*

The impact of the end of the Cold War period on Turkey's foreign and security policies was felt not only in the bilateral relations with its neighbors but also in the long-standing institutional affiliations with the EU and NATO. Western European countries wanted to seize the opportunity that emerged out of a series of dramatic events taking place in Central and Eastern European countries, which resulted in the collapse of the Warsaw Pact and the disintegration of the Soviet Union. Hence, the idea of deepening and enlarging the European integration toward the east to embrace as much European nations as possible has gained prominence in the EU circles. There were, however, political, military, economic, financial, social, and cultural dimensions of the process of expansion of the European integration. The political and military dimensions of the enlargement process were probably the most delicate ones that had to be handled with utmost care, because most of the Central and Eastern European nations such as Poland, the Czech Republic, Slovakia, Hungary, Lithuania, Latvia, and Estonia, which were envisaged to become members of the EU soon, were used to belong to the Warsaw Pact or to the Soviet Union. These countries were still heavily concerned with the possible consequences of the negative reaction of the Russian Federation to EU's eastward enlargement because the European integration process would be realized at the expense of the disintegration of what was left of the Russian zones of influence in Central and Eastern Europe. Anticipating the difficulties of eastward expansion, Western European members of NATO, which were also the leading members of the EU, wished to use the Alliance as a shield against the possible responses of Russia. Thus, the prospective members of the EU in Central and Eastern Europe and in the Baltic region were first invited to join NATO.

The collapse of the Warsaw Pact had also brought with it questions about the future of the North Atlantic Alliance. In the absence of the Warsaw Pact and the Soviet Union, the possibility of a confrontation between the military blocs was eliminated. Thus, it was argued that the *raison d'être* of NATO had disappeared. But, since nowhere in the text of the founding document of the Alliance (i.e., Washington Treaty of 1949) was there any country specifically mentioned as the enemy, the disappearance of the Warsaw Pact and the Soviet Union did not automatically require the termination of the mission that was successfully accomplished by NATO for decades. NATO's mission during the Cold War was to protect the "Western lifestyle" (i.e., democratic regimes and market economies) against armed attacks from outside. Abolishing of the communist threat, however, took place at almost the same time when new threats and challenges to Western lifestyle were on the steep rise. New threats and challenges were identified as ethnic, religious, and sectarian conflicts in the immediate neighborhood of the EU, as well as international terrorism that recognized no boundaries. Under these circumstances, NATO was welcomed to survive provided that the Alliance could adapt itself to the new political and military environment and the challenges arising thereof. This time, NATO's area of responsibility would go beyond the territories of its traditional members in Western Europe and North America, especially after the terrorist attacks on September 11, 2001.

REDEFINITION OF TURKEY'S PLACE IN EUROPE

Since the end of the Cold War, NATO has undergone a comprehensive transformation process, including several rounds of expansion toward the former Warsaw Pact countries. NATO's eastward expansion also perfectly coincided with the EU's policy to enlarge toward the east. As a result of the developments taking place in Central and Eastern Europe, the Western European countries and the United States have started to assign a much greater importance to the transition process in these countries from communist regimes to open democratic societies. Hence, the abolishing of the communist threat emanating from the excessive military capabilities of the Warsaw Pact and the Soviet Union has diminished the geostrategic and the geopolitical value of Turkey in the eyes of most European and American analysts. Therefore, Turkey's relations with its long-standing allies in Europe and in North America had to be redefined.

Turkey's Relations with Western Europe in Retrospect

Turkey's relations with Europe have usually been problematic due to a long history of confrontation since the Ottoman times. A series of battles between the European armies and the Ottoman army resulting in the establishment of a Turkish rule in the European territories, especially in the fifteenth through the seventeenth centuries, have left deep traces in the minds of both sides. The siege of Vienna, the heart of the Austrian Habsburg Monarchy, in 1529 and 1532, is still remembered by the European politicians who, from time to time, make references to this event when they try to explain the sources of difficulties experienced in the bilateral relations. The orientation of the young Republic of Turkey toward the West and the manifold attempts to improve bilateral relations have yielded positive results during the Presidency of Atatürk. Later on, Turkey's policy of "nonbelligerency" during World War II under the Presidency of İsmet İnönü and the eventual membership of Turkey in NATO in 1952 have given boost to the relations with the West. Turkey's geopolitical and geostrategic importance has been an essential factor in determining both the scope and the content of this relationship. Yet, political and economic developments in Europe and in Turkey have also greatly affected the pace of relations throughout the Cold War period and in its aftermath.

Turkey's Relations with Western Europe in the 1960s

When in 1957 the EEC was established with the signing of the Treaty of Rome, Turkey displayed its interest in the idea of being part of the European integration. Greece's application to the EEC in 1959 for Associate Membership urged Turkey to follow suit immediately. Ankara Treaty was signed between the EEC and Turkey in 1963, which gave Turkey a perspective for full membership. It was interesting to note that the same European nations had dragged their feet to admit Turkey in NATO at the beginning. France and the United Kingdom, in particular, had suggested that Turkey undertake a role within a separate security structure composed of the Middle Eastern nations. The United States, however, had a different role in mind for Turkey within the context of its *Containment* policy toward the Soviet Union. Turkey's heroic performance during the Korean War, between 1950 and 1953, shoulder to shoulder with the American soldiers, was presented by the United States to the European members of the Alliance as a proof of what Turkey could do for the defense of the North Atlantic Area. Hence, a decade later, Western European nations did not object to Turkey's application to the EEC for Associate Membership.

The early 1960s were indeed interesting years from the perspective of both Turkey and Western Europe. A military coup d'état took place in Turkey on May 27, 1960, resulting in the execution of Prime Minister Adnan Menderes, Foreign Minister Fatin Rüştü Zorlu, and the Minister of Finance Hasan Polatkan. In the international arena, Turkey also faced serious challenges, such as the Greek Cypriot attempt in 1963 to change the founding Constitution of the Republic of Cyprus, which was established in 1960 under the guarantorship of the United Kingdom, Turkey, and Greece. Turkey's reaction to the Greek Cypriot *fait accompli* with a limited air operation over the island, however, prompted the bitter letter of the U.S. President Lyndon Johnson to İsmet İnönü, who was then Prime Minister, reminding Turkey that such acts would not be tolerated by the rest of the North Atlantic Alliance.

Against all these odds, Turkey's application to the EEC on July 31, 1959 to become an Associate Member, only two months after the application of Greece, was accepted, and the Ankara Treaty was signed on September 12, 1963. By giving a membership perspective to the Turks, Europeans thought that intensification of Turkey's ties with the West would help consolidate its transition to a more democratic regime within the framework of the political and economic institutions of Europe. But, it would not be wrong to argue that Turkey's geopolitical and geostrategic importance provided a much greater incentive for the Western European members of NATO to accept the application of Turkey, because, in the 1960s, NATO was undergoing a dramatic shift in its strategy from "massive retaliation" to "flexible response," as far as the Soviet threat was concerned, placing more emphasis on the conventional capabilities of the Alliance.

In the 1950s, the strategy of "massive retaliation" was thought by the United States to deter Soviet aggression with the threat of use of disproportionate amount of force in retaliation. Massive retaliation strategy relied heavily on the nuclear weapons capability of the United States, which was at the time far more superior to that of the Soviet Union. Nevertheless, American preponderance in the nuclear weapons area could not stop the Soviet designs on the Korean Peninsula. In order to prevent a similar event, especially in Western Europe, the Eisenhower administration in the United States adopted the massive retaliation doctrine, which had a number of caveats, too. First and foremost, in case of a Soviet aggression with conventional weapons, the U.S. president would be left with no option other than retaliating with nuclear weapons that would have devastating effects. The political and moral responsibility of such a decision would be very costly. Secondly, since no clear-cut threshold was declared by the United States regarding the level of Soviet aggression, neither the Soviet nor the American leadership would have a clear idea as to whether the attack of the Soviets would be responded with U.S. nuclear weapons. In the absence of clarity of minds on either side, the Soviets could very well be panicked, and with the anticipation of a likely American nuclear retaliation, under the pressure of "use it or lose it" principle, they could preempt in using their nuclear forces against the United States, while the latter might have made no such decision.

The massive retaliation strategy was also open to misinterpretation, misperception, and miscalculation, thus carrying the risk of leading to an inadvertent nuclear warfare whose effects could be catastrophic. Bearing these in mind, especially in the wake of the Cuban Missile Crisis of 1962, the Kennedy administration developed the "flexible response" strategy, which envisaged responding to a possible Soviet aggression with proportionate military power.

Hence, if the Soviets launched an offensive with conventional forces, NATO would respond in kind by resorting to its conventional forces. But, if the Soviets went one level up and used their tactical nuclear weapons, then NATO would retaliate in kind with its tactical nuclear weapons, and so on. The flexible response strategy adopted first by the United States soon became the prevailing strategy of the North Atlantic Alliance.

The underlying principle of the flexible response doctrine was to retard the pace of developments during a crisis situation so as to gain more time for diplomacy to solve the differences short of use of armed forces, especially nuclear weapons. Turkey's geostrategic location and its military force posture was perfectly suitable to play a significant role to retard or to diminish the scale of a possible Soviet offensive on Western Europe. With the bulk of its military capabilities deployed toward the Soviet border, Turkey managed to tie-down hundreds of thousands of Soviet troops in the Caucasus, making it difficult for the Red Army to launch a decisive attack on Western Europe through the West German territory. Thus, giving a membership perspective to Turkey in its pursuit to become a part of the Western European integration would enhance the position of Turkey vis-à-vis its colossal neighbor in the east.

Turkey's Relations with Western Europe in the 1970s

The positive mood in Europe toward Turkey has started to change in the 1970s, mainly due to two major factors. First was the domestic political developments in Turkey. In 1971, the Turkish military intervened in politics for the second time by issuing a memorandum publicly, which harshly criticized the Süleyman Demirel government for its conduct of economic and political affairs in the country. In response to the generals' memorandum, Prime Minister Demirel resigned promptly, with a view to preventing a possible coup d'état similar to the one that took place only 11 years ago. The reaction of the Western European countries, which were already very critical about the role of the Turkish military in domestic politics, this time was rather harsh in their stance toward Turkey. A series of short-lived caretaker governments governed Turkey for a few years. Even after the general elections in 1974, the political turmoil in the country yielded three-party coalition governments one after another. The mere fact that a total of 14 governments were formed in Turkey during the 1970s should be an indicator of the political chaos in the country.

The second factor was the Détente period, which had eased the tension between the East and the West, reducing the reliance of Western Europe on the flank countries, such as Turkey, which would have to absorb the first wave of attack that could be launched by the Soviet Union. Even though the strategic importance of Turkey for the United States remained pretty much the same because of the extent of its interest toward the region from a much wider perspective, including the Middle East and the Gulf regions, Western European states saw no merit in promoting Turkey's position in Europe any further.

The first half of the 1970s had also witnessed two major developments in the international arena. One was the lowering of the production quotas and raising the price of oil by the OPEC, most important of which were Arab countries, in the aftermath of the Yom Kippur War in October 1973. The war was fought between Israel and the coalition of Arab states led by Egypt and Syria. Saudi Arabia imposed oil embargo against the United States and the Netherlands because of helping Israel during the war. The price of oil quadrupled shortly after, putting excessive pressure on the treasuries of the European states, which were heavily dependent on the oil imported from the Gulf region. Hence, the Western Europeans have turned inward and became heavily concerned with their economic problems.

The other development was Turkey's military intervention in Cyprus in July 1974 against the coup staged by the Greek Cypriot extreme nationalists, encouraged by the military Junta in Athens, who wished to annex the island to Greece. The armed conflict between the Turkish Army and the Greek Cypriot National Guard lasted for about a month with an intermission and finally came to a halt thanks to the United Nations–sponsored cease-fire. Even though Greece did not actively involve in fightings on the island, some confrontations took place on the Aegean Sea and in the air. As a reaction to the inactivity of NATO to take any action to prevent Turkey from launching an amphibious operation on the island, Greece withdrew from the military wing of the Alliance. Although failed to punish Turkey through the Alliance, Greece managed to mobilize its powerful lobby in the U.S. Senate to impose an arms embargo on Turkey between 1975 and 1978 during the Jimmy Carter administration.

These developments have further deteriorated the standing of Turkey vis-à-vis its bid for membership in the European institutions. Added to these was the strong disagreement between Turkey and the Western European states over the terms of the Customs Union Treaty, which would be the ultimate stage in the process of Turkey's integration to Europe. In 1971 Turkey had signed the Additional Protocol, which would regulate the transition to the customs union between Turkey and the EEC. This process has created a lot of difficulties in Turkey where the economy was far from being competitive with foreign goods and services. Hence, economic policies in Turkey, long-based on import substitution, made it extremely difficult to get the consent of the private sector as well as most of the public sector to put into effect the rules and regulations within the context of the customs union that would have to govern the Turkish economy in the years ahead.

Economic difficulties that were experienced in the second half of the 1970s, both in Turkey and abroad, coincided with the domestic political turmoil due to the mounting anarchy within the Turkish society. The chaotic situation emanating from the deeply rooted ideological confrontation between the leftist and the rightist factions caused Turkish politicians to turn inward, just like the Europeans did in response to the OPEC crisis and the Détente period. These inevitable changes in the political and economic atmosphere both in Turkey and in Europe caused a certain degree of alienation between the two. Then Prime Minister Bülent Ecevit finally decided to suspend indefinitely Turkey's aspirations to becoming a full member of the European Community (EC).

Turkey's Relations with Western Europe in the 1980s

If one could give a "passing" grade to the performance of Turkey in its relations with Western Europe in the 1960s and "probation" in the 1970s, a "failing" grade would have to be given for most of the 1980s. The military coup d'état that took place on September 12, 1980, staged by the then top-ranking generals in response to the deteriorating economic, political, and security situation in the country, has deeply affected Turkey's relations with Western Europe. Some politicians in Europe have even suggested to suspend Turkey's membership in the Council of Europe and to cut off all economic and political interactions with Turkey. Hopefully, the severity of the relations has not gone that far. With the November 1983 general elections, returning to the democratic practice in Turkey also helped the eventual normalization process of the relations with Western Europe, albeit at a much slower pace and also without much in the substance.

In the international arena, the Islamic revolution in Iran and the Soviet invasion of Afghanistan in 1979 have dissipated the positive mood in the East-West relations that was experienced thanks to the Détente period. Turkey's strategic significance, which was diminished in the eyes of its Western allies, was remembered. Nevertheless, the priorities of the Western European countries were not deeply affected by these developments. Radicalization of Iran and the Soviet presence in Afghanistan were considered by the Europeans as developments that mattered more to the United States. Only toward the mid-1980s that the return to Cold War rhetoric between the Americans and the Russians, centered on the "Star Wars" debate emanating from the SDI of the Ronald Reagan administration in the United States, seemed to have bothered the Europeans to some extent. Yet, in the second half of the 1980s, the Western European countries were much more concerned with the political future of the Soviet Union, which was undergoing unprecedented developments in the aftermath of the passing of Leonid Brezhnev who was in power for nearly two decades from 1964 to 1982 as the Secretary-General of the Soviet Communist Party. After Brezhnev, the office of the Secretary-General of the Soviet Communist Party was assumed first by Yuri Andropov and then by Konstantin Cernenko for very short periods who also passed away one after another. Then, the rise of Mikhail Gorbachev to power in the Soviet Union in 1985, and his positive and constructive approach toward the relations with the West in general, raised hopes in Western Europe for a more peaceful future. As such, Turkey's importance started to be diminished in the eyes of the European strategists within the context of the East-West confrontation.

Aside from the conjunctural developments taking place in the international arena, one factor has deeply and negatively affected the pace of Turkey's relations with the EC in the 1980s and onward. Greece, which had applied to the EEC in 1975 for full membership, realized its goal in 1981. Even though Greece was far from meeting many of the economic and also political criteria for membership, the return to democracy by overthrowing the military Junta in Athens following Turkey's intervention in Cyprus in July 1974 and the successful negotiation strategy of the Greek politicians and diplomats have accelerated the pace of the accession talks with their European counterparts. In order to achieve full membership at an early date, Greek politicians have accepted almost all of the conditions imposed on them and made the necessary adjustments to their legal and financial systems so as to close the phases of negotiations speedily. Once admitted in the EC, Greece used its rights and privileges stemming from its full membership to renegotiate many of the issues that were wrapped up earlier. More importantly, Greece used the privilege of its full membership in the EC for blockading literally every single inch of advancement between Turkey and the Community. The coming of the Pan-Hellenic Socialist Party (PASOK) to power in Greece under the leadership of Andreas Papandreou with the October 18, 1981 general elections has been particularly influential in the aggressive policies adopted toward Turkey. According to the Greek Premier Papandreou, the threat posed to Greece was not coming from the north (i.e., Warsaw Pact members Bulgaria, Romania, and the Soviet Union) but it was coming from the east (i.e., NATO ally Turkey). This categorization of the threat perception of Greece explains the nature of bilateral relations then.

In April 1987, Turkey submitted its formal application to the EC for full membership referring to its right documented in the Ankara Treaty that was signed in 1963 and entered into force in 1964. After more than two-and-a-half years later, the EC replied to Turkey in December 1989 by saying that even though the EC acknowledged Turkey's right to apply for full membership, it was not an obligation for the Community to accept Turkey's application, especially in the midst of the dramatic developments taking place in Central and Eastern Europe to which they had to give utmost priority. The answer of the EC also underlined that Turkey had serious deficiencies in its democracy, human rights, and in the treatment of its minorities. Turkey was also suggested to solve its problems with Greece and Cyprus, hinting at the difficulties that Turkey would otherwise encounter in its bid for full membership. In short, the answer of the EC in December 1989 was a refusal of Turkey's application in April 1987.

Turkey's Relations with Europe in the Post–Cold War Period

The great transformations that took place in the Central and Eastern European countries prompted the EC to take a series of decisions in order to seize the moment. During the summit meeting of the EC in Maastricht, the Netherlands, in December 1991, it was decided to open the Treaty on European Union to signature of the members of the Community. The Treaty, also known as the Maastricht Treaty, was signed on February 7, 1992 and entered into force on November 1, 1993. The Maastricht Treaty brought about a number of changes in Europe, the most important of which was the transition from EC to EU. Hence, the EU would aspire to becoming a powerful actor in the world scene by means of unification of not only the economic and financial policies but also, and more importantly, the foreign and security policies of its members. In order to properly exploit the window of opportunity that was opening with the collapse of the Warsaw Pact and the disintegration of the Soviet Union, EU drew up a long-term plan that would guide the process of expansion of the European integration toward the east. It was decided that the expansion process should be realized in phases that would prepare the former Warsaw Pact countries as well as some of the former Soviet republics to full membership. Accordingly, a set of criteria was developed during the summit meeting of the EU in Copenhagen, Denmark, held in June 1993, with a view to assisting the transformation of the former communist regimes to open democratic societies and their transition to EU membership.

The EU's criteria for membership, which are often referred to as the Copenhagen criteria, consisted of mainly three sets of requirements, including the political as well as economic criteria, and the adoption of the *Acquis Communautaire* involving the legislation of the Union. The political criteria required the presence of functional democratic governance enabling all citizens of the country to participate in the political decision on an equal basis from the level of municipalities to the national government. Accordingly, all citizens would have the right to participate in the elections, to establish political parties without any obstructions from the state, and to express personal opinions freely. In the same vein, the rule of law should prevail in the governance meaning that government authority could be exercised in accordance to laws and regulations. Human rights were given a special place in the political criteria of the EU emphasizing that human rights were inalienable rights of all human beings, including the right to life, the right to be prosecuted only according to the laws that exist, and the right to be free from torture. Respect for and protection of minorities, as a separate chapter in the political criteria, required that the members of national minorities should be able to maintain their distinctive culture and practices, including their language, without suffering any discrimination.

The economic criteria for membership required the candidate countries to have a functioning market economy as well as the capacity to cope with competitive pressure and market forces within the Union, and the ability to take on the obligations of membership, including adherence to the aims of political, economic, and monetary union. Finally, all candidate countries were required with the Copenhagen criteria to enact legislation in order to bring their laws into line with the body of European law built up over the history of the Union, which was known as the *Acquis Communautaire*. In preparing each candidate state to full membership, the *Acquis* is divided into separate chapters, each dealing with different policy areas. Furthermore, it was also decided during the summit meeting in Madrid, Spain in 1995 that while it is important that EC legislation is transposed into national legislation, it is even more important that the legislation is implemented effectively through appropriate administrative and judicial structures. This was seen as a prerequisite of the mutual trust required by EU membership.

Those states which would be given a membership perspective would have to prepare a national program, including a timetable explaining how and when the implementation of the tasks so required by the Copenhagen criteria. The EU would assist the implementation standing by the candidate countries in order to overcome political, economic, and financial problems that may arise out of the quick transformation process. The EU has undergone three rounds of expansion in the post–Cold War period. The first round that took place in 1995 incorporated the so-called "neutral" states during the Cold War period, namely Austria, Finland, and Sweden. They were both politically and economically more than ready to become full members of the EU. In 2004, ten more countries became the members of the EU, including the Czech Republic, Estonia, Hungary, Lithuania, Latvia, Malta, Poland, Slovakia, Slovenia, and Cyprus. This second round of expansion has not been that smooth or easy, and it had serious implications for Turkey in many respects. Finally, the third round of expansion took place with the entry of Bulgaria and Romania into the EU on January 1, 2007.

Transformation of the Cyprus Problem

One of the implications of the process of expansion of the EU integration toward the east for Turkey has been the transformation of the Cyprus problem that has a long history. After the creation of the Republic of Cyprus in 1960 following the Zurich and London conferences under the aegis of the United Kingdom, Greece, and Turkey as guarantor powers, in 1963 and in 1974 Greek Cypriots made attempts to annex the island to Greece. A *status quo* was reached especially after Turkey's military intervention in July 1974. Intercommunal talks were carried out between the Greek-Cypriot and Turkish-Cypriot leaderships sponsored by the United Nations as well as the two motherlands, namely Greece and Turkey. Due to the complexity of the issues involved and the historical defects in the mind-sets of both sides, no real progress has been achieved. After becoming a full member of the EEC in 1981, Greece wanted to take the issue from the platform of the United Nations to the platform of Europe. However, with the exception of the United Kingdom, other European nations wanted to stay away from getting heavily involved in the Cyprus problem in those years. Yet, they displayed their solidarity with Greece whenever needed and asked Turkey to play a more constructive role in the resolution of the conflict on the island.

With the dramatic changes taking place in the Central and Eastern Europe, the attitude of the EU toward the Cyprus problem also started to change. Greece wanted to benefit from the expansion project of the EU toward the east and wished to include Cyprus into the project. At first, the EU did not very much welcome the Greek initiative taking into consideration its implications for their relations with Turkey. The tacit understanding within the EU was that Cyprus should not become even a candidate for membership without the resolution of the problem between the Turks and the Greeks. Countries like France, Germany, Britain, and the Netherlands have even made explicit statements to that effect. However, Greece declared that it would blockade the entire expansion process by using its veto right if Cyprus were not added to the list of prospective members. Indeed, according to the 1960 founding Constitution, the Republic of Cyprus could not become a member of any international organization without getting the consent of all three guarantor countries, one of which was Turkey. Therefore, Turkey reminded both the Greeks and the British and asked the EU to turn down the Greek Cypriot application to become a full member of the EU. Turkey's request was not accepted by the majority of the members of the EU. Those who refused to accept Turkey's claims that Greek Cypriots had no right to apply to the EU according to 1960 Constitution argued that neither the Constitution was in force anymore nor the EU could be regarded as an international organization.

But the real reason behind objection to Turkey's attempts to prevent Greek Cypriot's accession to the EU was different. Leading members of the EU, such as Germany in the first place, which were heavily committed to eastward expansion that would embrace countries like Poland, Hungary, and Czech Republic, would not want to take the risk of refusal or the delay of their membership at once. Hence, the Greek policy of using the process of expansion of the European integration as a leverage to achieve one of its long-standing goals to bring the Cyprus problem into the platform of the EU proved successful.

One of the principal reasons for Germany's powerful support given to the membership of the Eastern and Southeastern European countries stemmed from historical considerations. Prussians and Russians have fought each other for centuries leaving deep traces in their respective mind-sets. Hence, the states in between the German and Russian territories have always been of high strategic significance where each actor wanted to exert its own influence. The situation that emerged in the post–World War II period was a clear manifestation of such strategic calculation of the Soviet leadership. The Soviet Union not only split the German state into West Germany and East Germany but also expanded its zone of influence to the eastern borders of West Germany. Once the reunification of the two German states was achieved thanks to the dramatic developments that took place in Central and Eastern Europe leading to the fall of the Berlin Wall, Germany also wanted to take advantage of the disappearance of the Soviet Union from the stage of international politics so as to take the historical revenge from the Soviet leadership.

Considering the significance of membership of Poland, Hungary, and others to the EU, nothing would be allowed to prevent this from happening. Since Greece was a member of the EU with the right to veto the expansion process and since Turkey was not a member and its membership was neither soon nor desired by most of the European nations, Germany could not take the risk of leaving the Central and Eastern European countries outside of the enlargement process. Hence, Germany and others decided to yield to the blackmail of Greece to accept Cyprus to the EU, instead of putting pressure on Greece to wait until the resolution of the Cyprus problem between the Turks and the Greeks on the island as well as on both sides of the Aegean Sea.

Debate over the European Security and Defense Policy

Cyprus was not the only bone of contention between the EU and Turkey in the post–Cold War political environment. Dramatic changes that occurred in and around Europe caused drastic changes in the perceptions of the European states as regards the threats to their interests. The war that broke out in the territories of the former Yugoslavia has shown to the Europeans that uniting their political and economic power was not enough for them to become a powerful entity in world politics or to stop the atrocities and the war crimes committed by the Serbs, first in Bosnia-Herzegovina and later in Kosovo. They also needed to unite their military power. In the aftermath of the Washington summit meeting of the Alliance in April 1999, NATO enlarged with the admission of the Czech Republic, Hungary, and Poland. Then, the EU also intensified its efforts to create a European Security and Defense Identity (ESDI), or the so-called "European Army," whose decision-making would be under the strict control of the Union.[1]

The European Army was envisaged to have the capability to deploy 60,000 troops anywhere in the world within one month, with these being able to conduct military operations with full force, if necessary, and to sustain themselves for at least one year. In other words, the EU wanted to have a military capability with a global reach in order to protect the interests of the Union wherever deemed necessary on the globe. Although some individual declarations hinted at the existence of a more ambitious desire, particularly among the French and

German diplomatic, political, and security elite—a desire to become a "global superpower"—these ambitions did not seem to be shared by other members of the Union, especially the Nordic countries, which were known as "welfare states." Nor were such ambitions substantiated by the political realities of the world at that time.

In order to avoid duplication of forces in the same geographical area, the EU requested the authorization, once and for all, to have automatic and uninterrupted access, if and when necessary, to the military assets of NATO to which they have already made their individual contributions as members of the Alliance. However, the NATO Charter requires unanimity amongst members in order for such an authorization to be given to the European Army. At this point, Turkey, as a nonmember of the EU, has made it clear that it would not give its unconditional approval to such a request, which would mean losing its control over the use of NATO assets in the future military operations of the EU. This was because Turkey feared that EU-led operations might well contradict its supreme national interests.

There was good reason to believe in such concerns as 13 out of the 16 worldwide conflict scenarios drawn up by NATO's contingency planners involved regions in the periphery of Turkey, such as Bosnia-Herzegovina, Sandjak, Kosovo, Albania, Macedonia, Nagorno-Karabagh in Azerbaijan, Chechnya, Abkhazia in Georgia, Georgia-South Ossetia, northern Iraq, Iran, Syria, Cyprus, Vojvodina, Privlaka, and Belarus, many of which could require direct involvement by Turkey. In such a case, EU intervention in conflicts in the immediate neighborhood of Turkey without Ankara's active participation both in the planning and in the operational phases could not only severely damage Turkey's interests but also threaten its security. What was more worrying was the possibility of an EU military intervention going out of control at one point during the conflict and paving the way for an Article 5 contingency, which would formally pull the non-EU members of NATO as a whole into the conflict. The fundamental commitment of all members of the Alliance to each other's security is enshrined in Article 5 of the North Atlantic Treaty, which states that an attack against one member country is considered as an attack against all. The Alliance's integrated military structure and common defense planning procedures underpin this commitment to collective defense. They are at the heart of the Alliance's strength and credibility. Turkey, as required by its Article 5 commitments, would have to become involved in a conflict that it had no responsibility for.

When looked at from the perspective of the EU, the quest for an independent military power was quite understandable. A sovereign political entity (the EU in this case) that has a parliament, a ministerial council, and a full-fledged bureaucracy, as well as a flag and a banknote in circulation (the Euro), has the right, in theory, to make a claim to establish a military unit of its own. Otherwise, its sovereignty would be called into question. However, if that political entity has to depend on others' military assets and capabilities, it must acknowledge the need to share the decision-making authority, as well as the command and control, with those who somehow contribute to its capabilities. The divergence of opinion on the autonomy of decision-making in European Security and Defense Policy (ESDP) between Turkey and the EU stemmed from this very point. Whereas the EU did not want to give away even a tiny portion of its authority over the decision-making autonomy of the European Army, arguing that it was a matter of principle, Turkey insisted on being admitted to the decision-making mechanism whenever NATO assets would be called into action, and especially when the EU conducted military operations in Turkey's immediate neighborhood.

The United States, as the most powerful country in NATO, did not mind allowing the EU to have assured access to the assets of the Alliance if and when the European Army needed. The United States also urged Turkey to adopt a similar attitude and not to follow a stubborn policy against the claims of the EU, on the grounds that such inflexibility by Turkey might force the EU to head its own way, which would end up with the dissolution of the Alliance. Thus, the U.S. authorities strived hard to find a middle way between Turkey and the EU, none of which wanted to step back. Eventually, a solution was found by paying due attention to Turkey's serious concerns and to its supreme interests, primarily in the Aegean and in the eastern Mediterranean. Turkey was given guarantees by the United States and the United Kingdom, of which the latter was acknowledged as representing the EU's position, that the European Army would not be used in contingencies involving the Aegean as well as the eastern Mediterranean. In other words, the EU's army would not interfere in problems between Turkey and Greece, both in the Aegean and in Cyprus.

Most Turkish officials believed the problem was resolved for Turkey. Notwithstanding the relaxed approach of Turkish politicians in particular, and without the issuance of any formal approval by the EU, the significance of the deal may evaporate if and when Greek Cypriot leadership asks for the amendment of the agreement between Turkey and EU negotiated back in the early 2000s. Until such time that Turkey feels more secure and more confident that its supreme national interests in the Aegean and in the eastern Mediterranean will not be hurt by Greece and/or Greek Cypriots, Turkish opposition toward the European security designs covering the region is highly likely to continue.

The Long Road Ahead toward EU Membership

Membership in the EU has long been a state policy in Turkey though not much had been specifically accomplished to that extent. Successive governments had undertaken cosmetic initiatives particularly at the times of election. More than four decades after the signing of the 1963 Ankara Agreement with the EEC,

Turkey was finally deemed eligible in October 2004 to begin the accession negotiations. By then, Turkey strove to comply with the Copenhagen political criteria that were designed to guide the former Eastern Bloc countries toward full membership. The usual process for full membership requires the national legislative bodies of each member state to approve admission after the completion of negotiations. But, in the case of Turkey, unlike any other candidate, referendums may be called particularly in countries like Greece, Cyprus, and France, where opposition to Turkey's membership is strongest. For instance, in the words of Alain Juppé, the former Prime Minister of France, in case of Turkey's eventual membership, the EU will not be the EU of their dreams. Juppé also believes that if and when Turkey becomes a member of the EU, they should rethink about the future of Europe, and a new architecture with the EU will emerge.[2] This kind of challenge will make Turkey's membership all the more difficult, if not impossible.[3]

There are several issues that make Europeans feel very uneasy about Turkey's membership. These may be categorized under four broad headings: political, economic, cultural, and military. With regard to political issues, Europeans are primarily concerned with the decision-making process in the EU that will certainly become further complicated with the inclusion of Turkey. Because of its population of 73 million and high birth rate, the number of seats that Turkey will occupy in the European Parliament will equal those of the leading members of the Union such as Germany, France, Britain, and Italy. Many Europeans see such an eventuality as a nightmare, particularly in view of their concerns about the level of democratic culture in Turkey, which they see as inadequate to meet the European standards.[4]

Economic issues are no less frightening for the Europeans, again primarily due to Turkey's population, which is more than the total of the new members; even the biggest, Poland, has only half of Turkey's population. While the EU is undergoing economic and financial difficulties in digesting the new members, it has serious concerns about Turkey's economic infrastructure, which is underdeveloped by European standards and less competitive in world markets. And upgrading the industrial and service sectors in Turkey may require a lot of investment. However, the greatest difficulty may be the Turkish agricultural sector, which will certainly need huge subsidies that the EU cannot afford. Added to these is a worry that the Euro will be negatively affected by Turkey's relatively weaker financial system.

Most analysts argue that neither the political nor the economic problems constitute the major stumbling blocks for Turkey's eventual membership in the EU. To them, cultural issues are more sensitive problems, as they pertain to religious and traditional differences between Turkey and the rest of Europe. They may not be resolved in the foreseeable future. In the post-9/11 world, differences over cultural issues have sharpened and moved to the point of confrontation. Europeans are getting more and more religious and more fearful and intolerant of Muslims as a reaction to some of the crimes committed by Islamic figures in the Middle East, such as the beheading of European aid workers and business-men in Iraq and the slaughter of Theo van Gogh, the Dutch filmmaker, on the streets of Amsterdam on broad daylight. These events and others will most certainly add further to anti-Islamic sentiments in Europe; that may well have a direct bearing on Turkey, whose population is predominantly Muslim.[5] In addi-tion, bad memoirs of the past since the Ottoman times still resonate within European society and contribute to the unpopular image of Turks and Turkey.

As for the security and defense issues, there are already problems between Turkey and some of the EU members such as Greece and Cyprus. Neither the Aegean problems with Greece nor the Cyprus issue has been resolved, even after the powerful intervention of United Nations Secretary-General Kofi Annan with a plan in 2004 for the creation of a federal state on the island. Turkey's recogni-tion of the whole island of Cyprus remains a problem; this would entail aban-doning the self-proclaimed Turkish Republic of Northern Cyprus, which is recognized only by Turkey. Likewise, there is strong reaction within Turkish soci-ety to the normalization of relations with Armenia. Even though Turkey formally recognized Armenia after the breakup of the Soviet Union, diplomatic relations have not yet been established. In other arenas, the Europeans are critical of Turkey's relations with the United States and Israel. There is fear that Turkey will be the Trojan horse of the United States, while its relations with Israel are seri-ously criticized, especially since the military cooperation agreement of 1996.[6] In addition to all of these problems, Turkey's relations with its Middle Eastern neighbors like Syria, Iraq, and Iran are seen as problematic; Europeans worry about upsetting whatever level of harmony they have achieved with these coun-tries. Taking all these into account, it could be argued that, in the words of Zbigniew Brzezinski, "the European Union will delay for as long as it can a clear-cut commitment to open its doors to Turkey."[7] Even if a certain degree of loose commitment can be achieved on some of Turkey's security concerns, it is unlikely that Turkey and the EU will see eye-to-eye when it comes to dealing with the problems emanating from Turkey's Middle Eastern neighbors.

TURKEY AND NATO IN THE POST–COLD WAR ERA

Turkey used to be the first line of defense of the West against the threats emanat-ing from the Soviet Union. Therefore, Turkey had great strategic importance for the West. In many respect, Turkey's membership in NATO and its military capa-bilities constituting the first line of defense against possible Soviet aggression were indispensible for the security of the West. However, the collapse of the Warsaw Pact followed by the disintegration of the Soviet Union eliminated the threat of a military confrontation in Europe. As such, Turkey lost its strategic value particu-larly for the European members of NATO. Turkey's strategic value was also diminished for the United States but to a lesser extent because a series of challenging developments, among others, the invasion of Kuwait by Iraq in August 1990 and the ensuing crisis, which finally resulted in a limited war in the Middle East, necessitated Turkey's active involvement in the proceedings. The abolishing of the communist threat to the West also brought with it severe criticism about the continuation of NATO. Hence, both NATO and Turkey, being one of the significant members of the Alliance, entered a period of soul searching.

Soul Searching for a New and Significant Role in the Alliance

Membership in NATO meant to most Turks much more than being part of a powerful military alliance. NATO signified Western values that were started to be adopted by the Turks since their earlier encounters with the European powers especially in the fifteenth century and onward. NATO also signified the climax of Turkey's membership in the Western institutions as an equal and noble partner. Hence, the disappearance of such an organization and the diminishing of its significance were not the kind of developments that the Turkish security and political elite desired to see. Turkey, therefore, was actively involved in the deliberations within the Alliance that aimed to cast new roles to NATO.

There was indeed a clear need for a powerful military actor in the turbulent times that followed the demise of the bipolar international system. The lifting of the pressure of the Cold War on the states on both sides of the *Iron Curtain* that had prevented them from getting involved in local disputes with the fear of escalation to a superpower confrontation paved the way to the eruption of conflicts here and there in the Eurasian landscape. Atrocities in the Balkans stemming from the secessionist desire of the former republics of the Socialist Federal Republic of Yugoslavia, such as Croatia, Slovenia, and Bosnia-Herzegovina, have long been the primary concern of the Alliance. Ethnic nationalism pursued by the Serbs against the other ethnic and religious communities that constituted the Yugoslav population led to the collapse of Yugoslavia along the ethnic lines. NATO helped to put an end to the bloody conflicts in Bosnia and Kosovo, and also prevented a civil war in Macedonia between the ethnic Albanians and Macedonians. In order to maintain peace and stability in these places NATO established stability forces. In addition to the Balkans, NATO also assumed a stabilizing role in Afghanistan, Iraq, and in the Darfur region of Sudan.

Turkey undertook an active role in most of the post–Cold War peace operations led either by the United Nations or by NATO. Turkish commitment to peace operations is reaffirmed in the *White Paper 2000* issued by the Ministry of National Defense. It is stated in the *White Paper 2000* that Turkey provides support to the Peace Operations carried out under the sanctions or control of the United Nations, NATO, or the OSCE for world and regional peace, in the direction of the principle of "peace at home, peace in the world" as once laid out by Atatürk.[8]

In the Balkans, Turkey participated in the UN Protection Force in Bosnia-Herzegovina (UNPROFOR) from 1993 to 1995, Implementation Force (IFOR) and Stabilization Force (SFOR) in Bosnia-Herzegovina (1996–), Combined Police Force in Bosnia-Herzegovina (1995), UN Preventive Deployment Force in Macedonia (1995–), International Police Task Force in Bosnia-Herzegovina (1997–), Operation Alba in Albania (1997), Kosovo Verification Force (1998–99), and Kosovo Force (2001–present). The Turkish Land Forces participated in UN peacekeeping operations in Bosnia with a brigade. The Navy participated in Operation Sharp Guard in the Adriatic, whose mission was to monitor and impose the arms embargo on former Yugoslavia. The Air Force joined NATO's Operation Deny Flight in Bosnia and Operation Allied Force in Kosovo with a squadron of F-16 aircraft.[9]

NATO also established a comprehensive framework with a view to advancing dialogue and cooperation with the former Eastern Bloc countries and the former Soviet republics to overcome the divisions of the Cold War period as well as to extend security and stability beyond the traditional NATO territories. For this purpose the Partnership for Peace (PfP) program was launched in 1994. Turkey also contributes to NATO's PfP programs enthusiastically by participating in PfP's military and naval exercises in the region. Turkey also established a PfP Training Center in Ankara in June 1998 whose mission is to provide qualitative training and education support to partners in accordance with NATO and PfP general principles and interoperability objectives.

In the face of the changing nature of challenges and threats to international peace, security, and stability, during the summit meeting of the Alliance in Prague, Czech Republic held in November 2002, NATO decided to undergo the necessary transformation and modernization processes so as to be able to deal with the twenty-first-century threats, international terrorism being at the forefront. Turkey also took an initiative in this field and established the Centre of Excellence Defence Against Terrorism in Ankara in June 2005. The Centre is accredited to NATO and has international staff who work on the conceptual and theoretical dimensions of the fight against terrorism. NATO is also taking on new operations and missions to bring peace to Afghanistan, to assist Iraq, and to help the African Union to bring peace to the Darfur region. Turkey has contributed actively to these missions as well.

In the aftermath of the September 11 attacks sponsored by Al-Qaeda, the United States invoked Article 5 of NATO's Charter and launched a military operation, Operation Enduring Freedom, against the Taliban regime, which provided all sorts of logistical support to Al-Qaeda. When Taliban rule in Afghanistan came to an end, it became possible to launch international initiatives to rebuild the country and to send a multinational peacekeeping force to Afghanistan. Turkey showed its willingness to participate in the multinational peacekeeping force for the reconstruction of Afghanistan. Turkish government decided to contribute to the campaign by sending a unit of Special Forces to work with American troops in humanitarian operations and to train the Northern Alliance fighters. Within this framework, Turkey assumed the lead-nation role and took over the command of the International Security Assistance Force (ISAF) in June 2002 for a period of six months to assist the Afghan government and the international community in maintaining security. The decision of the Turkish government on April 29, 2002 was taken in accordance with the United Nations Resolution 1413 dated May 23, 2002. After taking command of ISAF II, Turkey increased the number of its soldiers to 1,400 making it the largest contingent in the peacekeeping force reinforced with combat support and service officers commissioned in the ISAF Headquarters and Kabul Airport. Normally, Turkey should have handed over command of ISAF on December 20, 2002, but no country was ready to make this commitment. So, the UNSC extended Turkish leadership until February 10, 2003. Turkey handed over leadership to the joint command of Germany and the Netherlands on February 10, 2003. After turning over command, Turkey has continued to support ISAF with a 180-man military unit. In May 2004, Turkey sent 3 helicopters and 56 flight and maintenance personnel to work in ISAF. After taking command of ISAF VII once more on February 13, 2005, Turkey increased the number of its soldiers from 240 to 1,600 in Kabul. Moreover, from January 2004 to August 2006, Turkey's former Minister of Foreign Affairs and the former Speaker of the TGNA Hikmet Çetin served as the Senior Civilian Representative of NATO in Kabul. Hikmet Çetin benefited largely from the privileges of the long lasting Turkish-Afghan friendship in furthering the Alliance's goal of establishing peace and stability in Afghanistan.[10]

Motivation for Turkey to Contribute to Peace Operations

Turkey's decision to send troops abroad with a view to contributing to the multinational peace operation in various parts of the globe stems from a number of factors. These can be grouped into three main categories: the security-related factors, domestic political factors, and the ideational factors.

Security-Related Concerns of Turkey

Among the troubled regions that emerged with the end of the East-West tension, the Balkans has been a fertile ground for conflicts that have characterized the fundamental change in the political and security environment in the region in the post–Cold War era. Turkey attached importance to the creation of an atmosphere of understanding and peaceful cohabitation through closer ties among the Balkan countries, which would lead to the preservation of peace and stability in the region. Thus, Turkey's approach to the conflicts in the Balkans has not been confined to merely the cessation of hostilities but has also pursued a policy aimed at creating a durable climate of understanding conducive to cooperation across the region. In this respect, Turkey has been at the forefront of international efforts to settle the Bosnian and Kosovo conflicts,[11] because the eruption of bloody conflicts in the territory of the former Yugoslavia raised concerns about the possible spillover toward the borders of Turkey. It was feared that the fighting may spread to Muslim areas of Sandjak on the Serbian Montenegro border and from there to Kosovo. Albania might also intervene to protect the ethnic Albanians in Kosovo. As the Republic of Macedonia has a 30 percent Albanian population, it might join in. Greece might then assist Serbia, while Turkey and Bulgaria may enter to assist Bosnia.[12] In order to prevent such a likelihood, Turkey first resorted to the instruments of diplomacy and brought the issue before the attention of other nations in various platforms, including, among others, the CSCE and the Islamic Conference Organization (ICO). But, especially the Western European nations such as the United Kingdom and France in particular have tended to see the Serbian atrocities toward the other ethnic and religious groups in Yugoslavia as an unwanted but natural outcome of a civil war. Thus, mobilizing the world community to take military action to stop the Serbs has not been the case for several years. Western European nations considered such an intervention to be illegitimate and preferred to stay away for as long as possible. Had the region been rich in natural resources just like Kuwait, or if the majority of those suffering from bloody conflict had not been Muslim, the attitude of the leading European states might have been different, many observers believed. Once the United States weighed in and mobilized worldwide support starting from the United Nations platform, taking military action first to stop intercommunal hostilities and to make peace and then to maintain peace and stability in the region has become possible. Turkey, being a country which was long striving to find a way to get involved in the peacemaking efforts, did contribute with great enthusiasm to the multinational efforts.

Moreover, in response to Turkey's growing exposure to a constellation of hard and soft security threats, Turkey's security policy makers should have increasingly found it necessary to improve the operational capabilities of the TAF. Turkey's attainment of soft and hard military security capabilities would make it a more credible and influential power in the region. In parallel to the concept of forward defense, Turkish security policy makers should have found it necessary to transform the TAF from a conscript-based conventional army into a professionalizing army consisting of highly mobile and technologically equipped military units.[13] The presence of Turkish soldiers in peace operations could show Turkey's military capabilities to other countries contributing troops and to the world for deterrence. Turkey's role in the ISAF II can be considered as an important example of Turkey's command of a multinational peacekeeping force. The Turkish Army wanted to have the chance to prove that it could be successful as a regional power in order to assume greater responsibilities. Because peace operations demand special expertise, Turkey's involvement in peace operations in Somalia, Bosnia, Kosovo, and Afghanistan was hoped to increase the professionalization of the TAF. Through participating actively in the peace operation in Somalia, the Turkish Army would gain international experience in peace operations, which it could not gain during the Cold War era. It could also share its capabilities with other troop contributing countries and benefit from their experiences in peace operations.[14]

Historical and Cultural Ties with the Troubled Regions

A second reason why Turkey was heavily concerned with the events taking place in the Balkans was because of long history of relations with the people of the region. Having ruled the region for five centuries, Turks have had their imprints in almost all aspects of the history, society, art, culture, and religion of the Balkan nations. In particular, Bosnians and Kosovars have always been closer to Turks than other nations in the region and expected support from Turkey. Turks themselves are also an important ethnic minority in the region. Today, according to the 1994 census, about 77,000 Turks live in the Republic of Macedonia. In Kosovo, their number is estimated to be around 60,000, although the 1981 census put their number at around 11,000.[15] There are Turkish populations living in the Pristine, Gilan, Mitrovica, and Ipek regions. Many Bosnians, Kosovars, and Albanians in the region have relatives in Turkey, mostly in the big cities such as İstanbul, İzmir, and Bursa. From 1923 to 1990, more than 1.6 million people immigrated to Turkey, mostly from the Balkan countries. The flow of refugees, asylum seekers, and internally displaced persons also compelled Turkey to find ways to stop the flow and contribute to peace operations. With the outbreak of the war in the former Yugoslavia, hundreds of thousands of people became refugees. Turkey also experienced mass influxes of Albanians, Bosnian Muslims, and Turks between 1992 and 1995.[16] Hence, powerful lobbying groups drawn from communities that trace their origins to the Balkans put pressure on the Turkish governments to be more actively involved in the international efforts. Moreover, the cultural heritage of the Turks such as mosques and bridges built during the Ottoman rule was also at stake. Thus, Turkey could not be indifferent to the atrocities that also caused a lot of damage to these structures.

Ideational Factors

In addition to security-related concerns of Turkey and the historical and cultural ties with the troubled regions, ideational factors have also been important in motivating the Turkish decision-makers to be actively involved in the peace operations in the post–Cold War era. Back in the 1950s, Turkey contributed with a large brigade to the multinational force deployed in the Korean Peninsula in order to display its determination to share the same values with the Western nations against the communist threat. Turkey's participation in the Korean War is strongly believed to have paved the way to its membership in NATO, which was adamantly opposed by France and the United Kingdom at the beginning.

A similar logic also prevailed in the post–Cold War period at a time when Turkey's Western identity started to be called into question in the European circles. Once the threat of communism abolished, Turkey lost its perceived strategic value for the Western European members of NATO in particular, and it was started to be categorized as one of a number of countries where questions of national identity were actively debated during the 1990s. Turkey was classified as a torn country whose leaders typically wished to pursue a bandwagoning strategy and to make their countries members of the West but whose history, culture, and traditions were non-Western.[17] Notwithstanding such categorizations, by participating in the peace operations, Turkey not only showed that it was a security producing country but also a strong believer of the universal norms of the twenty-first century, such as the resolution of disputes by nonviolent ways, which were strongly upheld with much more enthusiasm especially in the Western world since the Paris Act of 1990.

NOTES

1. Mustafa Kibaroğlu, "Turkey's Triple-Trouble: ESDP, Cyprus, N. Iraq," *Insight Turkey* 4, no. 1 (January–March 2002): 49–58.

2. Mr. Juppé made these remarks during an international conference on "The US and Europe: Partnership or Competition" held at Boston University on November 16, 2004 in Boston, Massachusetts.

3. Mohammed Ayoob, "Turkey's Multiple Paradoxes," *Orbis* 48, no. 3 (Summer 2004): 451–63.

4. This view, which is common to most European elite, was reiterated by Mr. Giorgios Dimitrakopoulos, a Greek member of the European Parliament, during a private conversation at Harvard University on March 22, 2005. Mr. Dimitrakopoulos also added that, based on his personal observations, the Europeans most fear migration of Turks in large numbers.

5. Michael Bonner, "Turkey, The European Union and Paradigm Shifts," *Middle East Policy* 12, no. 1 (Spring 2005): 44–71.

6. Mustafa Kibaroğlu, "Turkey and Israel Strategize," *Middle East Quarterly* 9, no. 1 (Winter 2002): 61–65.

7. Zbigniew Brzezinski, "Hegemonic Quicksand," *National Interest,* no. 74 (Winter 2003/4): 7.

8. *White Paper 2000* at http://www.msb.gov.tr/Birimler/GNPP/html/GnPPDBeyazKitap.htm.

9. Uğur Güngör, "The Analysis of Turkey's Approach to Peace Operations" (PhD diss., Bilkent University, 2007).

10. Ibid.

11. "Synopsis of the Turkish Foreign Policy," Republic of Turkey, Ministry of Foreign Affairs, The Balkans, http://www.mfa.gov.tr/sub.en.mfa?91541430-f1dd-41d0-b6eb-e1a6cc3e556b.

12. Jane Sharp, "Intervention in Bosnia—The Case For," *World Today* 49, no. 2 (1993): 29–32.

13. Michael Hickok, "Hegemon Rising: The Gap between Turkish Strategy and Military Modernization," *Parameters: US Army War College* 30, no. 2 (2000): 105–20.

14. Güngör, "The Analysis of Turkey's Approach to Peace Operations."

15. Şule Kut, "Turks of Kosovo: What to Expect?" *Perceptions, Journal of International Affairs* 5, no. 3 (2000): 49–60.

16. Kemal Kirişçi, "Reconciling Refugee Protection with Combating Irregular Migration: Turkey and the EU," *Perceptions, Journal of International Affairs* 9, no. 2 (2004).

17. Samuel P. Huntington, "The Clash of Civilizations?" *Foreign Affairs* 72, no. 3 (1993): 433–35.

CHAPTER 6

Redefinition of Turkey's Relations with Its "Strategic Partners" United States and Israel in the Post-9/11 Period

After the creation of NATO with the signing of the Washington Treaty back in 1949, the United States has vigorously supported Turkey's desire for membership. Americans believed that, due to its geographical location, Turkey could play a very important role in their strategic vision for the post–World War II period. Western European allies were not equally enthusiastic about the idea. The defense of Turkey was the key issue of contention between Europeans and Americans as they did not have exactly the same list of enemy states against which the allied territories would have to be defended. Whereas the main concern of the Europeans was the Soviet threat, the scope of the Americans was much wider, encompassing countries in the Middle East, especially those hostile to Israel. The discrepancy between the views of Europeans and Americans concerning "which territory to defend against whom" has lingered on within the Alliance since Turkey's membership in 1952. Due to the selective attitude of the European allies in matters pertaining to the defense of Turkey, it was the Americans who most of the times prevailed in the discussions within the Alliance in these respects. As such, for many Turks, NATO meant the United States and vice versa, and the Turkish-American relations have evolved as *an alliance within the Alliance* all through the Cold War years.[1]

On the other hand, much has been said and written about Turkey's relations with Israel, which have grown fast and unprecedentedly in the post–Cold War period with regard to its scope and context. Political analysts in the world have differed over how to define this relationship. Depending on their assumptions, observers have called the Turkish-Israeli relationship an "axis," an "entente," even an "alliance." If an alliance requires formally documented and explicit commitments between two or more states, obliging them to assist one another in the event of an armed conflict, then the Turkish-Israeli relationship could not be categorized as an alliance. No formal document has been signed and no explicit commitment has been given that could be construed as obligating the two parties in this way. But a careful interpretation of the provisions of the document that they signed in 1996 suggested that it opened the door to a much enhanced cooperation between the two countries—a cooperation that could reach levels usually only reached by allies.[2]

Bearing these in mind, it becomes obvious that the scope and the intensity of the relations with the United States and Israel were well ahead of Turkey's strategic relations with other allies. Therefore, categorizing Turkey's relations with the United States and Israel as "strategic partnership," like many analysts and politicians do, may not be totally unfounded. However, one must also bear in mind that the term strategic partnership has far-reaching meanings regarding the expectations of "partners" from each other. One particular condition for a relationship to be identified as strategic partnership, between two or more nations, is to assess the world events almost identically and to decide on what kind of policies to pursue in very close coordination with one another. In this respect, one can easily identify the nature of relationship between the United States and the United Kingdom since World War II as strategic partnership. Similarly, the type of relations between Israel and the United States has long been one of strategic partnership. Considering these examples, even though Turkey and the United States were very close strategic allies, especially during the Cold War years, and a similar level was more or less reached in the relations between Turkey and Israel in the 1990s, defining these relationships as "strategic partnership" becomes contestable.

Moreover, in the aftermath of the September 11 attacks on the United States, the pace of events in the world, and particularly in Turkey's neighborhood, had a powerful impact on Turkey's foreign and security policies. Some of these events took place prior to and during the U.S. war in Iraq in March 2003, while others have been taking place since then in connection with the U.S. plans to transform the "Greater Middle East" region from radical regimes or dictatorships to moderate democracies and open societies. The geopolitical and geostrategic location of Turkey as well as its social and cultural peculiarities has almost unavoidably pulled her to the center stage of all of these developments. Nevertheless, Turkey's strategic relations with the United States and Israel are negatively affected from these developments due to the failure of the parties to find ways to act together, first when the United States wanted to station troops in Turkey's territory in its war against Saddam regime in Iraq. Then, the situation got even worse, let alone improve, between the two allies since the postwar occupation of Iraq by the United States. Similarly, diverging approaches of Turkey and Israel to the postwar restructuring of Iraq caused cooling of the strategic relations that had reached its climax only recently. Hence, considering the changing nature of the relations between Turkey and the United States as well as Turkey and Israel, it is necessary to analyze a series of events that have culminated in such a situation.

REDEFINITION OF TURKEY'S RELATIONS WITH THE UNITED STATES

Immediately after the September 11 attacks, all of the members of NATO have given their full support to the military campaign against the Taliban regime in Afghanistan by enacting Article 5 of the Washington Treaty. But, when Iraq was subsequently put on the target by the United States under the doctrine of preemptive use of force, most European allies refrained from giving their consent to another military intervention. Americans argued that the September 11 attacks have shown that they could not rely on the virtues of deterrence of their unmatched military capabilities against terrorist organizations. Neither could they wait until being attacked and then to retaliate. Hence, they contended that preemption might be necessary in some circumstances.

The discord between the two sides of the Atlantic on the military interventions in the Middle East continued and had direct bearings on Turkey in the post–September 11 period. Negative implications of such a dispute for Turkey have become clear in February 2003 when the Turkish government requested the North Atlantic Council, the highest decision-making body of NATO, to enact Article 4 of the Washington Treaty in order to take preliminary measures in case Article 5 would have to be put in operation against Iraq. France and Germany, in particular, opposed Turkey's request. Although not specifically mentioned in their statements, the Franco-German pact has implicitly referred to Article 1 of the Washington Treaty, which suggests that the allies should "refrain in their international relations from the threat or use of force in any manner inconsistent with the purposes of the United Nations." Bearing this in mind, it would be inconceivable for France or Germany, who opposed from the beginning the U.S. plans to use force against Iraq, to start discussing the measures for the defense of Turkey in a war that would break out because of another ally (i.e., the United States) whose threat of use of force would not be consistent with Article 1 of the very Treaty that created NATO. Turkish diplomats should have figured out the stance of France and Germany well in advance of bringing the issue before the North Atlantic Council. Nevertheless, that event caused fury in Turkey and underlined the value of relations with the United States as *the* key ally within the Alliance prior to the war in Iraq.

Impact of the Iraq War on Turkish-American Relations

Being the key ally, the United States had a lot of expectations from Turkey in its war against Saddam regime in Iraq, including formal requests concerning the stationing of large numbers of troops in Turkish territory. Many analysts agree that the request of the United States from Turkey to open its territory to allow stationing of a large number of American troops and to use Turkish seaports as well as airports from one end to the other has had serious consequences resulting in the deterioration of Turkish-American relations since 2003. A series of events that took place in that period are still being debated among the military-strategic analysts, politicians, and scholars, but not necessarily with enough information shared about the specifics of each stage of the negotiation process between Turkey and the United States prior to and during the war. It is, therefore, necessary to address some of the details of this process many of which may have been overlooked or even unnoticed in due course.

The U.S. Request for Basing Troops in Turkey and Its Consequences

In the days leading up to the Iraqi conflict, the United States and Turkey held extensive negotiations over the use of Turkish territory in aid of the U.S. campaign in Iraq. Basing tens of thousands of American troops on Turkey's soil was thought to be highly instrumental for the U.S. contingency planning in the war against Iraq. Representatives of two countries have conducted a series of negotiations first when there was a three-party coalition in Turkey, which was consisted of the Democratic Left Party (*Demokratik Sol Parti*—DSP) chaired by then Prime Minister Bülent Ecevit, the Nationalist Movement Party (*Milliyetçi Hareket Partisi*—MHP) chaired by Devlet Bahçeli, then Deputy Prime Minister, and the Motherland Party (*Anavatan Partisi*—ANAP) chaired by Mesut Yılmaz who did not take part in the Cabinet.

As a result of worsening of economic situation in Turkey following two severe financial crises in 2001 and 2002, the coalition partner MHP called for early elections to be held in November 2002. Many political analysts considered this to be a suicidal decision for the coalition, which ultimately led to its replacement by the newly established *Adalet ve Kalkınma Partisi* (AKP) chaired by Recep Tayyip Erdoğan who sworn in as a deputy first and then Prime Minister a few months later due to some legal technicalities that had to be overcome with by-elections in February 2003. The new Turkish government resumed the negotiations from the point where they were stalled and decided to draft a resolution that would allow American Special Forces to be deployed in Turkey in order to cross the border into Iraqi territory as part of a plan to encircle the enemy forces together with the U.S. and the British troops that were already deployed in the south to march toward Baghdad.[3]

Many Americans assumed that Turkey would quickly agree to any U.S. proposal, and the Turkish government that was formed after November 2002 elections was harshly criticized both in and out of the country for "deliberately" drawing out the negotiations with the United States. The negotiations were conducted along three tracks: political, military, and economic. The Turkish government wanted to prevent the emergence of an independent Kurdish state in northern Iraq, to which the United States responded affirmatively. Negotiations on the military track concerned where Turkish troops could be deployed and how many would cross the border into northern Iraq without simultaneously disrupting U.S. military operations against Baghdad. Finally, on the economic track, negotiations were aimed at compensating Turkey for the economic damage a U.S.-led campaign against Iraq would cause. Although an understanding was reportedly reached on the political and military tracks, negotiations on the economic track never came to fruition. There was a lot of speculations about a US$6 billion deal, which would have been welcomed in Turkey's financial and commercial sectors.

Time was probably the most precious asset for both the Turks and the Americans in early 2003. Turkey was in need of hard currency, having suffered two severe debt crises in the past two years, and the United States was concerned about conducting a military campaign in the increasing heat of the Iraqi desert. "Hysteria" might be the word to describe the state of affairs in Ankara in the days leading up to the Iraqi conflict, and there was probably some of the same feeling in the air on Capitol Hill. Washington's attitude was expressed in political cartoon caricatures of all things Turkish that appeared in the U.S. media, including the *New York Times* and weekly magazines like *Time* and *Newsweek*. Some have held that these humiliating caricatures were responsible for the reversal of the attitude of most deputies of the Justice and Development Party (AKP), which held a two-thirds majority in the TGNA, and who had tabled the basing resolution before the parliamentarians—and who ultimately blockaded the way to the U.S. troop deployment in Turkey. That would be a simplistic assessment, however, of why Turkey turned down the U.S. request to use a combination of military bases and air and sea ports, in return for which a number of financial benefits would have flowed from Washington to Ankara.

The Essence of Disagreement

The seeds of the no vote were actually planted in March 1991, with the creation of the "safe havens" that allowed the return of the hundreds of thousands of Iraqi Kurds who had fled their country and sought refuge in Turkey and Iran. The Kurds feared being gassed by Saddam's air force, in a repeat of the massacre at Halabja in March 1988, in which 5,000 men, women, and children were killed. The so-called *no-fly zones,* established by the United States—one above the 36th parallel in the Iraqi north, the other below the 32nd (later the 33rd) parallel in the Shiite south—were considered by many Turks as a first step in a long-term U.S. plan to create an independent Kurdish state. Nevertheless, in 1991 permission was granted by the TGNA for U.S. aircraft to use the İncirlik

Air Base near Adana, Turkey, to enforce the no-fly zone, and that permission had been renewed every six months since.

Whenever the United States was accused of using the zone to help create a Kurdish state in northern Iraq, U.S. officials and their representatives in Ankara dismissed Turkish concerns by saying that U.S. authorities had no such intentions, and that they were observing Iraq's territorial integrity. But Turkish military circles and many of their like-minded political followers were very suspicious. The military, in particular, witnessed the close coordination of U.S. Special Forces and other U.S. agents and the Iraqi Kurdish militia throughout the 1990s. For instance, thousands of Iraqi Kurds went through a special training program on Guam where they learned, among other things, the fundamentals of administering a state bureaucracy, including the military. This caused deep resentment in the Turkish military. One former Chief of General Staff, Doğan Güreş, recalled in a live tv8 interview that he had sometimes given orders to check the engines of U.S. helicopters stationed on Turkish soil, and therefore subject to certain restrictions, to see if they were hot, an indication that they had been carrying out missions that did not have the approval of Turkish authorities. Similarly, former Prime Minister Bülent Ecevit told CNN Türk television channel that he had sincere doubts about the real intentions of the Americans with regard to the Kurds in Iraq.

But if Turkey had not trusted the Americans on the Kurdish issue since 1991, one may reasonably ask why the Grand National Assembly did not rescind its approval of the no-fly arrangements, first known as "Operation Provide Comfort I & II" and later as "Operation Northern Watch." As a result of these operations, an independent Kurdish political entity appeared in northern Iraq, becoming over the years a *de facto* state, with a parliament, ministries, a bureaucracy, a central bank, and its own currency. There were two reasons for continuing to permit the use of Turkish bases for these operations. One was the fear of a new wave of refugees from Iraq who had crossed the border into the Turkish territory. The Kurds in the north and the Shia in the south were encouraged by the U.S. President George Bush, the father, to rise up against Saddam's authority who was defeated in the war and forced to pull back his forces from the Kuwaiti territory in March 1991. So did the Kurds and the Shia, with the expectation that their revolt would be backed up by the Coalition Forces leading the way to the toppling of Saddam Hussein. However, they had forgotten one very important detail, which was the limited mandate that was granted to the Coalition Forces by the UNSC with Resolution 678 authorizing the use of military force against the Iraqi military. The authorization aimed at restoring the situation along the Iraqi-Kuwaiti border prior to the invasion in August 1990. Hence, Coalition Forces could not, in violation of the limited authorization, use force against the Iraqi forces once the job was done by expelling them out of Kuwait and a cease-fire was signed. Therefore, anticipating that no military support would come from the Coalition Forces, the Kurds and the Shia who had already revolted against Saddam began to flee their country so as to save their lives, which they felt were in danger.

The other, and maybe more compelling, reason why Turkey continued to give permission, every six months for more than a decade, to the implementation of the no-fly zone by the U.S. and British Air Force taking off from the İncirlik base was the implicit approval by successive U.S. administrations of Turkey's sporadic but large-scale cross-border incursions into northern Iraq throughout the 1990s. These operations carried out in pursuit of the PKK terrorists, who had been waging a separatist war against Turkey since 1984, involved tens of thousands of troops with the close air support of the Turkish Air Force. The establishment of the no-fly zone had turned northern Iraq into a sanctuary for the PKK. Turkey's incursions were much criticized by the European countries, but the United States preferred to turn a blind eye to its ally's effort to fight the terrorists who were getting all sorts of logistical and military support from Syria and other countries in the region.[4]

Against this background, it would be naïve to argue that negotiations on the economic track, which were said to deadlock on the amount as well as the method of payment of U.S. aid, determined the fate of the resolution that would pave the way for basing American troops in Turkey. The deadlock was political. There were public rumors about secret U.S. plans for a Kurdish state, and Zalmay Khalilzad, President Bush's special representative, shuttled between Ankara and northern Iraq in search of a breakthrough. But he could not satisfy Turkish concerns; his Turkish counterparts insisted that the Turks (or Turkmen) in Iraq be included in Iraq's future political restructuring. A political role for the Turkmen was seen as a safety valve—a way to protect Turkey's vital interest in northern Iraq, by means of which efforts to create a Kurdish state could be rendered ineffective.

Turkish policy makers maintained that Iraq's Turkmen had always been oppressed, whether they lived in Saddam's Iraq (squeezed in between the two no-fly zones) or in Iraqi Kurdistan. Turkish negotiators wanted a political settlement that would enable the Turkmen to be represented in the "new Iraq" commensurate with their population, which was estimated to be roughly 2.5 million—more than double the official figure. But the Kurds in the north were not about to agree to a deal that would elevate the Turkmen to an almost equal status with themselves in the northern provinces, which they claimed to be "unarguably Kurdish." The noninclusion of the Turkmen in the meeting of Iraqi opposition groups in the northern city of Suleymaniyah—which took place on March 1, 2003 by coincidence the very day the TGNA voted on the troop-basing resolution—reinforced the doubts of many deputies. The resolution failed with 264 yes votes, 250 no votes, and 19 abstaining, because it required the approval of an absolute majority of the 550-member Parliament.

Allegations of Turkey's Secret Plans over Mosul and Kirkuk

There has been much speculation about why Turkey was reluctant to allow the U.S. troops to put their feet on the Turkish soil. Some argued that Turkey wanted more money from the U.S. treasury and thus resorted to oriental bargaining techniques with a view to capitalizing on the country's estate value. Some went on even further to claim that Turkey had hidden desires concerning the oil-rich Mosul and Kirkuk provinces in northern Iraq, which were governed by the Turks for centuries until World War I, then lost to the British. Hence, it was alleged that Turkey was conducting secret negotiations with the United States to that effect. None of these allegations was even slightly close to the truth. With respect to the bargaining issue, it suffices to say that money talk with foreigners was traditionally unpopular among Turkish politicians, especially in times of crisis or war. Representatives of a warrior culture would only be ashamed if they traded security of their people with money, regardless of the amount of cash at stake or the level of economic hardship in the country. Therefore, the first claim was totally out of question.[5]

The claims of a secret deal with the United States to annex Mosul and Kirkuk to Turkey were also unfounded. It is true that the Mosul province of the Ottoman Empire, which covered the entire territory that is now known as northern Iraq, including the cities like Kirkuk, Erbil, and Suleymaniyah, was part of the National Pact that was declared by the first Turkish Parliament in 1920 during the War of Liberation led by Mustafa Kemal against the occupying powers. The Mosul problem was one of the unresolved issues at the Lausanne negotiations that paved the way to the foundation of modern Republic of Turkey. During the negotiations, it was agreed to form a commission under the auspices of the League of Nations in 1924 with a view to finding a compromising solution between the British and the Turks who had divergent views on the status of the Mosul province. Turks claimed that Mosul was inherently a Turkish city, while the British maintained, on the contrary, that the demographic structure of the region did not substantiate Turkey's claims. Finally, after long deliberations, the Council of the League of Nations decided in 1926 to rely on the commission's report that literally was completely in line with the position of the British in this debate.[6] Since then, no matter how difficult it may have been for many Turks to acknowledge such a decision, it is a fact of life and has been observed fully by Turkey, provided all the other parties concerned behaved similarly. That is, no ethnic and/or religious group should claim sovereignty over the region in mention.

Hence, Turkish policy makers have kept their temper even during the repulsive behavior of Kurdish Peshmerghas in these cities in the immediate aftermath of the fall of Saddam regime. Had the Turks really had secret desires about Mosul and Kirkuk, the atrocities of Kurdish militia in these cities could very well serve

Turkey's alleged objectives to launch a large-scale military operation into northern Iraq at a time when the U.S. troops were still far from the region. But since such an irresponsible act would have further complicated the already tense relations of the parties concerned, Turkey acted with wisdom as expected.

Post–March 1, 2003 Resolution Period

The failure of the troop-basing resolution in the Turkish Parliament upset the prewar strategies of the Pentagon and caused fractures in the relations of the two long-standing allies. Misunderstanding and miscalculations by the two countries had created profound tensions that were then thought to be highly likely to endure. The failure to implement this prewar strategy forced the American administration to put into practice an alternative plan, albeit much slower than it was asserted, which heavily relied on the militia-like units, namely the Peshmerghas formed by the Kurdish groups in the northern sectors of Iraq, acting under the leadership of Mesout Barzani and Jalal Talabani.

In the absence of Turkey's active contribution to the U.S. military campaign against Saddam Hussein, the result of the war has been an absolute disappointment for many Turks for basically two reasons. First, Turkey's relations with its decades-old "staunch ally," namely the United States, suffered serious ruptures almost at all fronts. Second, the outcome that was most unwanted by Turkey (i.e., the prevalence of Kurdish groups concentrated in the north in the political restructuring of Iraq over the other ethnic/religious groups that are spread all over the country) has almost happened. Hence, decision-makers, civilian and military bureaucrats, and all concerned body of intellectuals in Turkey started to assess the outcome and tried to figure out as to what went wrong and what then could be done in order to reverse the course of undesirable developments, as well as to repair the relations with the United States.

Concerns of Turkey about Internal Threats

Having said what was *not* the reason why Turkey did not cooperate with the United States, it may be appropriate to state here as to what the real concerns of the Turks were, indeed. Since its foundation, the Republic of Turkey has faced challenges from inside as well as outside. Apart from the challenges from outside, two major internal threats have always been at the top of the security agenda of the Turkish policy makers, be they civilian or military. First is "religious fundamentalism," which is strongly believed to aim at reconstituting the Sheria order in the country as well as to bring back the caliphate, both of which were abolished by Atatürk. Second is "ethnic separatism" especially by a small fraction of Kurds living mostly in the southeastern districts of the country. The crisis as well as the war in Iraq could have very well triggered events in both of these fields and could have rendered Turkey into a zone of internal conflict.[7]

There were mass demonstrations countrywide particularly around the mosques against the governmental policies that would seemingly rank Turkey among the coalition powers siding with the United States whose president had once mentioned "crusade" against the Muslim world.[8] The constituents of the single-party government in power formed by the AKP are mostly active practitioners of Islam. The AKP was widely believed to be a continuation of the former Islamic parties, namely the Welfare Party (*Refah Partisi*—RP) and the Virtue Party (*Fazilet Partisi*—FP), with slight deviations and some makeup. The *Refah* Party was banned with a decision of the Turkish Constitutional Court on February 15, 1998. Its successor, the *Fazilet* Party, faced the same problem and it was banned with a decision of the Court taken on June 22, 2001. Therefore, it would be to nobody's surprise if the government encountered serious difficulty in convincing its deputies to vote in favor of the troop-basing resolution. So it happened. The result was a failure in the parliamentary voting of the troop-basing resolution.

On the other hand, at the beginning of the crisis in the fall of 2002, the military adopted the utmost caution in its stance vis-à-vis the issue of U.S. troop deployment in Turkey so as not to make any statement that could ignite mass reactions against the security units in the country. Things might have well gotten out of hand with the provocations of some factions and some organizations. A cold-blooded approach and a relatively low-profile attitude was determined to be the position of the TAF in order to preserve its credibility among the Turkish society as an institution that has long been seen as the "guarantor" of the secular and republican regime in the country and the "weapon of last resort" against the so-called fundamentalists who desired to "take the revenge" from the followers of Atatürk's revolutionary principles.

In addition to concerns over various sketches of religious extremist groups, issues like territorial integrity and internal stability of the country were no less important to the military. Having fought against the insurgencies of the Kurdish separatist organization, namely the PKK, for nearly two decades, and having suffered thousands of casualties in these fights, the Army was seriously concerned with the possibility of proclamation of a Kurdish state in the northern districts of the neighboring Iraqi territory. Even short of full sovereignty in the foreseeable future, any form of autonomy that would be gained by the well-organized U.S.-backed Kurdish groups in Iraq was feared to pave the way to full sovereignty in the medium to long term that could also be followed by certain claims on Turkey, such as territory and compensation.

Further Negotiations with the Americans

The Turkish military was indeed willing to take part in the Coalition formed by the United States in order to secure a seat for Turkey around the table that would shape postwar Iraq. Yet, due attention was paid so as not to be seen as "war mongers" within the Turkish society for the very reasons cited above. Hence, military experts conducted painstaking negotiations with their American counterparts, which resulted on February 8, 2003 in a Memorandum of Understanding (MOU) that documented in more than a hundred pages the "rules of engagement" that the parties would observe with regard to the respective positions of their troops to be stationed in the Iraqi territory.[9] Turkish and American diplomats had intense negotiations for several weeks. Major issues of contention were the number and the sites of American troops to be deployed in Turkey and the Turkish troops in northern Iraq. United States did not want to jeopardize a potential strategic alliance with the Kurdish groups in northern Iraq by allowing Turkish troops into their sectors. But, Turkey made U.S. troop-basing resolution conditional upon a similar permit for Turkish troops to cross the Iraqi border.

The MOU could not be put in practice because of the disapproval of the resolution in the Turkish Parliament on March 1, 2003. A serious implication of the absence of a set of rules of engagement between Turkey and the United States was seen on July 4, 2003 when American soldiers detained a dozen of Turkish Special Forces who were operating in northern Iraq. The presence of some 1,500 Turkish troops was not at all unknown to the United States ever since they were stationed in northern Iraq in March 1995, when the first large-scale Turkish military operation was conducted in the pursuit of PKK terrorists into the Iraqi territory. Never, in the bilateral relations, has the military presence of Turkey in northern Iraq been a serious issue between Turkey and the United States. However, the tide has turned with the failure of the troop-basing resolution to get the approval from the Turkish Parliament. The general mood among the political and academic circles was that, had the resolution not been disapproved, such unwanted developments would not have taken place. The lack of clear-cut engagement rules between the parties was only a time bomb, and it went off on the 4th of July. Paradoxically, the detention of Turkish soldiers for some 60 hours did also provide an opportunity to take a deep breath to cool down as well as to reassess the state of affairs between Turkey and the United States because there was then a "delicate balance of anger" between the two allies. A fresh start was thought to be possible, and the subject then could be to help the United States out in its dealings with the Iraqi debacle.

Due to the possibility of unwanted developments in northern Iraq which could end up with the Kurds having the upper hand in the restructuring of the country, the Turkish government, briefed by the General Staff and the Foreign Ministry officials, got involved in further negotiations with the Americans in the autumn of 2003. In these negotiations, the objective was to secure feasible guaranties from the United States that the Kurds would not prevail in the politics of postwar Iraq, especially in the north where a significant Turkmen population was living alongside the Kurds. The overwhelming majority of the population of Iraq consists of Muslims, of whom some 65 percent are Shiites and about 30 percent are Sunnis. Christians constitute 3 percent of the total population. When it comes to ethnical formation of the population, Arabs constitute 70 percent of the total population, while the Kurds constitute 15–20 percent. Turkmen and other groups constitute 10 percent of the population.

The pace and the tone of negotiations were dramatically different than the previous ones. Until then, almost a constant proportion of Turkish population was against sending troops to Iraq where atrocities were mounting, including the deadly attacks on the United Nations buildings and its personnel resulting in losses of lives. Eventually, a growing number of people started to acknowledge that the only way to prevent the future damage that would be caused to Turkey's interests by the chaotic environment in Iraq would be to help the United States stabilize the country as quickly as possible and to secure a promise in return from the United States that no Kurdish state would be allowed in northern Iraq in the years ahead.

There were also other serious concerns such as the status of the Turkmen in Iraq and their future constitutional rights. The new Constitution of Iraq was an issue yet to be worked out by experts from inside and outside the country. Turkey was deeply concerned with whether the Constitution would have loopholes or shortcomings in keeping the Iraqi people together in the decades, if not years to come. Another major issue of concern to Turkey was the threat of PKK, which was using the Kandil Mountain on the Iraq-Iran border as a sanctuary for its approximately 5,000 members. Turkish and American experts have come together frequently to work out a feasible plan for the elimination of the threat posed by the PKK. Yet, there were a number of difficulties in taking further effective steps right away. First, and foremost, the Turkish Parliament had passed a bill in August 2003 that gave the opportunity to the PKK members to be free if they gave up their arms and surrendered, provided that they were not involved in killings in the past. The "amnesty law" expired on February 6, 2004. Still a combined military operation against the PKK might have potentially created a lot many troubles for the United States in the political domain both at home and abroad. Secondly, a military operation against the group of terrorists on the mountains is estimated to necessitate some 30,000 U.S. troops that had to be allocated to conduct combat operations for more than a month, which were also likely to suffer hundreds of casualties. The United States, however, did have barely a single soldier to spare for a prolonged military operation whose political objective and military benefits were not very clear to most Americans.

Such concerns notwithstanding, the Turkish military had made its pledge to send troops to Iraq implicitly conditional upon the swift measures to be taken by the United States against the PKK terrorists stationed in northern Iraq. The United States did yield to this claim, especially at a time when there were not many countries volunteering to send troops for the stabilization of Iraq and maintaining peace and security in the country. Some allies of the United States feared heavy casualties, while some others were concerned with the legitimacy principle and sought a new UN resolution. Up until mid-October 2003, Turkey seemed to have the upper hand in the negotiations with the United States with the capability of making a generous contribution in terms of number of troops and the courage to take over the most dangerous zones where the American soldiers were under incessant attacks every day. On October 7, 2003 the Turkish Parliament approved the resolution that would allow sending troops into the Iraqi territory. Then the United States faced a dilemma.

On the one hand, deploying Turkish troops in Iraq would facilitate controlling the most difficult sectors of the country where U.S. soldiers were being killed or seriously wounded daily. This in turn would heat up domestic politics in America and strengthen the hands of those who challenged President George W. Bush in the run up to the presidential elections in November 2004. The Turkish military had gained invaluable experience as well as expertise in prolonged low-intensity warfare in rough conditions during its fight against the PKK and also learned a lot and proved itself in peacekeeping and nation-building efforts in Bosnia, Kosovo, and lastly in Afghanistan. Hence, Turkey's offer could not be easily turned down by the American administration.

On the other hand, the northern Iraq, which was a relatively quieter place when compared to the rest of the country, could be seriously disturbed with the Turkish flag flying in sectors near the Kurdish-controlled zones. A Turkish troop deployment in Iraq (possibly to the northwest of Baghdad) would necessitate establishing a logistical supply route from Turkey to the deployment area cutting through northern Iraq mostly controlled by the Kurdish Peshmerghas. Such an eventuality was said to be by no means acceptable to the Kurdish leaders who threatened both Turkey and the United States with the possibility of armed clashes if Turkish troops entered into northern Iraq, which they claimed to be "Iraqi Kurdistan." Then Turkish Deputy Chief of General Staff General Ilker Başbuğ stated quite clearly on October 13, 2003 during a press meeting in response to such threats that the Turkish soldiers would retaliate in kind if and when they are attacked no matter by whom.[10] Such statements, one after another, have put further strain on the decision then yet to be taken in Washington, D.C., as to whether Turkish troops should be deployed in Iraq as part of the stabilization force or not.

When it became clear for the United States that a new UNSC resolution could be approved and that it would satisfy the condition of legitimacy for a number of countries, especially in the Muslim world, a series of statements were started to be made from the high levels of the U.S. administration that sending Turkish troops to Iraq could be risky. The UNSC adopted the Resolution 1511 on October 16, 2003 that provided necessary legal ground to send troops to Iraq for restoring security and stability in the country. Until then, the U.S. administration seemed to turn a blind eye to the opposition to any Turkish military presence in Iraq that was voiced fiercely among the Kurds as well as the Arab world. But as a result of the crossfire of words between Turks and the Kurds, the United States asked Turkey to stay on its side of the border.

Impact of the "Greater Middle East" Project on Turkey-U.S. Relations

In addition to the developments in Iraq, the U.S. policy to transform the "Greater Middle East" also had a negative impact on the Turkish-American relations. According to many analysts, the U.S. wars in Afghanistan and in Iraq, following the September 11 attacks on the World Trade Center and the Pentagon, constitute important stages of a bigger strategic objective commonly known as the transformation of the Greater Middle Eastern region from radical regimes and dictatorships to moderate democracies and open societies. When looked from the Western capitals, and especially from Washington, D.C., the region extending from North Africa well into the heartlands of Central Asia is viewed as having certain common characteristics that are believed to give rise to radicalism, and more importantly, terrorism aiming to destroy Western civilization. The "Greater Middle East" goes far beyond the classical delineation of the Middle East that comprises countries like Egypt, Israel, Jordan, Saudi Arabia, Syria, Iraq, and Iran, and encompasses more countries like Morocco in the west and Uzbekistan in the east, and Caucasian Muslim nations in the north and Sudan in the south. Islam, with its different interpretations and applications in different nations having different regimes, is observed to be at the very core of the common characteristics of the majority of the nations falling within this geographical region. In view of Western analysts, the combination of the version of Islam and the type of regime gains prominence concerning the categorization of the threats these states pose to Western civilization. Seen from this perspective, while some states and their regimes in the "Greater Middle East," such as Syria and Iran, are perceived as posing a significant threat, others, indeed one, namely Turkey, is considered as having the potential to act as a "model" for the rest of the states in the region.

Turkey's encounters with Western civilizations are not new. Turks have lived and also ruled in large territories in Europe for centuries. Even though most of the ruling elite and the overwhelming majority of the population in the Ottoman Empire as well as in Turkey have been Muslim, religion has not been the dominant factor in the administration. Islam is one of the constituents of Turkish identity. There have been times when this particular aspect of Turkish identity was tried to be pushed to the fore in the domestic political domain, but internal checks and balances system worked and made the necessary adjustments as required from the institutions of a secular democratic regime founded by Atatürk in the 1920s.

Nevertheless, developments in the post–September 11 era underlined the Middle Eastern aspects of Turkey's identity among Western powers. Notwithstanding the expectation of Europeans and Americans of Turkey in regard to its capacity to offer a model for the states in the Greater Middle Eastern region to emulate in their efforts to transform themselves into liberal democracies, such an argument was seen by Turks to erode the credentials of Turkey's Western identity. The more the suggestion that Turkey offer a successful example to the peaceful cohabitation between Islam and democracy, the more alerted Turkey's secular elites felt. To these elites, Turkey is first and foremost a secular state in which Islam should not be mentioned to define the state's identity. The U.S. claims that Islam and democracy could coexist suggests that Islam is a social force shaping people's identity. Seen from this perspective, the legitimacy of the ideational approach toward the West has increasingly been contested particularly on the part of Turkey's Kemalist security elites who are staunch believers in, and followers of, the principles of Mustafa Kemal Atatürk and the reforms that he introduced to the Turkish nation during the state-building process in the 1920s.

The Greater Middle East project of the United States has also contributed to the rise of nationalism and Western skepticism in Turkey. A wide margin of Turkish public opinion now shares a feeling of growing "anti-Americanism." The rise in anti-Americanism is driven by the gap between Turkey's expectations from the United Sates and the way the United States has responded to them, particularly concerning northern Iraq. During the Iraq war in March 2003, U.S. President Bush remarked at one point that he "told the Turks not to send troops into northern Iraq." Five years later, during Turkey's limited operation to destroy an important base of PKK terrorists inside northern Iraq in February 2008, he made a similar statement telling that "the Turks should get out." No other recent U.S. president would have used such an undiplomatic language toward a "staunch ally," as the father Bush once pronounced during his term in the White House. In a similar situation, former U.S. presidents would have been careful to say "we advised our Turkish allies" or "our Turkish friends."

It is clear that the United States faces a dilemma in its relations with Turkey. On the one hand, the United States wants to see Turkey playing a significant role in its Greater Middle East project by becoming a role model for the Islamic states and Muslim communities around the world. On the other hand, Turkey's serious concerns about the developments in northern Iraq, including the claims for an independent Kurdish state as well as the PKK terrorism, which finds refuge in the region, are not taken seriously into consideration by the United States as much as the Turkish authorities would like to see. Unless the United States and Turkey find ways to satisfy each other's expectations regarding their (grand) strategic objectives, the United States is likely to face this dilemma so long as it remains the occupying power in Iraq.

U.S. Occupation in Iraq and the Future of Turkish-American Relations

Many years of U.S. occupation in Iraq have had two major effects on Turkey: a deterioration in Turkish-American relations and the transformation, rather than abolition, of perceived threats from Iraq. Their common denominator is Turkey's serious concerns about the aspirations of Iraqi Kurds to independence. From Turkey's perspective, the future will to a great extent be shaped by the pace of events on these issues. The failure of the Turkish Parliament to pass a resolution that would allow the stationing of some 60,000 U.S. troops on Turkish territory demoted Turkey in the eyes of the Bush administration. Furthermore, the development provided justification for the United States to elevate the status of the Kurds in northern Iraq to that of "strategic partner" in the region. Considering that the U.S. interest in the Kurds had already taken a dramatic turn with the 1991 Gulf War, the degree of commitment the United States shows in fulfilling the expectations of the Kurds in Iraq and in neighboring countries, such as Iran, Syria, and Turkey, will determine the scope and content of Turkish-American relations in the future.

Since the beginning of the U.S. occupation in Iraq, despite sporadic and short-term improvements in relations between Turkey and the United States, especially at times of high-level visits, U.S. policy in Iraq appears much more sensitive to meeting the demands of the Kurdish authority than those of its longtime NATO ally. An example of this was the unanticipated and much resented attitude of the United States during Turkey's ground operation against PKK strongholds in northern Iraq in February 2008. Even though the White House and the Pentagon were in advance provided with detailed information about the scale and purpose of the operation, the statements of U.S. President George Bush and Secretary of Defense Robert Gates that "the Turks should get out" underlined the fact that Washington considered the Kurds in northern Iraq as its primary strategic ally.

The value of the Kurds to the United States emanates from a number of factors. First, the Kurds are key to Iraqi integration or indeed disintegration. If the United States wants to "transform the greater Middle East," it has to be successful in Iraq so as to set a precedent for the rest of the region. Without the consent of the Kurds, Iraq will not stay united (even if it has already in fact disintegrated). Second, the Kurds control large oil and gas fields, especially in and around the Kirkuk and Mosul districts that are likely to be exploited by American companies. Third, Kurdish northern Iraq lies between Turkey's relatively rich water resources, namely the Tigris and the Euphrates rivers, and U.S. allies in the region, including Israel, Jordan, Saudi Arabia, and other Gulf monarchies. Fourth, the geographical location of Kurdish northern Iraq provides Israel with a "forward defense capability" against threats from Iran and potentially from Pakistan, who have long-range missiles that may carry warheads with WMD. Fifth, the Kurds are among the most secular groups in the entire Islamic world. As such, in the age of America's "global war on terror" that is based on the neoconservative belief that Islamic radicalism feeds terrorism around the world, a Muslim Kurdish community that can ally itself with the West becomes indispensable.[11]

Against this background, unless a change of mind occurs in Washington's approach toward Ankara, it may not be a mere pessimistic estimate to argue that in the future the military-strategic significance of Turkey for the United States will be diminished; Iraq will become the forward defense post of the United States for future contingencies in the Middle East and a launch pad for power projection in Central Asia, if need be; and the United States will probably maintain troops in Iraqi territory and operate military bases on long-term contracts, which will undermine the indispensability of İncirlik and other military installations in Turkey. All of these suggest that the general nature of Turkish-American relations may not improve and might even become worse.

Still, U.S. strategists will no doubt bear in mind that the greatest challenge to U.S. security will come from the threat posed by international terrorism. And no military capability—no matter how great—can prevent or deter acts of terrorism. The most important instrument will be reliable intelligence. At that point, Turkey will be seen again as an invaluable partner, given its location, cultural, religious, and linguistic common denominators with other civilizations in the Greater Middle Eastern region, as well as its centuries-old expertise in military affairs, including intelligence-gathering capabilities. If and when the U.S. administrations are able to take a wider perspective on world affairs and see where Turkey fits into their strategic calculations, attaining the level of strategic partnership may be possible and rewarding for both parties. If not, Turkey's attempts to prevent certain developments in Iraq may well lead to confrontation with the United States that may delay its attempt at building a new Iraqi state and thus "bringing democracy to the Middle East."

REDEFINITION OF TURKEY'S RELATIONS WITH ISRAEL

Turkey and Israel enjoyed an almost perfect relationship throughout the 1990s that amazed their friends, yet bothered their rivals. However, the U.S. war in Iraq in 2003 revealed that the two long-standing allies did indeed have contradictory objectives and concerns with respect to the future restructuring of Iraq.

Clashing Interest of Turkey and Israel over Northern Iraq

When the United States set on to achieve its political goals, such as to establish a democratic regime in Iraq, the political climate between Turkey and Israel started to deteriorate, because attaining this particular goal of the United States necessitated paving the way to free elections in the country in order to form a representative body of the Iraqi people as the first step. Such an initiative, however, has deeply affected and shaken the highly sensitive fabric of the Iraqi society. Various groups that form a rather complex demographic structure of Iraq started to come forth with such claims that could hardly be met altogether even in the advanced democratic countries. To cite a few, for democracies, secularism is a highly crucial condition without which the rule of reason and wisdom cannot be fully achieved within the society. Nevertheless, the Shia clerics in Iraq insisted for the ultimate decisions with regard to the administration of the country, including the penal code as well as the civil code, and the making of the domestic and foreign policies to be in conformity with Sheria. Such a demand contradicted with democratic aspirations, because there is no room for either negotiation or bargaining for certain claims coming from different sectors of a society ruled by Sheria, which requires its followers (the *Ummah*) to strictly abide by the verses of God. On the other hand, Kurds who barely constitute some 20 percent of the Iraqi society, which is now divided into 18 different administrative sectors, insisted on having the capability to veto, if need be, any forthcoming constitution if it did not satisfy their goal of autonomy and eventual independence. This was also in contradiction with established democratic principles, because the will of the overwhelming majority would be taken hostage by the aspirations of a minority group, which in turn might trigger other minority groups such as the Turkmen, Assyrians, and others to make claims for similar rights and privileges. Hence, Turkey started to feel uneasy about a possible array of political developments in its neighbor. The possibility of Iraq falling apart and the emergence of an independent Kurdish entity in northern Iraq thus became a major source of wary for Turkish statesmen and the military alike.

Notwithstanding the fears of Turkey, such an eventuality might even be favorable for Israel. In other words, while Turkey, once Israel's strategic ally, was searching for ways to prevent the creation of a Kurdish state out of the Iraqi territory, Israel could prefer to see a powerful autonomous Kurdish authority, or even an independent state in northern Iraq. Since, speculative though it may be, a Kurdish self-rule in Iraq with which Israel could conclude, among others, a comprehensive military cooperation agreement could be highly instrumental for its security. Such an agreement would enable Israel to build a forward defense capability against potential and active threats emanating from countries like Iran, Pakistan, and beyond, in the medium to long term. Therefore, it is quite understandable why Israeli authorities in particular, and the Jewish community in the United States in general, give support, or at least do not oppose (as much as the Turks would like to see), the efforts of the Kurdish groups lobbying both in Iraq and elsewhere to achieve their grandiose objective, namely the creation of an independent Kurdistan.

Moreover, the moral affinity between the Jews and the Kurds, of which the former managed to have its own state after long and painstaking deliberations,

need to be reminded here. There are approximately 160,000 Jewish Kurds
(or Kurdish Jews) who are the citizens of Israel most of whose ancestors had emi-
grated from Iraq decades ago. Some of these Kurdish Jews are buying lands and
other intangibles and invest in northern Iraq. One should, therefore, acknowledge
the very facts and the reasons behind the moral support, if anything else, given to
the Kurds among the Jews in general. However, even this kind of a support alone
constituted a particular reason for the deterioration of the Turkish-Israeli relations.

Origins of Interest of Israel in Northern Iraq

While Turkish policy makers and the military were so heavily preoccupied
with the contingencies in Iraq and trying to take every chance to keep Turkey's
marginal capability to control the pace of events, the approach of the Israeli
policy makers to the developments seems to be dramatically different than that
of their Turkish friends. Beyond being a moral issue for the Jews, the geostrategic
value of northern districts of Iraq for the security of Israel can be compared to
nothing else.[12] Patrick Clawson of the Washington Institute for Near East Policy
argued, "Israel's overwhelming national-security concern must be Iran. Given
that a presence in Kurdistan would give Israel a way to monitor the Iranian
nuclear effort, it would be negligent for the Israelis not to be there."[13] Similarly,
a former American senior intelligence official argued that the Israelis' tie to
Kurdistan would be of greater value than their growing alliance with Turkey.[14]
On the same subject, a former Israeli intelligence officer said, "we love Turkey
but got to keep the pressure on Iran...the Kurds were the last surviving group
close to the United States with any say in Iraq. The only question was how to
square it with Turkey."[15]

Weapons of Mass Destruction Capabilities of Iran and Pakistan

The threat of Iranian as well as Pakistani ballistic missiles that could be tipped
with all sorts of WMD, whose ranges can cover any point in the Mediterranean,
looms large. Iran is believed to possess chemical weapons and ongoing research
programs focusing on the production of biological agents, and an advanced
nuclear program revealed in 2002.[16] It goes without saying that the Iranian clergy
is deeply hostile to Israel. Bearing in mind the military capabilities displayed by
Iran with a series of test-firings of 1,350 kilometer-range Sahab-3 ballistic missiles
since 1998, Israel has good reason to fear a surprise or even maybe a suicidal
nuclear first-strike from Iran. The Israelis believe that Iran wants nuclear weapons
to further and bolster its flagging revolution, to provide an alternative to Egyptian
secular moderation, and to challenge the military supremacy of Israel and the
United States in the Middle East. According to an Israeli officer "when the
Iranians have enough fuel for enrichment and the technology for it, it's over."[17]

Israeli analysts have similar concerns with regard to the Pakistani nuclear weapons and ballistic missile capability. Even though at present Pakistan is believed to be preoccupied with the threat posed by the Indian nuclear capability, the war on Afghanistan has shown to the world the degree of "Talibanization of the Pakistani Army," which has a good deal of nukes at stock. The more the radical Islamic groups seize control of the Pakistani army, the greater will be the threat posed to Israel by that country,[18] because a radical Islamic leadership may then turn its face from the east (i.e., India) to the west (i.e., Israel). This is by no means a scenario that can be taken lightly by Israel being a country vulnerable to long-range ballistic missile attacks that can be tipped with nuclear warheads, because of the geographical limitations and demographic structure of the country.[19]

One must bear in mind that, in case a ballistic missile is fired from Iran toward Israel, regarding the distances involved, which is approximately 1,100 kilometers, and the velocity of the missiles, which is in the order of 4 kilometers per second in their terminal phases, the total flight time of such a missile would last only a couple of minutes after launch. Regarding the limitations of even the most sophisticated antiballistic missile shields to intercept all of the incoming missiles and the very short duration of the time needed for an enemy missile to reach its destination, it is essential for Israel to be able to prevent such attacks before they occur. This can be done at various stages. The best is through gathering timely intelligence that would enable special units to preempt in order to render the enemy capabilities ineffective. Israel relies on its spy satellite Ofek-6 to increase surveillance over Iran to be able to have more early warning in case of a surprise attack.[20] Should intelligence units fail to detect timely such a desire of the possible enemies of Israel, the next best mode of action from the Israeli perspective would be to destroy the missiles in their most vulnerable positions (i.e., on the launching pad) or in the early phase of the launch (i.e., the boost phase).

In order to be able to destroy incoming ballistic missiles, Israeli military units should be stationed in areas nearby the enemy missile launchers and must act very swiftly on a very short notice. Be they missile shields on the ground or be they aircraft loaded with air-to-surface or air-to-air antiballistic missiles to take out the enemy missiles, Israel needs to use the Turkish air bases and/or the Turkish airspace neighboring Iran. The military cooperation agreement of 1996 between Turkey and Israel allows such contingencies.[21] One may therefore think that Israel should be satisfied with these guarantees. However, this was not the case especially after September 11, 2001.

Israel's Doubts about Turkey's Future Cooperation

The tragic events on September 11 are believed, in the non-Muslim world in particular, to have demonstrated the potential of a clash between civilizations, religious motifs being at the forefront.[22] The degree of trauma experienced on that specific day has unavoidably and deeply affected the mind-sets of policy makers in the Christian as well as the Jewish world. Hence, one must admit that, as against the political controversies of the past, now an age of religious dispositions seems to open. Israel, being a Jewish state, and Turkey with its predominantly Muslim population found themselves distanced from each other under the impact of the centrifugal forces exerting upon them due to the rapidly changing conjuncture.

Israel's toughened stance toward the Palestinians and the serial assassinations of top Hamas leaders in the spring of 2004, which was declared by Israeli officials as being their adopted strategy in the fight against terror, have created strong reactions in some factions within the Turkish society. Large-scale demonstrations were staged, especially following the Friday prayers in the mosques of big cities like İstanbul and Ankara where Israeli flags were burned. Moreover, a couple of innocent Jewish-Turkish citizens were killed in insanity by radical Islamists for no reason other than their mere religious identity. Amid such horrible developments taking place in Turkey in relation to Israel, the Turkish Prime Minister Recep Tayyip Erdoğan added further and unprecedented strain on the pace of already tense relations with his bitter statements toward Israel. Tayyip Erdoğan harshly criticized Israeli security units in his public speeches here and there for their "indiscriminate killings in Palestine and not using caution." He went on to blame his Israeli counterpart Ariel Sharon for retaliating to suicide bombings by committing state terror against innocent Palestinians. In an interview with the conservative Israeli newspaper *Haaretz,* Prime Minister Erdoğan said in June 2004 that the Israelis were treating the Palestinians similar to the way they themselves were treated 500 years ago. Turkish Premier further added by saying that the Turks extended a helping hand to the victimized Jews in Spain during the Inquisition, whereas today the Palestinians are the victims and the Israelis are bombing civilians from helicopters killing children, women, and the elderly and demolishing buildings.

Against this background, it would not be difficult to understand the reasons why Israeli decision-makers would not want to depend on Turkey in the protection of their country against possible nuclear missile attacks from Iran and beyond. Israeli diplomats and policy makers are concerned with the question of "who could guarantee that Turkey would allow Israel to use its territory or its airspace for example in the future in case missiles attack from Iran or beyond is imminent?" Hence, Israel felt the need to look for another ally in the region that would serve the very same purpose with much less unknowns into the future. The best candidate would be the Kurds in northern Iraq who are not fundamentalists, nor are they likely to have a political system or a bureaucratic mechanism that may create frictions vis-à-vis the expectations of the United States or Israel particularly in the military domain, because the Kurds will be indebted to those who will have contributed, in one way or another, to achieving their ultimate objective of creating an independent state of theirs.

The Estate Value of Northern Iraq for Israel

The estate value of northern Iraq stems from its position along the Iranian frontier. When that territory was under the control of Saddam in the 1980s and 1990s, Turkey's southeast served the very purpose of flying along the Syrian, Iraqi, and Iranian borders, and thereby sending these capitals the message that their strategic assets were within the reach of Israeli Air Force. Having been liberated from Saddam's rule, the northern Iraq itself became accessible to the United States, and therefore Israel, the latter being a potential ally of the Kurds. It would only be a matter of formality to station forward defense units of Israel such as Arrow missiles as well as the F-16 fighter aircraft in northern Iraq in the years to come, if and when Israel decides to enter into contractual relations with the Kurdish entity that is gradually fledging. Then, Israeli analysts and policy makers will not have to worry about the direction of domestic politics and the public sentiment in Turkey as to whether the next government would honor the highly sensitive security and defense arrangements between the two countries in the decades to come.

Future of Turkish-Israeli Relations

There is indeed no serious reason for Israelis to doubt the commitment of a significant proportion of the Turkish population to the preservation of parliamentarian democracy in the country. There is equally no reason to believe that the powerful institutions in Turkey, the military being at the forefront as well as academia, nongovernmental organizations, and various interest groups may ever compromise the secular characteristic of the republican regime. The stance of the Turkish military is particularly important in this respect because the agreement that was reached between the military establishments of Israel and Turkey back in 1996 and the security guarantees thereof will remain in force as long as both parties desire so. Therefore, Israel's misgivings about Turkey's assurances in dealing with the threats on the horizon are unfounded.

Even though reciprocal visits of top politicians on both sides continued according to schedule, the cool atmosphere in Turkish-Israeli relations lasted for nearly half a decade and a number of attempts at political reconciliation have not borne much fruit. For instance, news in May 2008 that Turkey was playing a facilitator role between Israel and Syria over the last few years has created some speculation as to whether such a development would help revive Turkish-Israeli relations. However, it would be optimistic to have such expectations, basically for three reasons. First, Israel and Syria have several backchannels whereby they communicate to whatever extent is required by the two parties. Second, the

United States has been playing a mediator's role for a long time, regardless of Syria's standing on the list of "terrorist states" maintained by the State Department. Third, even though there has been a normalization process in Turkish-Syrian relations since 1998—when Turkey coerced Syria to halt its support to the PKK—not much has been achieved in substance between the two nations other than reciprocal high-level visits.

It is also questionable whether arms sales agreed upon during the visit of Israeli Defense Minister Ehud Barak in February 2008 will be enough to elevate relations between Turkey and Israel to the level where they were in the late 1990s, largely because there is a major difference between then and a decade later regarding the degree of commonality in the threat perceptions of the two nations. Compared to the 1990s, the threats perceived by Turkey's political leaders from their Middle Eastern neighbors have seemingly diminished. For instance, in 2008 Iran's nuclear program is not considered to be a major threat to Turkey. This can be understood from Prime Minister Erdoğan's statements emphasizing that Iran has the right to develop nuclear technology so long as it do not exploit these capabilities for weapons purposes. Turkey's relations with Syria are also far from problematic. While there is much to be done, Turkey and Syria have had peaceful and friendly relations for more than a decade after the crisis over the issue support to PKK terrorism. As for Iraq—so far as the central authority in Baghdad is concerned—relations can be seen as improving rather fast. Even though the presence of PKK terrorists in the northern districts of Iraq controlled by the Kurdish Regional Government has cast a shadow on Turkish-Iraqi relations, the level of threat perceived from Iraq can in no way be compared to the threat posed by the Saddam regime.

Israel's threat perception, on the other hand, has not undergone similar improvements, with the exception of abolishing the military threat of the Saddam regime. However, the future of Iraq is still uncertain. On the Syrian front, there may have been a slight decline in the threat perceived by Israel with the coming to power of Beshar Assad, who seems to be a more pragmatic leader than his father Hafez, ruler of Syria for nearly three decades. But the support of Syrian authorities to Hamas and the role of Syrian intelligence in domestic political conflicts in Lebanon constitute major threats to the security of Israel. Above all, Israel is concerned with the threat posed by Iran's nuclear program, especially with the statements of the top Iranian leadership who suggest "the destruction of the Zionist regime."

Against this background and in the absence of the powerful glue of common threat perceptions by Turkey and Israel, it remains to be seen how far relations can be advanced and whether they can reach the strategic level again. Moreover, the deterioration of Israel's image in the Turkish public eye, a by-product of the post-9/11 trauma experienced in bilateral relations, will continue to be a major factor in the ongoing Turkish-Israeli relationship.[23]

NOTES

1. Mustafa Kibaroğlu, "La Turquie, les États-Unis et l'OTAN : une alliance dans l'Alliance" [Turkey, the US and NATO: An Alliance Within the Alliance], *Questions Internationales,* no. 12 (March–April 2005): 30–32.

2. Mustafa Kibaroğlu, "Turkey and Israel Strategize," *Middle East Quarterly* 9, no. 1 (Winter 2002): 61–65.

3. David A. Sanger and Dexter Filkins, "US Is Pessimistic Turks Will Accept the Deal on Iraq," *New York Times,* February 20, 2003, A1 and A13.

4. Mustafa Kibaroğlu, "Turkey Says No," *Bulletin of the Atomic Scientists* 59, no. 4 (July/ August 2003): 22–25.

5. Interview with Ambassador Yaşar Yakış, then Turkish Foreign Minister, March 2003, Bilkent University, Ankara. Foreign Minister Yakış had presided the Turkish delegation during the early phase of the negotiations with their American counterparts in January and February 2003.

6. David Fromkin, *A Peace to End All Peace: The Fall of the Ottoman Empire and the Creation of Modern Middle East* (New York: Avon Book, 1989).

7. Mustafa Kibaroğlu, "Clash of Interest over Northern Iraq Drives Turkish-Israeli Alliance to a Crossroads," *Middle East Journal* 59, no. 2 (Spring 2005): 246–64.

8. George W. Bush, "Address to a Joint Session of Congress and the American People," September 20, 2001. For the original script of President Bush's address, see www .whitehouse.gov.

9. Memorandum of Understanding between the Government of Turkey and the Government of the United States of America on the Establishment and Implementation of Basic Policy, Principles, Procedures and to Determine the Status of Forces to Be Provisionally Deployed in Turkey for the Purposes of Possible Operations Toward Iraq.

10. İlnur Çevik, "The Spheres of Interest of the Military," *Turkish Daily News,* October 14, 2003.

11. Mustafa Kibaroğlu, "Kurds Hold the Key for Both Turkey and the US," www.bitterlemons-international.org, March 2008.

12. Seymour M. Hersh, "Israeli Agents Operating in Iraq, Iran and Syria," *Democracy Now,* June 22, 2004, http://www.democracynow.org/2004/6/22/seymour_hersh_israeli_agents _operating_in; Seymour M. Hersh, "As June 30th Approaches Israel Looks to the Kurds," *New Yorker,* June 28, 2004.

13. Seymour Hersh, *Chain of Command: The Road from 9/11 to Abu Ghraib* (New York: Harper Collins Publishers, 2004), 351–60.

14. Ibid.

15. Ibid.

16. Mustafa Kibaroğlu, "Good for the Shah, Banned for the Mullahs: The West and Iran's Quest for Nuclear Power," *Middle East Journal* 60, no. 2 (Spring 2006): 207–32. Şebnem Udum, "Missile Proliferation in the Middle East: Turkey and Missile Defense," *Turkish Studies* 4, no. 3 (Autumn 2003): 71–102.

17. Steven Erlanger, "Israeli Spy Satellite Ditches after Takeoff," *International Herald Tribune,* September 7, 2004, p. 5.

18. Mohammed E. Ahrari, *Jihadi Groups, Nuclear Pakistan and the New Great Game* (Carlisle, PA: US Army War College Strategic Studies Institute, 2001).

19. Interview with late Ze'ev Schiff, formerly senior journalist and military affairs editor with Israeli newspaper *Haaretz,* July 2001, İstanbul.

20. Erlanger, "Israeli Spy Satellite Ditches after Takeoff."

21. Interviews with General Çevik Bir (Retired), May 2001 in Ankara and January 2005 in İstanbul. General Çevik Bir was among the drafters of the 1996 military agreement between Turkey and Israel as the Deputy Chief of Staff of the TAF in the mid-1990s.

22. Samuel Huntington, "The Clash of Civilizations," *Foreign Affairs* 72, no. 3 (Summer 1993).

23. Mustafa Kibaroğlu, "New Tests for Turkey's Evolving Security Relationship with Israel," www.jamestown.org, posted in February 2008.

CHAPTER 7

The State of Affairs in Turkey's Relations with Its Neighbors

This book covered so far a great deal of issues pertaining to Turkey's foreign and security policies since the foundation of the Republic. The evolution of these policies is studied in phases taking into consideration the turning points in history, such as World War II, the bipolar international system that emerged in its aftermath, the collapse of the Soviet Union, and the terrorist attacks on 9/11. Turkish policy makers tried to adapt to the changing conditions in the international system. This has not been an easy task, because in addition to the changing international environment that compelled states to adopt certain policies, the nature of Turkey's relations with its neighbors sometimes forced the Turkish decision-makers to pursue policies that deviated from the systemic alignment, as has been the case in Cyprus.

Throughout the republican history, there has been continuity as well as change in Turkey's foreign and security policies especially with regard to its neighbors. Experts in the field of International Relations admit that Turkey is located in a difficult neighborhood. Relations with Greece, Armenia, Iran, Iraq, and Syria constitute the lion's share in the preoccupation of Turkish diplomats, politicians, and the civil and military security analysts. Therefore, Turkey's relations with these countries will be taken under the scope of this final chapter. Instead of giving a full account of the history of bilateral relations in a chronological order, the emphasis will be placed on the most troubling issues. To state a few, the Cyprus issue and the problems in the Aegean Sea constitute the major bones of contention between Turkey and Greece. Similarly, the Armenian allegations of "genocide" concerning the events of 1915 in eastern Anatolia continue to poison the relations between Turkey and Armenia. On the other hand, Turkey's troubled relations with its Middle Eastern neighbors, namely Iran and Syria, are seemingly improving, while major issues, such as the nuclear ambitions of Iran and the unwavering attitude of Syria with its claims on the waters of the Euphrates and Tigris rivers, preserve their potential for future conflicts. Regarding Iraq, however, instability and chaos in the country and the *de facto* partitioning of the Iraqi territory among the Sunni and the Shi'a Arabs, and the Kurds cause serious concerns in Turkey. Moreover, the presence of the PKK terrorists in northern Iraq, controlled by the Iraqi Kurds, who declare time and again their aspirations to independence, is no less distressing from Turkey's perspective. Hence, the following sections will try to explain what lies behind these and other problems that create obstacles in front of developing much better relations between Turkey and its neighbors.

RELATIONS WITH GREECE

Relations with Greece has been one of the thorniest issues that needs to be dealt with in a continuum by Turkish civil and military officers as well as politicians and diplomats. A well-known Turkish career diplomat, Ambassador Şükrü Elekdağ, had once told the authors that he had to allocate approximately one-third of his time in office in his nearly four-decade career in the Turkish Ministry of Foreign Affairs to matters related to Greece and Cyprus. Many more figures who had similar experiences can also be mentioned here. This example alone should indicate the significance as well as the weight of the relations with Greece for Turkey.

The history of Greek-Turkish relations features all sorts of colors from bright to dark instigating, at times, hope and despair. There is a wide array of opinions and perspectives of scholars, historians, intellectuals, and the average person on the street concerning the nature of the Greek-Turkish relations. On the one end of the spectrum are those who believe that the Turks and the Greeks are indeed potentially friendly nations separated with the Aegean Sea. Thus, with a little help to build confidence between them, many of the obstacles in front of achieving a lasting peace and stability can be overcome. Notwithstanding this optimistic approach, those on the other end of the spectrum contend that there is a never-ending rivalry between the two nations emanating from their diametrically opposing cultures. Hence, they suggest that caution should prevail in the relations between Turkey and Greece.

Historical Dimension of the Relations

The two major areas of conflict between Greece and Turkey are the Aegean Sea and the Cyprus island in the eastern Mediterranean. Regarding the Aegean Sea, since the 1830s, when Greece won its independence from the Ottoman Empire, the Hellenic state has continuously expanded its borders at the expense of the Turkish territories in the Balkans and in the Aegean. Moreover, Greece invaded the western districts of Turkey following World War I. Regarding Cyprus, history goes back to earlier ages. Cyprus was invaded in 1571 by the Ottoman Empire and the Turkish rule was consolidated in the next centuries while also respecting the local religious and ethnic diversity. The administration of the island was left to Great Britain during the Berlin Congress of 1878 convened in the aftermath of the Russo-Turkish War. The idea was to gain the support of the British Empire to prevent the expansion of the Russian influence toward the Aegean and the eastern Mediterranean. Even though the parties had agreed that Cyprus would remain as the Ottoman territory, the island was annexed to Britain when the Ottoman Empire entered World War I on the side of Germany.

Cyprus was not an issue during the Lausanne peace negotiations that followed the Turkish victory in the War of Liberation against the occupying powers in 1922. Cyprus, with its location in the eastern Mediterranean on the trade routes to India, had a geostrategic value for Great Britain, and in 1925 Cyprus was declared a Crown colony. But, in the aftermath of World War II, Britain decided to withdraw from most of its colonies. Anticipating such a development, the Greek Cypriots launched an armed struggle, in coordination with the motherland Greece, against the colonial rule of Britain with the hope of annexing (*Enosis*) the island to Greece. To this end, Greek Cypriots formed the National Organization of Cypriot Fighters (*Ethniki Organosis Kyprion Agoniston*—EOKA) under the leadership of George Grivas. The armed struggle intensified after the Suez Canal crisis in 1956 when Britain minimized its military presence in the eastern Mediterranean.

Greek Cypriot atrocities deeply affected the status and the security of the Turkish Cypriots who had been living on the island for ages. The EOKA's armed struggle lasted until 1960. The island was granted independence as a result of the Zurich and London Agreements in 1959 and 1960, respectively, with Turkey, Greece, and the United Kingdom being the "guarantors" of the constitutional state formed with the name of the Republic of Cyprus. Soon after, in 1963, the Greek Cypriot leadership took a unilateral initiative to change some 13 articles of the Founding Constitution, which meant a huge loss of rights and privileges of the Turks in Cyprus. In protest at such a move of Greek Cypriot leadership, the Turkish Cypriot ministers withdrew from the government. Atrocities began with killings of Turkish Cypriots in December 1963 on Christmas Eve, and Turkey felt compelled to intervene, albeit in a limited manner. A squadron of Turkish military aircraft flew over the island at very low altitudes to display Turkey's determination to protect the rights of the Turkish population on the island.

At that time, Turkey did not have enough military capabilities of its own to launch an amphibious operation on the island. Moreover, then U.S. President Lyndon Johnson sent a bitter letter to the Turkish Premier İsmet İnönü and advised him not to use in Cyprus the military equipment or the weapons systems that were given to Turkey within the context of its NATO liabilities. The "Johnson letter" was not only a serious blow to Turkish-American relations but also a wake-up call for the Turkish political and security elite about the degree of Turkey's dependency on other countries in matters pertaining to its security and sovereignty.

The Turkish military and security elite had no doubt that the Greek Cypriots would never give up the idea of *Enosis* and, therefore, they would certainly make another trial in the future. Taking this possibility into consideration, Turkey embarked on building up the necessary force structure all by itself. A brigade of mountain commandos was formed near the city of Bolu in northwestern Turkey specifically for this purpose so be able to fight whenever necessary in the mountainous territory of Greek Cyprus. Landing ships were also built for a large-scale amphibious operation. It was then only a matter of time for the Greek Cypriots to create another provocation that would compel Turkey to intervene, this time with a more comprehensive military capability at its disposal. In the summer of 1974, encouraged by a military government in Athens, the Greek Cypriot National Guard staged a coup with the aim of uniting Cyprus with Greece. Turks saw the coup as another manifestation of the *Megali Idea,* the Greek dream of reconstituting the Byzantine Empire, which was lost to the Ottomans in 1453. The first thing Prime Minister Bülent Ecevit did was to call on the other guarantor states, namely Britain and Greece, to intervene politically in order to stop the EOKA fighters who had started to attack Turkish Cypriots. Britain refrained from getting involved by saying that although it had the right to intervene as a guarantor state, it was not obliged to do so. In other words, Britain saw intervention as "a right but not an obligation." The meeting of Turkish and Greek prime ministers in Bern, Switzerland did not yield a result either, and the Turkish military, which was ready for such a contingency, intervened in Cyprus on July 20, 1974. Fighting lasted for several weeks. A cease-fire was reached to give another chance to diplomatic interventions. However, no solution was found. Turkey continued its operations for another short while and then stopped. Since then, the island remains divided along the "Green Line" passing through Nicosia, the capital city. Even though the Republic of Cyprus could not be restored on the 1963 Constitutional grounds, with Turks and Greeks both represented, the presence of Turkish troops on the island put a halt to the civil war between the two communities that had resulted in mass killings. Turkish military presence since then is also seen by the Turks as guaranteeing their security and stability.

Origins of the Greek-Turkish Dispute

The recent history of Greek-Turkish relations is full of incidents in the Aegean and in the related airspace, some of which have brought the two countries close to war. Although war between modern democracies is unlikely, an unintentional armed clash might escalate to all-out warfare. Contentious issues between Greece and Turkey, apart from their respective position vis-à-vis the Cyprus problem, consist of, mainly, the delimitation of the territorial waters, the continental shelves, and the airspace mostly in the Aegean region; the demilitarized status of the islands; and the status of some islands, islets, and rocks in the Aegean Sea whose affiliations are yet to be determined. Hence, there is a host of problems between Greece and Turkey that must be resolved in some ways so as to establish fair and lasting peace and to bring stability to the relations. That said, the most important problem is the deep disagreement between the two nations about whether there is a set of problems, as advocated by Turkey, that must be treated as a package, or is there only one problem, as asserted by Greece, which is the continental shelf problem, and the way to resolve it would be to take the issue to the International Court of Justice (ICJ) in the Hague. According to Greece, all other "so-called problematic issues" are indeed its "sovereign issues" and that they cannot be negotiated with other countries. It must be clear from such an attitude that, even if a Turkish government would be ready to do everything necessary to solve the problems in the Aegean, such as the expansion of the territorial waters above its current levels, which is six miles for both countries, or to put an end to the airspace violations, there is no such possibility to discuss these matters simply because of the fact that Greece does not consider them as matters that can even be negotiated. In the absence of even a common definition of the problems, or *the* problem, it becomes highly difficult to be hopeful that peace and lasting stability in the Aegean can be reached in the foreseeable future.

Even in the case of the dispute over the continental shelf in the Aegean, which is acknowledged by Greece to be the only problem that can be negotiated with Turkey, Greece suggests that Turkey should take the issue to the Hague, if it so wishes. But, for a dispute to be brought before the ICJ, parties to the dispute must first agree on what they disagree by documenting their points of disagreements, and then they must ask for the jurisdiction of the Court. Then the Court takes a decision, which binds the parties so applied to it. No country can take an issue before the Court all by itself. Moreover, Turkey did not yet recognize the competence of the ICJ in looking into the matters pertaining to Turkey. Hence, in the absence of bilateral negotiations in the area of continental shelf dispute, which is an issue that unavoidably encompasses the territorial waters issue that Greece rejects to talk about on the grounds of sovereignty principle, Turkey cannot take the issue to the Hague. Yet, even if Turkey recognizes the competence of the Court and, with or without Greece on board, takes the continental shelf dispute to the ICJ, Greece, on the other hand, has reservations on the competence of the Court as regards the matters relating to its national defense. It is clear that continental shelf issue is related to national defense issues in successive stages, because it is directly related to the territorial waters issue that has direct relevance to national defense matters. Then, again, there will be a deadlock in the resolution of this dispute.

This specific case alone shows how complicated are the problems between Turkey and Greece and that they are interrelated with one another. Especially the link between the Cyprus problem and the problem(s) in the Aegean is particularly important to recognize. The common understanding in the world as well as in Turkey is that "if the Cyprus problem can be resolved, then Turkey and Greece can easily solve their differences in the Aegean." However, this is not the case, and the truth is the exact opposite of what is commonly believed. It must be acknowledged that the Cyprus problem is taken hostage by the problems between Turkey and Greece, and without the resolution of these problems, any attempt to solve the Cyprus problem may either yield temporary solutions and will make no good to achieve a lasting peace, or it may aggravate the situation in the eastern Mediterranean and in the Aegean even further in the following stages.

The Link Between Cyprus and the Aegean Problems

There have been a series of negotiations to find a solution to the Cyprus problem either directly between the Greek and Turkish Cypriot leaders or with the involvement of the Secretary-Generals of the United Nations or their special representatives and envoys. Thus far, it was not possible to come up with a workable solution that would satisfy the Turks and the Greeks both on the island and also in the motherlands Greece and Turkey, because the Cyprus problem is part of a bigger set of problems between Turkey and Greece. Therefore, understanding the origins of the dispute as they pertain, among others, to the situation in the sea and in the air becomes highly crucial. What follows is the true reason behind the dispute, which, however, may not be heard from the official circles in Turkey.

Since the July 1974 attempt of the Greek Cypriots to realize their goal to annex Cyprus to Greece (*Enosis*), the political and security elite in Turkey have paid the utmost attention whenever Greek politicians and government office-holders have suggested that Greek territory should be enlarged in the east to include Cyprus, or even İstanbul, the latter being the capital of Orthodoxy, the principal religion of Greece. With the lessons drawn from historical experiences, Turkey's security elite have always been concerned that Greek decision-makers could decide to stage a surprise attack on Turkey when the time is deemed ripe—for instance, if Turkey were deeply immersed in serious conflicts with its rivals in the Middle East.

From a military perspective, Greece has a strategic advantage over Turkey because several Greek islands in the Aegean Sea, only a few miles off the Turkish coast, have small-scale air bases. While scenarios of a surprise attack are quite unlikely in the current political environment both in the Aegean and in the world, the military capabilities of Greece in the islands that should have remained demilitarized according to the Lausanne Treaty are yet a matter of concern especially for the Turkish military elite. Therefore, what is more likely and of more serious concern for Turkish political and security elite is the possibility of a unilateral move by a Greek government to extend Greece's territorial waters above the current limit of six miles. The Law of the Sea Convention, which was signed in 1982 and entered into force in 1994, gives right to the states parties to the Convention to extend their territorial waters up to 12 miles in high seas. But, the geographical situation in the Aegean Sea where there are some 3,000 Greek islands in a relatively narrow area does barely fit the definition and the terms of the Convention in this regard. Nevertheless, the Greek Parliament was hasty to empower the Greek governments on June 1, 1995 with the right to declare extension of Greek territorial waters above six miles up to 12 miles whenever they deemed appropriate. In response to this move of the Greek Parliament, the TGNA convened on June 8, 1995 and declared that a decision of Greece to extend its territorial waters in the Aegean beyond six miles would not be acceptable and, should this happen, Turkey would take necessary measures, including military ones, to counter the situation. Turkey's reaction was simple but a decisive one by declaring that it would not recognize a *fait accompli* that could result in a hot confrontation between the two countries. This was understood, and presented as such, in the international arena as *casus belli*.

The reason behind Turkey's stubborn opposition to the extension of the territorial waters must be clarified here. At the present situation with the 6-mile limit in the territorial waters on both sides of the Aegean, approximately 43.5 percent of the Aegean Sea is the sovereign territory of Greece due to the thousands of Greek islands spread all over the region. Turkey's sovereignty is only approximately 8 percent. If one assumes for a moment that both Turkey and Greece decide to increase simultaneously their territorial waters to 12 miles, then the area that will fall within Greek sovereignty will increase to 71.5 percent, whereas Turkey's sovereign territory in the Aegean Sea will become 9 percent with only one unit increase. In other words, for one unit increase in the territorial waters of Turkey, there will be 28 units increase in the Greek territorial waters in case of 12-mile application. Moreover, Turkish ships will have to ask for permission from Greece to sail between two Turkish cities such as İstanbul and İzmir. These are not the types of situations that sovereign states would like to see limiting their freedoms as well as damaging their military and economic interests.

Greece harshly criticized Turkey with its *casus belli* statement on the grounds that such an attitude would run contrary to the founding principles of the United Nations Charter, which outlaw the use or the threat of use of force in Article 2 paragraph 4. Indeed, the wording of Turkey's statement did not include explicit references to the "cause of war." But the attitudes of both sides may unavoidably lead to a confrontation in successive stages should they insist on their declared policies, because if Greece decides to put its decision into effect and officially declare its territorial waters above the current six miles level, then Turkey will still consider the zone between the current six miles and the self-proclaimed additional Greek territorial waters as international waterways and will continue to send ships (civil or military) to this area without asking permission from the Greek authorities. Notwithstanding Turkey's negligence, the Greek coast guard, claiming sovereignty on the expanded territorial waters, will have to engage Turkish ships. Then, Greek authorities will have to make a hard decision. They will either have to turn a blind eye to the passage of Turkish ships without permission from the expanded Greek territorial waters, but unrecognized by Turkey. However, this will be a humiliating option for Greece. Or, they will have to engage the Turkish ships with Greek naval forces.

Similar situation exists in the airspace between the two countries as Greece claims sovereignty in 10-mile airspace while Turkey does not recognize above six miles. Normally airspace is the area strictly above the territorial waters, which is currently six miles for both Greece and Turkey in the Aegean. Greece is the only country in the world whose claim for sovereignty in the airspace far exceeds its territorial waters. Because of such a claim of the Greek administration, Turkish aircraft are frequently engaged by the Greek military aircraft between the 6 and 10 miles. Therefore, "dog fights" occur between the Greek and Turkish fighter aircraft, which sometimes end with the losses of aircraft as well as lives on both sides. In the sea, such an engagement may end up with opening fire by the Greek coast guard or naval forces on Turkish ships, which will be allegedly "violating Greece's sovereign territorial waters." It is not difficult to imagine what may come next.

Hence, the Turks believe that only the threat of a strong penalty prevents Greece from resorting to a surprise attack or to extend its territorial waters above the current level. To put it straight, as an effective retaliation to a Greek *fait accompli* in the Aegean, that penalty will be a Turkish invasion of the Greek sectors of Cyprus. The 40,000 mechanized and well-trained troops stationed in the Turkish-controlled sectors of Cyprus are capable of invading the rest of the island, if need be.

Turkey's "Deterrent" and Stability in the Eastern Mediterranean

A Turkish threat to take over Cyprus should be considered as analogous to the "second-strike capability" possessed by the United States and the Soviet Union during the Cold War. The presence of thousands of nuclear missiles in the arsenals of the United States and the Soviet Union that were deployed in safe and secure platforms such as long-range bomber aircraft, nuclear submarines, and underground silos (i.e., the triad) lent confidence to both sides that even if one of the parties launched a large-scale nuclear missile attack, the party that would be attacked would still be able to retain a significant number of missiles in the triad that would enable it to strike back causing an unacceptable damage to the party that attacked first. Hence, the ability to ride out an enemy attack and then retaliate was acknowledged to be key to maintaining stability between the two superpowers. By the same token, Turkish political and security elite believe that Turkey's ability to invade the whole of Cyprus, only in retaliation to a Greek move in the Aegean, so far helped maintain the strategic balance of power with Greece. This has provided the Turkish political decision-makers with a strong sense of security. Hence any attempt, political or military, that may upset the long-established balance in the Aegean may result in undesired consequences.

Seen from this perspective, in late 1996, the Greek Cypriot plan to deploy Russian-origin sophisticated air defense systems on the island, namely the S-300, posed an unprecedented challenge to Turkey's "strategic deterrent" and brought Turkey and Greece to the brink of war once again. Turkey insisted that Greek Cypriot administration withdraw its decision because the presence of such an elaborate air defense system would pose a challenge to the supremacy of the Turkish Air Force in the eastern Mediterranean. Turkey conducted maneuvers in Cyprus and in the eastern Mediterranean displaying its ability to attack the missile launcher sites and its determination to do so in case S-300 missile systems are deployed on the island. After long deliberations with the involvement of particularly the United States, which has become seriously concerned with the possibility of a confrontation between two of its allies, the Greek Cypriot administration was convinced to shelve its desire to own a highly sophisticated air defense system. The S-300 missile launchers and other related equipment and trucks that were bought from Russia by the Greek Cypriots were stored in a depot on the Greek island Crete in 1998.

The Future of Turkish-Greek Relations

In contrast to such periods when Turks and Greeks came to the brink of war, there have been times when hopes have flourished as well. For instance in 2003, an initiative was taken by the then United Nations Secretary-General Kofi Annan who came up with a set of ideas first and then a comprehensive plan, generally known as the "Annan Plan," with a view to overcoming obstacles in front of reconstituting the Republic of Cyprus of the 1960s. Unlike his predecessors, Kofi Annan and his good offices were much more heavily involved in the deliberations on both sides of the Green Line in Cyprus and also in both capitals in Greece and Turkey. Meanwhile, the change in the government in Turkey with the November 2002 general elections and the coming of liberal-conservative Justice and Development Party (AKP) to power with the rhetoric to solve the long-standing disputes of Turkey with its neighbors has also injected fresh impetus to the negotiations within the context of the Annan Plan. The Turkish Premier Recep Tayyip Erdoğan stated, as an indication of his determination to solve the Cyprus problem, that Turkey would be "always one step ahead" in coming up with proposals so as to find breakthroughs in the resolution of the problems. The AKP government's attitude was harshly criticized by many circles in Turkey for selling out the Turks on the island and also for severely damaging Turkey's supreme national interests. However, the negotiations were carried on and culminated in a final document that would be put to vote on both sides of the Green Line in Cyprus. It was agreed in the Annan Plan, among others, that the Republic of Cyprus would be formed again by both the Greek and the Turkish Cypriots with differing percentages in terms of representation commensurate with their population rates; the united Cyprus would become a member of the EU; and the Turkish military presence would be brought down to the level of a division composed of some 650 soldiers that would have only a symbolic meaning in terms of the guarantorship of Turkey, a condition that was also put in the first Founding Treaty of 1960.

The Annan Plan was put to referendum in the Greek and the Turkish sectors of Cyprus on April 24, 2004. The results of the referenda were astonishing. On the Turkish side of Cyprus, the Annan Plan was accepted with some 65 percent of the votes, whereas Greek Cypriots voted against the Annan Plan with an overwhelming majority of some 76 percent. Hence, according to the terms of agreement, the Annan Plan was declared "null and void" meaning that it would be treated as if it has never been discussed or negotiated.

The motives behind the "yes" and "no" votes of the respective parties vary significantly. On the Turkish side, caution prevailed, at first, regarding the intentions behind such a comprehensive plan that would require the Turks to make a lot of concessions, which were adamantly opposed by them in the past. However, the possibility of becoming the citizens of the unified Cyprus, thereby joining the EU, has become a powerful incentive for most of the Turkish Cypriots to endorse the Annan Plan. Moreover, the AKP government, in line with its policy "to solve Turkey's bilateral disputes with its neighbors," launched a comprehensive campaign in support of the Plan using the media very effectively with the support of liberal intellectual circles. As such, the proponents of the Plan managed to mobilize enough support, which was not there until several months ago.

On the Greek side of Cyprus, however, the administration in general, and the Greek Cypriot leader Tassos Papadopoulos in particular, launched a negative campaign against the Plan as if it was not them who had negotiated the Plan and agreed to put to a vote. On the eve of the referendum, in his televised address to the Greek Cypriot people, with tears in his eyes, Papadopoulos asked the Greek community to cast "no" vote. So did the three-quarters of the Greek Cypriots and the Plan failed to enter into force despite the approval of the Turks. There was no penalty applied for the Greek Cypriots for turning down the

Annan Plan, whereas the Turkish Cypriots was punished by not being admitted to the EU. It is indeed understandable as to why the Greek Cypriots have refused the Plan. Because, had the Plan been approved, it would have consolidated the partially Turkish character of the Republic of Cyprus, which would not be acceptable to the nationalist-conservative Greeks both in Cyprus and in Greece. Hellenism does in no way tolerate Turkish character of Cyprus or of the Cypriot community. Hence, so long as the Turks remain on the island, it is highly likely that the Greeks will continue their attempts to cleanse the island from the Turks, in one way or another. This, of course, is an issue open to speculation and also subject to all sorts of dangerous scenarios in the future.

Despite the refusal of the UN-sponsored Annan Plan, Greek Cyprus is admitted to the EU as of January 1, 2005. Since then, both Greece and the Greek Cyprus use their privileges and rights within the EU to impose conditions on Turkey in its accession negotiations with the European Commission. One last requirement of the EU from Turkey was to open its sea and airports to Greek Cypriot naval vessels and aircraft in accordance with the fullest implementation of the Customs Union between Turkey and the EU, which entered into force in 1995. Even though the AKP government signed the Additional Protocol that envisages granting such permissions to the Greek Cypriot vessels, the issue is yet to be brought before the Grand National Assembly for ratification. There is enormous pressure on the government by the opposition groups who argue that ratification of the Protocol will simply mean the recognition of Greek Cyprus as the only representative of all the Cypriots, including some 150,000 Turks, who live in the island, and also the renunciation of the Turkish Republic of Northern Cyprus, which proclaimed sovereignty in 1983 and was recognized only by Turkey. Short of ratification of the Additional Protocol in such a way to encompass Greek Cypriot vessels, the European Commission decided in December 2006 to suspend the accession negotiation process with Turkey on 8 of the 35 chapters, putting a *de facto* halt to Turkey's European vocation.

History has proven that Turks and Greeks are better off when peace and cooperation prevail in their bilateral relations, as has been the case in the 1930s during the time of Mustafa Kemal Atatürk and Elefterios Venizelos, the great leaders of Turkey and Greece, respectively. It must be remembered that Venizelos had nominated Atatürk for the Nobel Peace Prize in 1934. This must be an indication of the degree of trust of the two statesmen in each other and the caliber of their leadership. One may argue that at that time neither Cyprus was an issue, nor was there the Law of the Sea Convention that would provoke Greece to opt for increasing its territorial waters, and that reaching such a level of friendship and cooperation would be easy in the absence of complicated matters relating to their sovereignty and their supreme national interests. Yet, one may also argue that, even in the presence of these and other problems, being the great leaders of two nations who managed to leave a bloody history behind them, Venizelos and Atatürk would have found ways to solve their differences to reach a fair and lasting peace by respecting each other's needs as well as vulnerabilities. They would not see the nature of Turkish-Greek relations as "zero sum game," meaning one's gain being the other's loss. They would rather consider the relations as "win-win" situation where both parties would gain. Conditions exist for this to happen, so long as the parties look to the future without being stuck in history, most part of which may be distorted. But, it takes leadership, wisdom, and courage to solve such thorny issues, which will be to the benefit of both nations in the long-term if peace is achieved.

RELATIONS WITH ARMENIA

Turkey recognized the Republic of Armenia on December 16, 1991 together with other former Soviet republics in the Caucasus and Central Asia who declared independence from the Soviet Union. But, Turkey did not establish diplomatic relations with Armenia since then due to a number of reasons, including the allegations of "genocide" and the efforts of the Armenian Diaspora for worldwide recognition of the allegations; claims for territory and compensation from Turkey for the 1915 events; and the Armenian occupation of some 20 percent of the Azerbaijani territory in the Karabakh region.

Armenians, those who live in Armenia as well as the members of the Diaspora, claim that the Ottoman Empire should be held responsible for the death of more than a million Armenians back in 1915 because of its policy of relocation (or "deportation," as argued by Armenians) of the entire Armenian population living in eastern and southeastern Anatolia. Armenians commemorate this event, every year on April 24, which they claim should be recognized by the international community as "genocide." Notwithstanding the Armenian claims, Turkey and an overwhelming majority of the Turks do not accept these allegations. On the contrary, Turks claim that it was indeed the Armenian gang members who, in collaboration with the Russian army against which the Ottoman army was fighting, actually killed hundreds of thousands of Turks living in the same region. Both sides claim to have undeniable evidences in support of their allegations whose authenticity, however, is disputed by the other side.

This particular issue that creates a stumbling block in front of establishing good neighborly relations between Turkey and Armenia requires ample space for an elaborate discussion. However, neither the scope nor the purpose of the book permits discussing the allegations and counter-allegations at sufficient length as much as the gravity of the subject matter would require. Considering that there is a plethora of books and articles on this issue that are available for the interested readers and researchers, this section of the book will place the emphasis on the implications of the allegations for the current state of affairs and the future of the relations between Turkey and Armenia.

Impact of Allegations of "Genocide" on Turkish-Armenian Relations

The debate on the Armenian allegations of "genocide" does not only center on whether there was genocide or not. There is also a debate about whether the events of 1915 could be labeled as "genocide" or not. The term genocide is defined clearly in the "United Nations Convention on the Prevention and Punishment of the Crime of Genocide" approved by the General Assembly of the United Nations in its resolution of December 9, 1948. The Convention took effect on January 11, 1951. Turkey signed and ratified the Convention according to which the definition of the crime of genocide consists of three elements. First, there has to be a national, ethnic, racial, or religious group. Second, this group has to be subjected to certain acts listed in the convention, such as the "*murder of the members of the group, and forced transfer of the children of one group into another group and subjecting the members of a group to conditions which will eventually bring about their physical destruction.*" Third, there has to be "*an intent of destroying,*" in part or in whole, the said group.[1] Those who acknowledge that tragic events have occurred during the displacement of large groups of Armenians but refuse to accept the Armenian allegations of "genocide" mainly refer to this definition. They underline the fact that the Ottoman administration who ordered the displacement had no intentions whatsoever to destroy an entire population of Armenian community who were the subjects of the Ottoman Empire.

The State of Affairs in the Ottoman Empire in 1915

For a lay reader, publications propagating the Armenian allegations of "genocide" may create an impression that the Ottoman administration had carefully planned and executed the systematic killings of the Armenians who were living inside the imperial territories. However, one should ask if that was the case. Moreover, one should also ask whether that could be the case at all, given the political, economic, and military conditions that the Ottoman Empire was passing through in 1915. Hence, it is necessary to understand how and why the tragic events that claimed the lives of hundreds of thousands of people have happened.

The Ottoman Empire, once almighty, which ruled on three continents extending from Central Europe to the Persian Gulf and North Africa and turned the Black Sea and the Mediterranean Sea to "Turkish lakes" with its invincible armada, entered a stagnation period starting with the eighteenth century due to the inability of the sultanate to keep pace with the scientific and technological innovations that benefited the European powers to a large extent. The situation did not improve in the successive centuries either. With the flame of nationalism that set the imperial structures to fire across the European continent in the nineteenth century, the Ottoman Empire as well started to fall apart. European powers began to see the Ottoman Empire as the "sick man of Europe." Their number one concern was the so-called "Eastern question," meaning the question of who would take over the rule from the Ottomans in the Balkans and especially in the Middle East—or the "fertile crescent" as coined by the Chicago University professor James H. Breasted at the turn of the twentieth century—once the Empire collapsed.

The defeats in the Italo-Turkish War in 1911–12 and the Balkan Wars in 1912–13, followed by the heavy preoccupation with World War I since 1914 and onward, have not only depleted what was left in the Ottoman treasury, but the central authority was much weakened paving the way to a chaotic situation in Anatolia, the heartland of the Empire, as well. With the fear of further deterioration of the situation in the countryside, several measures were taken by Talat Pasha, then Minister of the Interior, who ordered the displacement (*Tehcir Law*) of the Armenians who were suspected of collaborating with Russia against which the Ottoman Empire was fighting in the Caucasus.

There is confusion over the policy of the Ottoman Empire concerning the displacement of the Armenians as to whether it was "relocation" as argued by the Turks or "deportation" as argued by the Armenians. Unlike many have argued, *Tehcir* does not mean "deportation," because *Tehcir* had envisaged the relocation of the Armenians from eastern Anatolia, which was a war-zone between the Turks and the Russians, to Syria, which was still an Ottoman territory. Considering that the term "deportation" means forcing people to cross the national boundaries into another state, then forcing the Armenians to go to Syria, which was still a sovereign territory of the Ottoman Empire, cannot be identified as deportation. Relocation better describes the situation. Nevertheless, the gravity of the tragic consequences of the decision of the Ottoman administration does not change even if one agrees upon the meaning of *Tehcir*.

Turning back to the debate as to whether the Ottoman Empire had acted with "an intent of destroying" the entire Armenian community living within the imperial borders, one must bear in mind that, since the Athenian massacre of Melos during the Peloponnesian Wars in antic times, to the massacre of the Sioux Indians by the Americans, or to the "holocaust" committed by the Nazi Germany, history teaches that such crimes against humanity have been committed deliberately by the ruling powers during the height of their military strength and also when their self-confidence was the highest. In the case of the Ottoman Empire, one can hardly argue that was the case. In 1915 the Ottoman Empire was getting closer to its total collapse after decades of dramatic decline. More specifically, in April 1915, when the Armenian "genocide" has allegedly taken place in eastern Anatolia, the Ottoman Empire was trying to defend the most strategic parts of its remaining territory in western Anatolia, namely the Dardanelles Straits, in the War of Gallipoli against the great powers such as the British and the French. The fighting at Gallipoli was so intense that there were bullets found in the ruins of the war, which were hit by other bullets in the air. Tens of thousands of Turks were killed during the war at Gallipoli, which miraculously turned out to be a victory under the command of Mustafa Kemal. Considering that the distance between the two theaters in eastern and western Anatolia was approximately 2,000 kilometers, the allegations of systematic killing of the Armenians on one side while defending the country on the other side at exactly the same time sound illogical, if anything else.

It is, therefore, extremely difficult to agree with the allegations that the Ottoman administration, itself being devastated with consecutive wars on all fronts, had executed a plan with the intent of destroying the Armenians. At this point, only the historians and competent researchers may come up with an unequivocal answer as to whether that would still be possible, let alone being carried out. But, the Armenians claim that "everything is crystal clear, there is nothing to research on this matter, and the only thing that remains to be done is Turkey's formal recognition of the genocide." Such an attitude does not help neither to convince the Turks that their ancestors have committed a crime against humanity and, therefore, they should recognize it and compensate for the losses incurred by the Armenians nor to establish good neighborly relations between Armenia and Turkey that would be beneficial for both sides.

Views in the Turkish Public Domain

The Armenian allegations of "genocide" have been debated in the Turkish public domain, in the media, in scholarly circles as well as in politics with the participation of large segments of the society. It is not possible to say that the tone or the content of the debate is always satisfactory or to the point. But, considering the sensitivity of the subject matter, this is an understandable situation, at least for the time being. There are a number of reasons why such a debate takes place. First of all, an overwhelming majority of the Turks are proud of their past and they are not ashamed of their ancestors just because they are blamed by others for having committed a crime. Turks are ready to confront such allegations instead of turning a blind eye to the accusations, which they believe are unfounded.

Secondly, since the Helsinki Summit meeting of the EU in December 1999 where Turkey was officially declared a candidate country for full membership, this issue has been brought up more frequently either in the formal or informal statements of the European politicians or in the resolutions of the European Parliament. Moreover, several members of the EU have made Turkey's ultimate accession to the EU conditional upon its recognition of the "genocide" allegations. Hence, Turks are very well aware of the fact that, even if they did not wish to talk about the allegations today, they will have to face them in the future in case the accession negotiation talks with the EU Commission come to fruition and Turkey becomes ready to join the EU.

Third, several Turkish historians and intellectuals have made statements in support of the allegations, such as Halil Berktay, professor of history at Sabancı

University in İstanbul, and Orhan Pamuk, first Turkish Nobel Prize winner novelist. The controversial views of these popular figures triggered an additional interest on the subject matter and inflicted a debate in the Turkish public domain. The debate has become more heated since the assassination of Hrant Dink, a Turkish citizen of Armenian descent and an intellectual journalist, on January 19, 2007 by an "ultranationalist" youngster in broad daylight in the streets of İstanbul. Public reaction to the assassination was notable. It is worth mentioning here that tens of thousands of Turkish citizens from all walks of life and diverse backgrounds took to the streets and marched by carrying banners "we are all Hrant Dink" in protest of the assassination.

The meaning of all these is that there is a lot to be done to bring the historical facts to daylight in order to satisfy the conscious of the people. This can only be done by means of objective and systematic research through the primary documents and archives whose authenticity cannot be disputed. Scientists and scholars know very well how to do this job, and they should be allowed to do it. It is true that not all of the Ottoman archives or all other documents have been made available to the researchers yet. Some more time and effort is needed to prepare the ground for a scholarly research on this issue.

Nevertheless, Armenians flatly reject such a proposal, which they consider as humiliating them. They ask outright recognition of the "genocide" by Turkey, which they claim to have happened for sure in an undisputable manner. They also argue that they base their allegations on records and documents, which they claim to have been found through the scientific research and study of the respectable Armenian scholars and researchers. However, Turks also have claims to the contrary regarding the credibility of the documents that are put forward by the Armenian scholars. World renowned scholars like Stanford Shaw, Justin McCarthy, and Heath Lowry claim in their books and articles to have proofs of the forgery or distortion in the documents forwarded by their Armenian colleagues. As such, it would be far too optimistic an attitude for the Armenians to expect the recognition of their allegations by the majority of the Turkish people while there is still much to be proven.

Any person who is in an impartial position, but yet interested in this subject, should ask the following questions and also try to figure out the answers: Considering that today there are approximately 40 sovereign member states of the United Nations who were once the subjects of the Ottoman Empire, how come these communities, who were ruled by the Turks for centuries on three continents, managed to protect their identity, language, religion, and their cultural heritage if the Turks had the intent of destroying other ethnic groups under their control just because they were different? One should also ask if the Armenians are that much confident of their cause, why they decline to let historians from all parts of the world, not just those who are party to the dispute, to conduct comprehensive research in the archives and documents. Let alone agreeing to such a proposal, the Armenian Diaspora, in coordination with the like-minded politicians, especially in European countries such as Switzerland and France, lobby in the parliaments to pass resolutions to prosecute those who decline to accept the genocide allegations. In democratic societies like France and Switzerland, for instance, if one argues that he or she does not believe that the Armenian genocide happened, that person will be prosecuted. It is an awkward situation to note that while these allegations create a lot of sensitivity and anger within the Turkish society, Turks still manage to discuss it by and large in open forums in the universities and in the media, the same subject cannot be discussed in the same manner in advanced democratic countries or in Armenia.

The Future of Turkish-Armenian Relations

In the presence of the genocide allegations hanging on the Turks as the Damocles's sword, it is not easy to be highly optimistic about the future pace of bilateral relations. Turks cannot, and probably will not, accept the allegations of "genocide" just because the Armenians or other nationals, who are not allowed to be informed about the Turkish counterarguments, want them to do so. Unless the precondition of recognition of the allegations is lifted, the future prospects of the relations will also be hanging in the air. There is indeed a considerable potential to do business between Armenia and Turkey. Armenia is a landlocked country encircled by Turkey, Azerbaijan, and Georgia. So long as Armenia occupies some 20 percent of the Azerbaijani territory in the Karabakh region, it would be far too optimistic a view to expect even incremental improvements in the relations between the two nations. Georgia, on the other hand, is not in an open confrontation with Armenia. However, the presence of Russian soldiers in the two Russian military bases in Georgia, one of which is in the Armenian-populated part of the country, is a serious cause of concern for Georgian authorities. Moreover, the intensification of the relations between Georgia and Turkey toward the late 1990s also marred the Armenian-Georgian relations ever since. The BTC oil pipeline crossing Azerbaijan, Georgia, and Turkey has been seen as a deliberate attempt of these countries to hold Armenia out. The Armenian population, which is barely above three million, is reducing due to a high rate of migrations to Europe and North America. There is a huge rate of unemployment especially among the younger generation due to the economic situation, which is not promising either. There are proposals that are put forth by the international community as well as several pressure groups in Turkey to open border gates between Turkey and Armenia to facilitate trade between two countries. Should this happen, Armenia's *de facto* isolation will be greatly reduced and its economy will prosper creating many more job opportunities on both sides of the border. However, insistence of Armenia for Turkey's *a priori* recognition of the "genocide" allegations makes it all the more difficult to advance any such proposal in the public domain or in the decision-making circles in Turkey.

In response to the stubborn attitude of Armenia, Turkey also came up with its conditions to start even thinking about proposals like opening the borders. Turkey wants Armenia to agree to establishing a commission composed of internationally recognized historians and scholars to investigate the events that have taken place in 1915 so as to be able to judge what exactly has happened. In addition to that, Turkey also wants Armenia to withdraw from the Karabakh region. In none of these conditions did Armenia show any inclination to move even an inch toward a compromise. Neither did Turkey show any inclination toward the recognition of the Armenian allegations. Hence, the relations are ostensibly deadlocked. But, there is a certain degree of "trade" between Turkey and Armenia. There are reports on the media that some 70,000 Armenians have found works, albeit illegally, in Turkey, mostly in İstanbul. There are almost regular flights between Yerevan, the capital of Armenia, and İstanbul every day. The presence of small Armenian community who are the citizens of Turkey is a facilitating factor in having even this much of interaction between the two nations. Needless to say, this is not enough. Considering the depth of the history of the two very old nations who have been living side by side for more than a thousand years, it is unfortunate that the shared history has not been conducive to the betterment of the relations. It is, of course, not necessarily the history itself that divided the two countries, but the different interpretations, if not distortion, of history that set the two nations apart.

RELATIONS WITH IRAN

Turks and Iranians have a long history of relations characterized mostly with rivalry. Until the eighteenth century, the main reason of tension in the Turkish-Iranian relations was the struggle between the Safavid Persian Shiism and the Sunni tradition of Islam embraced by the Ottoman Empire.[2] The peace accord between the Persian and the Ottoman empires reached with the Treaty of Kasr-ı Shirin in 1639 succeeded in reducing tensions.[3] Each party recognized that sovereign states could be part of the Islamic world community even if their interpretations of Islam did not match.

Recent History of Turkish-Iranian Relations

During the twentieth century, Iran's relations with Turkey remained peaceful, although not always amicable. In the first half of the twentieth century, there have been commonalities as well as divergences in Iranian and Turkish foreign policies. The most important difference was the fact that Turkey was ruled along the lines of the republican constitutionalism established by Mustafa Kemal Atatürk, whereas Iran was ruled according to an absolutist monarchy led by Reza Shah.[4] Although the political systems of Turkey and Iran were divergent, the fact that both countries experienced fragmentation on the domestic level and foreign occupation resulted in a common concern in both countries' ruling regime that was to consolidate their domestic power and to strengthen their regimes, at the same time trying to pursue an independent foreign policy. With those vital concerns in mind, neither Turkey nor Iran saw one another as immediate threat, therefore were not hostile toward each other.

During the Cold War years, both Turkey and Iran, fearing communist expansionism and Soviet influence in their domestic affairs, were within the pro-Western camp and designed their foreign policies accordingly. By joining the Central Treaty Organization (CENTO) as founding members, Turkey and Iran became regional allies. During the Détente period starting in the aftermath of the Cuban Missile Crisis, with the decrease in tensions between the two superpowers and in the international system, both Turkey and Iran could focus on regional problems and causes of concerns. Their efforts in cooperation on a bilateral or multilateral level were supported by the United States. In 1964 Iran and Turkey along with Pakistan founded the RCD grouping, which would later turn into the Economic Cooperation Organization (ECO) to promote economic, technical, and cultural cooperation among members although the organization failed in achieving concrete outcomes.[5] At the time, Turkey perceived Iran as a friendly power within the Western camp, and most importantly, Iran was seen as a *status quo* power, not willing to jeopardize Turkey's position in the region or its security.

The 1979 Islamic Revolution in Iran shook the stability of Turkish-Iranian relations. The ambition of the clerical leadership in Iran to export its fundamentalist principles to secular and democratic Turkey caused serious tension in the bilateral relations, because the Republic of Turkey was created in 1923 as a secular state. The adoption and perpetuation of secular principles by the Turkish population, who are predominantly Muslim, has since been a highly sensitive issue in domestic politics. Another issue rose between Turkey and Iran when in the mid-1980s Turkey became the target of the PKK terrorism. Turkish officials suspected that Iran was supporting the PKK or turning a blind eye to PKK terrorists that used Iranian territory to stage attacks on Turkey through the inadequately controlled Turkish-Iranian borders. Turkish officials also accused Iran with interfering in Turkey's domestic affairs and with conducting attacks on Iranians living in Turkey. On the other hand, Iran was accusing Turkey of harboring antirevolutionary forces, such as the *Mujaheddin-e Khalq* (People's Warriors).[6] Moreover, in the early 1990s, the competition between Turkey and Iran over the "leadership" of the former Soviet republics in the Caucasus and Central Asia, which had cultural and religious common denominators with both Turkey and Iran, further strained their relations. Turkey has been supported by the Western countries, especially the United States, which feared the spread of political Islam in the area, in providing a model to the former Soviet republics.[7]

In the 1990s, Iran's image in Turkey was associated with a "dark regime" trying to cause instability in Turkey with a view to paving the way to a similar (i.e., Islamic) revolutionary movement. Turkish secular elite blamed Iran for supporting religious extremist groups in Turkey. They also held Iran responsible for a series of assassinations that claimed the lives of a number of prominent secular intellectuals who, in their writings and speeches, had pointed out the dangers of the Iranian fundamentalist Mullahs' designs over Turkey. The tension between Iran and Turkey in the political domain has heightened with the participation of the Iranian ambassador to Ankara in the so-called "Jerusalem night" on January 31, 1997 that was organized by the Mayor of Sincan, namely Bekir Yıldız, in a middle-sized town in the suburbs of the capital, heavily populated with "religious" people. It was reported that the Iranian ambassador delivered fundamentalist messages to the audience, harshly criticized Turkey's secularism, and cursed Atatürk for founding the Turkish Republic on secular principles.

Shortly after this incident, on February 4, 1997, a convoy of main battle tanks and armored vehicles of the Turkish Army marched through the streets of Sincan. The purpose was to display the determination of the secular circles in the country, the armed forces being at the forefront, to defend the secular characteristic of the regime in Turkey. This event was also said to be responsible for sparking a series of developments and popular demonstrations that put an end to the two-party *Refah-Yol* government in June, the same year. The *Refah-Yol* government was formed by the Welfare Party (RP) from the Islamic wing, whose leader, Necmettin Erbakan, was the Prime Minister, and by the True Path Party (*Doğru Yol Partisi*—DYP) from the center-right and conservative wing, whose leader, Tansu Çiller, was the Deputy Prime Minister. The *Refah-Yol* government was the outcome of the democratically held elections in the spring of 1996 that resulted in the entrance of half a dozen parties to the Grand National Assembly who could hardly come together to form a coalition without the RP deputies, who were seen as the representatives of the "Islamist" factions in Turkey.

During his long career in politics, Erbakan was well known for his "Islamist" approach to politics. The Constitutional Court in the 1970s and the military coup leaders in the 1980s shut down his parties, the National Order Party (*Milli Nizam Partisi*—MNP) and the National Salvation Party (*Milli Selamet Partisi*—MSP), respectively. Yet, so long as Erbakan was perceived as representing only a small percentage of the Turkish population hoping to institute the Sheria law, he did not pose an imminent threat to the regime. However, his unpredicted rise to premiership and his hasty attempts to shift the direction of Turkey's mainstream foreign policy orientation from the Western world to the Islamic world were not tolerable for the "guardians of the regime" (i.e., the army). Erbakan's decision to pay his first official visit as the Prime Minister of Turkey to the Islamic fundamentalist Iran and his second visit to Colonel Qaddafi's authoritarian Libya has generated much reaction in Turkey's mainstream secular circles.

Such visits were out of the ordinary in the history of the Turkish Republic. He was, therefore, driven out of the office that he had stayed in only about a year, with a so-called postmodern coup. The Constitutional Court eventually shut down Erbakan's Welfare Party in January 1998 and its successor, the Virtue Party (FP), in June 2001,[8] both on the grounds that they "became the logistical head-quarters of the attempts of the Islamist factions in Turkey to overthrow the secular democratic regime that was founded on Atatürk's principles."

The Impact of 9/11 on Turkish-Iranian Relations

The Sincan incident alone shows how closely Iran's activities in Turkey were being monitored and how promptly and effectively the secular circles in the state structure confronted them. Nevertheless, in the post–September 11 period, Turkey adopted a substantially different attitude toward Iran. The political climate inside and outside of Turkey was dramatically different when compared to several years ago; the actors at the decision-making posts were entirely different, and Turkey's external relations were on a substantially different track with its neighbors. Following the events leading up to the U.S. invasion of Iraq in 2003, the relationship between Turkey and Iran has seemingly entered a new phase. Similar concerns about the probable consequences of the developments in Iraq may have motivated the two countries to converge their political stance with respect to the regional political issues. Since then, there has been an unprecedented rapprochement between Turkey and Iran resulting in an increase in the number of exchanges of high-level official visits.

Changing Perception of the United States and Israel

Until September 11, 2001, Turkey's relations with the United States were quite good, suffering only sporadically from some disagreements, yet serious ones, over the enforcement of the no-fly zone policy toward Iraq since 1991. The relations with Israel, on the other hand, were historically very good and reached their climax with the signing of a comprehensive military agreement in 1996. The role of Israel in Turkey's unprecedented pressure on Syria in the autumn of 1998 to cease its long-standing support to the PKK terrorist organization as well as to expel its leader Abdullah Öcalan out of Syria, resulting in his capture in Kenya, cannot be underestimated.

Notwithstanding the generally good nature of Turkey's historical relations with the United States and Israel, a series of developments that have taken place in the aftermath of the September 11 attacks have dramatically altered the vision of the world on both sides. According to many political analysts and statesmen alike, Turkish-American relations suffered an unprecedented blow with the failure of the resolution in the TGNA on March 1, 2003 that would have allowed the deployment of tens of thousands of U.S. troops in the Turkish territory as part of the strategy in the war against Iraq. Another serious blow to the bilateral relations came on July 4, 2003, when U.S. troops detained a dozen soldiers from the Turkish Special Forces who had been operating in the northern districts of Iraq specifically for intelligence collection and monitoring purposes for more than a decade with the knowledge of U.S. authorities. This shocking incident, which appalled the Turkish military authorities as well as the entire nation, has since been the very source of the skyrocketing anti-American feelings in almost every segment of Turkish society. Moreover, the obvious support by the United States of the Kurdish groups in northern Iraq, who are believed by many in Turkey to be only a few steps away from proclaiming independence, also damaged the bilateral relations that have never reached the pre–September 11 levels. Israel is also believed in Turkey to be closely linked with those U.S. policies toward Iraq in general and the Kurdish region in particular that ultimately hurt Turkey's vital interests in the region. Some analysts in Turkey go even further to assert that it is indeed Israel who dictates these policies to the United States, thanks to its influence on Capitol Hill by means of the powerful Jewish lobby.

Apart from such mainly "Nationalist" (*Ulusalcı*) interpretations of U.S. and Israeli policies toward the Middle East in general and Iraq in particular, there is also a separate "Islamist" interpretation of what is happening in and around Turkey, and why. The reactions of the Christian and Jewish populations to the September 11 attacks have resulted in an anti-Islamic rhetoric in the statements of many politicians and in the media in the West. In most cases, Islam is directly or indirectly associated with terrorism or, at best, with religious extremism as an antagonist to Western culture and as the "other." Such an approach has resulted in counter reactions in the Islamic world that triggered brutal demonstrations in Muslim countries against Christianity and Judaism and their representatives. The military offensives of the U.S. troops in Iraq that were covered extensively in the media of Islamic nations have also deeply affected public opinion and fueled anti-Americanism in these countries.

Changing Attitude of Turkish Government

Coming of the Justice and Development Party (AKP) to power in Turkey with an "Islamist" as well as "liberal-conservative" appeal at the November 2002 general elections cannot be fully explained without considering this background picture mentioned. Many in Turkey saw the AKP as a continuation of the Islamist parties, such as the MSP, the RP, and the FP, all of which were banned from politics and Recep Tayyip Erdoğan, the leader of the AKP and the Prime Minister, as being no different than Mr. Erbakan. The AKP government did not choose to confront the United States and Israel head on, at first, regarding foreign policy matters. However, deputies of the AKP and Prime Minister Erdoğan himself eventually started to make bitter statements about Israel and its policies toward the Palestinians and publicly criticized Israel for "committing state terror" following the assassinations of the spiritual leaders of Hamas and the demolition of Palestinians' houses in Gaza by the Israeli security forces. Moreover, despite the fact that Hamas was officially recognized as a terrorist organization by Turkish authorities, the Hamas leader-in-exile, Khaled Meshal, was given a warm reception in the AKP headquarters in Ankara in February 2005. These and other developments have apparently distanced Turkey from Israel under the AKP government.

The "Nationalists" in Turkey applaud the Iranian leadership and their "dignified" policies to protect Iran's rights and national interests against the "only superpower," namely the United States. They also suggest a similar attitude to the Turkish politicians who are harshly criticized by them for their inability to take measures, under pressure from the U.S. administration, against the Kurdish leaders or the PKK terrorists in northern Iraq. The "Islamists," on the other hand, support Iran's quest for nuclear power, which, in their view, terrifies Israel and will bring the Jewish state to the point of respecting their Muslim brothers in Palestine and elsewhere in the world. Negative feelings in the Turkish public domain toward these countries, which were Turkey's closest allies in the recent past, have not only resulted in the gradual worsening of bilateral relations at the governmental level but also caused Turks to lend huge support to other countries such as Iran, who defy U.S. and Israeli policies.

Attitudes in Turkey toward Iran's Nuclear Program

There is little wonder that public sentiments toward other nations affect the foreign policies of governments everywhere in the world. The AKP governments, since 2002, have also proved not to be exceptions to this rule by being reluctant to challenge Iran on the nuclear issue, due to the undeniable support in the Turkish public domain for Iran's nuclear program. However, governments have the primary duty to pursue the vital interests of their nations, which requires, among other things, avoiding emotional approaches to the formulation of foreign and security policies. Therefore, Turkey, even under the current AKP government, may be forced to change its reluctant attitude, if and when Iran advances its capabilities in the nuclear field and gets closer to, or passes, the threshold of nuclear weapons manufacturing capability.

Views of the Political-Security Elite

Turkey's official stance toward Iran's nuclear program is clear. Turkey recognizes the right of Iran, which is a member of the NPT, to develop nuclear technology, provided that it remains on a peaceful track and allows for the application of full-scope safeguards inspections by the International Atomic

Energy Agency (IAEA) in such a way that would lend the utmost confidence to the international community about its intentions. Statements to this effect have been made by the Turkish Premier Recep Tayyip Erdoğan on a number of occasions. For instance, in an interview with a Kuwaiti newspaper *El Anba* in March 2007, Erdoğan reiterated the diplomatic position of his government by saying, "states have the right to possess nuclear energy to utilize for peaceful purposes." Erdoğan also emphasized that Turkey has good neighborly relations with Iran and that the two countries have developed mechanisms for the purpose of cooperation in security issues. In response to a question posed by a journalist during the Munich Security Conference in February 2008 about "why Turkey did not seem to be worried about Iran's nuclear program," Prime Minister Erdoğan replied by saying, "our Iranian colleagues tell us that they want nuclear energy for peaceful purposes to satisfy their energy needs, not for weapons."

The consensus view among the Turkish political and security elite is that, contrary to its apparent low-profile stance, Turkey cannot stay aloof from Iran's nuclearization for long, even under the AKP government.[9] If and when unequivocal signs of Iran's efforts to advance its existing nuclear capability toward weaponization are received by Turkish authorities through various sources, it is highly likely that the issue will figure more frequently on the agenda of the National Security Council (NSC). The NSC, once a powerful institution that determined strict guidelines for governments as well as the entire state mechanism as to how to govern the country, has been transformed into a more Western-style advisory board on national security matters. The Council meets regularly every two months, and whenever necessary, with the participation of top representatives of the government, the armed forces, and other relevant departments of the state apparatus.

There have already been statements made on various occasions by leading figures in Turkey that express concern about Iran's nuclear program and its intentions. In an address to the Turkish War Colleges in İstanbul in April 2005, then Chief of Turkish General Staff Gen. Hilmi Özkök stated, "doubts about Iranian efforts to influence the regimes of the surrounding states had disturbed Turkey and has been responsible for the low level of relations between Turkey and Iran."[10] Similarly, then Minister of Foreign Affairs Abdullah Gül (became the President of the Republic in September 2007), in response to a motion in the TGNA in June 2006, stated, "the IAEA Director General's reports has revealed the fact that Iran concealed its nuclear program for years, which creates suspicions about Iran's intentions." After mentioning that Ankara was carefully observing the developments about the Iranian nuclear program that had gradually attained a more serious dimension, Gül said, "The emergence of the possibility of Iran's possessing a nuclear weapon disturbs Turkey as all the members of international society."

Perception in the Turkish Public Domain

Opinions in Turkey toward nuclear weapons in general and Iran's nuclear program in particular exhibit stark differences, depending on from which perspective one looks at the issues. While, on the one hand, serious concerns about the possible negative implications of Iran's growing nuclear capabilities are expressed by the security elite, on the other hand, a significant degree of support exists in the Turkish public domain for Iran's nuclear endeavors. Revelations about Iran's clandestine enrichment program in August 2002 inflicted a debate on the public domain, not only with its military-strategic implications, but also with its political implications for Turkey's domestic and foreign policies. From the public perspective, Iran's nuclear ambitions are mostly welcome among the Turks for a number of reasons. First, Iran's defiance of the U.S. pressure to halt its enrichment program is considered to be a dignified stance of a small country against a global hegemonic power. Second, Islam is seen as a common denominator between the Turks and the Iranians, and the emergence of another Muslim nation with atomic power after Pakistan against the Christian and Jewish bombs is considered a necessary equalizer. Third, and in relation to the second, due to anti-American and anti-Israeli sentiments, growing ever since the U.S. invasion of Iraq, anything that is seen as hurting American or Israeli interests is usually welcome. There are hundreds of Web sites, blogs, and chat rooms in which Turks exchange their views on whether Iran's nuclear ambitions constitute a threat to Turkey or not and whether Turkey should possess nuclear weapons or not. Regarding the degree of the perceived threat from Iran's nuclear aspirations, the majority of Turks do not believe that Iran, as a friendly Muslim nation, would want to threaten Turkey with its nuclear weapons, today or in the future, especially when Israel is considered Iran's prime target.

The Future of Turkish-Iranian Relations

Despite positive signs, it is still early to say that the pace of relations between Turkey and Iran will stay on the same track in the long term. The nature as well as the extent of Iran's nuclear program is highly likely to have a decisive impact on the future of Turkish-Iranian relations. There are too many unknown factors in this respect that require further cooperation of Iran with the international community and its neighbors in order to provide more transparency about its capabilities and intentions in advancing its nuclear program. On this particular issue, speaking at an international symposium on Middle East security issues convened in İstanbul on June 5, 2008, the Chief of General Staff Yaşar Büyükanıt stated that Iran's nuclear capabilities constitute the "number two security concern" for Turkey in the Middle Eastern context, the number one being the situation in Iraq.

General Büyükanıt's military perspective, which diverges to a certain extent
from the political perspective of the AKP government, is worthy of analyzing
seriously, because Turkey is one of the countries that will be most negatively
affected from Iran's nuclear weapons capability, if and when developed. This
may sound as an overstatement at first, but the following analysis may suggest
that it is not without substantiating arguments. If Iran builds a nuclear stockpile,
it will only add a new dimension to its already militarily superior position vis-à-
vis the Gulf States like Kuwait, Emirates, Qatar, and Saudi Arabia. Syria will
most likely remain as Iran's one and only ally in the region, primarily due to
geopolitical considerations, at least, for as long as the Assad dynasty, or a like-
minded ruler, remains in power. Relations between Iran and the former Soviet
republics in the Caucasus and Central Asia grow steadily in many areas ever since
they gained their independence. No serious bone of contention exists between
them and Iran, with the exception of the Azeri people's aspirations to "greater
Azerbaijan" on both sides of the Iranian-Azerbaijani border.[11] However, these
calls are not powerful enough that might trigger a secessionist movement in the
region, if Iran, with an Azeri clerical leader Ali Khamaney, develops nuclear
weapons. Russia, being the second largest nuclear power in the world, will not
be challenged by Iran even if it builds a small stockpile of nuclear weapons. Huge
imbalances that exist between the two countries aside, no major hostilities are
seen on the horizon. There is also a *patron-client* relationship between Russia
and Iran especially in the nuclear field which is likely to continue in the future
that will strengthen the hand of the former vis-à-vis the latter. Iran's would-be
nuclear weapons capability is not going to pose a serious challenge to Pakistan,
India, or China, either, because all three of them are nuclear powers already
and none of them has much to compete with Iran that might potentially lead
to a confrontation in the foreseeable future. On the contrary, China's and India's
dependency on Iran's oil and gas supplies is likely to increase, which will most
probably affect the pace of their bilateral relations in favor of Iran.

On the other hand, the hostile relationship between Iran and the United States
is likely to persist in the coming years so long as Iran insists carrying on its
nuclear program. Iran's support to Hezbollah and Hamas whose militants stage
attacks on Israeli targets and its alleged role in the instability in Iraq as well as
the Palestine problem have been among the other serious bones of contention
between Iran and the United States. But, the presence of a handful of nuclear
weapons in Iran's military arsenal will not alter its inferior position vis-à-vis the
United States for a long time to come. Similarly, Israel's nuclear capability will
remain, by all measure, to be a credible deterrent against a nuclear blackmail by
Iran. Moreover, in the Middle Eastern context, the Israeli nuclear capability
may not be considered separately from that of the United States anyway. As such,
Iran will not be able to have the upper hand in its relations with Israel just
because it will have nuclear weapons. By the same token, Iraq, where the

United States is building a new nation as its protectorate, will most likely be given strong positive security guarantees with a long-term commitment that will serve as a credible deterrent against Iran's would-be nuclear weapons capability.

Regarding Turkey, however, the presence of nuclear weapons in the Iranian military arsenal will upset the delicate balance that exists between the two nations, since the Treaty of Kasr-ı Shirin of 1639, in favor of Iran. The topographic and demographic characteristics of the region and the presence of more or less equal size military capabilities on both sides of the border have since forced the parties to refrain from confronting each other. Based on this analysis, one may conclude that the value added of nuclear weapons to Iran's political assets and military capabilities in its bilateral relations with other nations may be the highest in the case of Turkey.

While General Büyükanıt emphasized his concerns about Iran's accomplishments in the nuclear field, on the sidelines of the same international symposium in İstanbul on June 5, 2008, General İlker Başbuğ, Commander of the Land Forces, who would soon become the Chief of General Staff, underlined the significance of coordination with Iran in the fight against the PKK across the Iraqi border. This is an area where Turkey and Iran will have the ability to exploit more opportunities to cooperate in the future so long as the security situation in Iraq remains problematic. Even though high-ranking Turkish and Iranian military officers do not come together, at present, coordination (but not necessarily in cooperation) is taking place at lower levels. Both countries suffer from the PKK terrorism, because a branch of the PKK, namely the Party of Free Life of Kurdistan (*Partiya Jiyana Azad a Kurdistanê*—PJAK), operates in Iran fighting against the Islamic regime. Hence, it is in the interest of both Iran and Turkey to devise concerted strategies in order to achieve greater effectiveness in the fight against the PKK terrorism. It is interesting to note that the United States is known for supporting activities of PJAK with a view to staging a regime change in Iran, while at the same time its sister organization PKK is on the list of terrorist organizations maintained by the U.S. Department of State. Considering that Turkey and the United States are cooperating in the fight against the PKK terrorism, how this situation will affect Turkish-Iranian relations in the context of Iran's fight against the PJAK remains a problem.

In addition to military-strategic issues, another area of cooperation between Turkey and Iran is economics with particular emphasis on the oil and gas sectors. In August 1996, Turkey and Iran signed two important agreements. First was a US$23 billion agreement of gas supply from Iran to Turkey in addition to a gas pipeline construction project, and with a second agreement where parties decided to increase the bilateral trade in merchandise to US$2.5 billion a year. The implementation of these agreements has become problematic due to several reasons. First, the signature of the agreements coincided with a period in Turkish political history where the "first Islamic government" was formed by Necmettin

Erbakan whose "moderate Islamic" Welfare Party (RP) won the first rank in the 1995 general elections. This coincidence created an impression that the relations between Turkey and Iran were improving because of the ruling party's Islamic character. But, the agreements had been planned long before the RP came to power. Second, in relation with the first, was the U.S. concerns about whether a coalition of "Islamic" governments in this part of the world was emerging. Hence, the United States put pressure on Turkey not to go ahead with the gas deal. This has created frictions and delays in the implementation of the project. A third reason has been the attitude of the Iranian leadership to use the gas deal as leverage in its relations with Turkey. Whenever Turkey was approached by the United States to take on a tougher stance vis-à-vis Iran's nuclear program, Iran cut off the gas supplies in the middle of the winter season arguing that the cuts were due to technical reasons, an excuse that nobody believed.

Against this background, one may conclude that the pace of relations between Turkey and Iran is likely to fluctuate in the future as has been the case in the past. The attitude of the Turks toward Iran and the Iranian leadership has been an indicator of the political climate in Turkey. When the image of Iran ruled by the Mullahs was associated with a "dark regime" in the 1990s, the public sentiments in Turkey toward the Americans and Israelis were highly positive. Similarly, when Turkey's relations with Iran were strained in the same period, the strategic relations with Israel and the United States reached their peak in the post–Cold War period. However, in the post-9/11 period, the unusually high degree of popularity of Iran and the Iranian leadership in the Turkish public domain is among the indicators of the unprecedented levels of negative sentiments of the Turks toward the United States and Israel. On the other hand, in contrast to the warmth in the political atmosphere between the governments of Iran and Turkey, the reservations of the Turkish generals toward their Iranian counterparts can be an indicator of significance of the Westernization process for the secular elite. Hence, considering the rivalry between the Turks and the Iranians throughout the history, despite the fact that some common concerns exist as regards their national interests, the scope and the content of Turkish-Iranian relations may not go far beyond the present levels unless Turkey makes a radical turn in its relations with the West in general, and the United States in particular, even if they may not be at satisfactory levels either.

RELATIONS WITH IRAQ

Iraq was ruled by the Turks for more than four centuries since the capture of Baghdad and Basra in 1535 by the Ottoman Sultan Süleyman *the Magnificent.* The Ottomans divided the Iraqi territory into three provinces in terms of administrative units. Today's northern Iraq was the "Mosul province" of the Ottoman Empire. Similarly, today's southern Iraq was the "Basra province." The Baghdad province, on the other hand, was what is now known as the Sunni-dominated central and western parts of Iraq. During the dramatic years of decline, Ottoman Empire lost the Iraqi territory to Great Britain who took advantage of involvement of the Turks in World War I on the side of the Germans. British troops first landed in Basra in November 1914. After years of intense fighting, in 1917 Britain occupied all three Ottoman provinces, namely Basra, Baghdad, and Mosul. In the aftermath of the Great War, the mandate of these provinces were given to the British by the League of Nations.

Notwithstanding the decision of the League of Nations, especially the Mosul province was part of the National Pact of the young Turkish Parliament that was born out of the ashes of the collapsed empire. When Mustafa Kemal launched the War of Liberation against the occupying powers, the ultimate objective was to free the country and to restore the lands that belonged to the Turks, including the Mosul province.[12] However, regardless of the victory gained in the battlefield against the occupying powers, the Mosul province could not be annexed to Turkey during the Lausanne negotiations because of the adamant opposition of Great Britain. Following the long deliberations under the auspices of the League of Nations, whose impartiality was so much in doubt in the eyes of the Turks, in July 1926 Turkey agreed to sign a treaty with Iraq (literally ruled by the British) that constituted the current frontier between the two countries.[13] The Ankara Treaty was indeed implicitly conditional upon the territorial as well as the political integrity of Iraq. Should one or more of the groups that constitute the highly diverse fabric of the Iraqi society attempt to break up with the rest of the country, Turkey may feel like having the right to intervene due to historically acquired rights, such as a guarantorship of the integrity of Iraq. Recent developments taking place in Iraq since the fall of the Saddam regime do not at all convince the Turks that Iraq may stay politically or territorially integrated. The *de facto* partition of the country among the Kurds in the north, Sunnis in the middle, and the Shiite in the south may turn out to be a *de jure* situation unless a powerful political authority comes to the office and carry out the necessary legal, political, and constitutional reforms and the related arrangements rather quickly and completely.

Turkey's Interest in Iraq since the Gulf War of 1991

Turkey is one of the countries that closely monitor the developments in Iraq. However, Turkey's interest in these developments is not new. Since the first Gulf War in March 1991, Turkey has found itself dragged into this rough neighborhood. The creation of the so-called "no-fly zones" by the United States and Britain, without referring specifically to any United Nations resolutions, which denied the Iraqi military entering the large segments of the Iraqi territory both in the north and in the south, caused much political concern as well as serious security problems for Turkey in many respects.

In the aftermath of the short-lived war in Kuwait between the Coalition Forces and Iraq, hundreds of thousands of Iraqi Kurds had fled their country and sought refuge in Turkey and Iran. The creation of safe havens for the Iraqi Kurdish population turned out to become a serious security problem for Turkey for mainly two reasons. First, the northern sectors of the Iraqi territory that fell into the scope of the no-fly zone enforcement became a sanctuary for the PKK terrorists who used to wage guerilla warfare against the Turkish security forces since the mid-1980s with the objective of separating the southeastern parts of the country that was heavily populated with Kurdish citizens of Turkey. Saddam's forces had left a lot of light and heavy weaponry as well as their munitions behind them when they were forced to retreat from the region after the victory of the Coalition Forces led by the United States in 1991. The PKK terrorists not only seized these weapons and munitions but also benefited from the lack of authority in northern Iraq to gain many more recruits. They also increased their revenues by controlling the arms and drug trafficking between Central Asia and Europe during the first half of the 1990s.

Secondly, the consolidation of the Kurdish rule in the northern sectors of the Iraqi territory constituted another security problem for Turkey. Due to the incessant enforcement of the no-fly zone, the Kurdish groups have flourished by establishing a "Parliament" after a series of locally held elections, full-fledged administrative units including "ministries," hospitals, schools, a central bank and money in circulation. All of these and other such developments have paved the way to raising their voice to claim for an independent Kurdish state with the help of the outside powers such as the United States and the United Kingdom. In the immediate aftermath of the fall of Saddam regime, then British Premier Tony Blair said in a Parliamentary gathering in Britain that he would carefully pursue the aim of providing the Kurds with no less than they used to have over the last decade in terms of democratic rights and privileges, and that he would do his best to take the cause of the Kurds to the platform of the United Nations. The words of Tony Blair concerning his desire to take the Kurdish issue to the UN platforms reminds one the history of creation of the State of Israel.

Turkey's Concerns with an Independent Kurdish State

Turkey is seriously concerned with the possibility of declaration of independence by the Kurds in northern Iraq, because such an eventuality may set a bad precedent for the rest of Iraq as well as the entire region, which is indeed a mosaic of different ethnic and religious groups. Should the Kurds claim for their independent state, other ethnically and religiously diverse groups may very well follow suit that may render the whole Middle East into a chaotic situation. Scholars use the term "Balkanization of the Middle East" to point out to the possibilities that may follow once one of the ethnic groups within a multiethnic society claims independence from the rest of the country. The tragic events in the Balkans started when Croatia and Slovenia, strongly supported by Germany, proclaimed their independence from Yugoslavia, and others, such as Bosnia-Herzegovina and Kosovo, desired to follow suit.

Another reason why Turkey is concerned with the possibility of an independent Kurdish state in northern Iraq is because there is a significant Turkmen population in Iraq, around two million, most of whom live in northern Iraq. Turkmen people of Iraq have a long history in the region where they live. While some of them prefer to be called simply "the Turks of Iraq," some others wish to preserve their "Turkmen" identity which has deep-rooted kinship with the Turks but yet *sui generis*.[14] That said, the population of the Turkmen within the entire Iraqi society has long been a point of controversy among the concerned body of intellectuals. The figure that is mostly referred to by the Kurdish groups as well as the Western scholars in their statements is 500,000, whereas the Turkmen claim to have a population over three million constituting slightly more than 10 percent of the society. Considering the fact that the last population census was carried out back in 1957, and no reliable database has since been established to make accurate inferences into the demographic structure of Iraq, there is equal likelihood for both parties' claims to be substantially wrong. Some academic studies have attempted to be conducted, yet with imperfect and incomplete information, referring to available historical records as well as scholarly studies that survived the brutal regime of Saddam Hussein, suggest that a meaningful figure for the Turkmen population could be somewhere in around two million.[15]

Hence, proclamation of independence by the Kurds of Iraq whose population is approximately four million will surely put the Turkmen in a very disadvantageous position, because the Kurds in northern Iraq claim that the city of Kirkuk, which is very rich in oil reserves, should belong to the "Kurdistan Regional Government" (KRG), which is created after new Iraqi Constitution. According to Article 140 of the new Iraqi Constitution, the status of Kirkuk will be determined with a referendum following a normalization process and a population census that will determine those who will vote in the referendum. Turkey feels uneasy about this three-stage process that will determine the fate of Kirkuk and also the Turkmen. The so-called "normalization" process envisages the right to return of the Kurds back to their homes and villages where they used to live before they were displaced by the Saddam regime. Kurds pronounce figures like 50,000 of them were displaced in the 1970s. They also claim that the population of those who were displaced has grown to at least 300,000. The KRG provides strong incentives to the Kurds who live in other districts to go to Kirkuk. At the same time, the Kurdish paramilitary units, namely the Peshmerghas, brutalize the Turkmen and force them to flee Kirkuk. With such an attitude, the KRG aims to have the popular support at the referendum for annexing Kirkuk to the Kurdish region. Turkey has expressed its deep concerns with the developments taking place in the region, because from the standpoint of Turkey's historic claims and interests, just as the importance of the territorial integrity of Iraq, the political integrity of the country is essential. However, the Kurds defy Turkey's concerns and make statements that the Kurds alone have the right to determine the future of the Kurdish region, meaning northern Iraq.

The Future of Turkish-Iraqi Relations

The future of Turkish-Iraqi relations is uncertain and depends heavily on the security situation in Iraq. So long as instability and disorder persists, the central authority in Baghdad will not be able to lend confidence to the Turkish authorities that Iraq will preserve its territorial as well as political integrity. Therefore, Turkey is one of the countries which takes initiatives to bring all the concerned parties together, within the context of "Iraq's Neighbors Initiative," in order to discuss the future of Iraq as well as the measures that should be taken with the concerted efforts of the international community to bring security and stability to the country. In addition to such multilateral efforts, Turkey is trying to elevate its bilateral relations with Iraq to a higher level by means of respective state visits. Several treaties are signed in political and economic fields during these high-level encounters with a view to expanding the scope and the content of trade relations. The amount of investments in northern Iraq coming from Turkey is in the order of billion dollars every year. Construction projects for the infrastructure such as highways as well as superstructures such as airports in and around the big cities in northern Iraq like Irbil are undertaken by Turkish companies. Whether these investments will continue or soon be halted is hard to tell. Much depends on the security situation in Iraq in general, and the attitude of KRG toward Turkey in particular. Needless to say, the presence of the PKK terrorists in northern Iraq who not only find refuge and receive ample logistical support from within the region is an issue that continues to poison the relations. Iraq is rich enough to turn the desert into a paradise provided the security problems are resolved and peaceful relations are established with its neighbors. Iraqi people who have been suffering decades of misery under the rule of brutal regimes deserve much better and prosperous living conditions. For this to happen, both Iraq's neighbors must do their utmost to help the Iraqi people stand on their feet and the Iraqi authorities, be they Sunni or Shi'a Arabs or Kurds, should not let the territories under their jurisdiction to become a source of insecurity for their neighbors either.

RELATIONS WITH SYRIA

Just like Iraq, Syria as well was under the Turkish rule for centuries. Following the defeat of the Ottoman Empire in World War I, the mandate of the Ottoman territories in Syria were given to France by the League of Nations in 1920. In the aftermath of World War II, as a result of the withdrawal of the war-weary great powers like France and Great Britain from their colonies in the Middle East, Syria gained its independence in 1946. During the French mandate, Turkey's relations with Syria were limited. However, Atatürk, before his passing, managed to prepare the political and diplomatic conditions for the eventual annexation of the Hatay province to Turkey in the run up to the Great War. Hatay has since been one of the bones of contention between Turkey and Syria, which never recognized the annexation that was a result of a secret French-Turkish deal. In the post–World War II period, Turkey, being a member of NATO, refrained from getting involved in Middle Eastern politics. Turkey's rather distanced policy toward the Middle East also affected its stance vis-à-vis Syria. Yet, Hatay continued to be an issue.

Strained Relations between Turkey and Syria since 1970s

Starting with the 1970s, Turkish-Syrian relations started to be strained due to basically two reasons. One was the dispute over the ways and means of using the waters of the Euphrates and Tigris rivers both of which have their origins in Turkey. The other and somewhat related issue that poisoned the bilateral relations was Syria's support to terrorist organizations such as ASALA and the PKK in its territory or in the territories of Lebanon under the Syrian control.

The Armenian terrorist organization ASALA is responsible for the assassination of more than 30 Turkish diplomats, including ambassadors, consuls, counselors, and representatives in foreign countries like the United States, Canada, Australia, France, Switzerland, the Netherlands, Austria, Greece, Portugal, Spain, the Vatican, Bulgaria, Belgium, Yugoslavia, Lebanon, Iran, and Iraq between 1973 and 1994. Most of the assassinations were staged between 1979 and 1984. After years of intense diplomatic initiatives, Turkey finally managed to mobilize international support to put an end to the attacks of ASALA in the mid-1980s. The diminishing of the ASALA terror coincides with the rising of the PKK terrorism, which is known as a Kurdish separatist organization. Like ASALA, the PKK as well received support from Syria. The PKK terrorists were trained in the Syrian-controlled Bekaa Valley in Lebanon. PKK terrorism, which claimed the lives of thousands of civilians as well as security personnel, has negatively affected the security situation in Turkey's southeast where grandiose irrigation projects were started since the mid-1970s.

Syria was very much disturbed with the Southeastern Anatolia Project (GAP, its Turkish acronym) that aimed to irrigate huge lands in Turkey's southeast to boost agricultural and social development. Considering that the GAP would heavily depend on the use of the waters of the Euphrates and the Tigris rivers, the two downstream riparian states, namely Syria and Iraq, anticipated serious cuts in the amount of waters that they would receive from these rivers and adopted a rather hostile attitude toward Turkey. Hence, the link between Turkey's GAP and the Syrian support to the PKK terrorism becomes clear, even though the Turkish authorities do not want to acknowledge such a connection.

Origins of Dispute over the Waters of the Euphrates and Tigris Rivers

The Euphrates and the Tigris rivers originate in a particular topographic and climatic zone and end up in quite a different one. The basin is characterized by high mountains to the north and to the west, and extensive lowlands in the south and in the east. The two rivers begin, scarcely 30 kilometers from each other, in a relatively cool and humid zone with rugged 3,000-meter high mountains and are visited by autumn and spring rains, and winter snows. From there, the two rivers run separately onto a wide, flat, hot, and poorly drained plain. In their middle courses, they diverge hundreds of kilometers apart, yet meet again near the end of their journey in the Shatt al-Arab, and discharge together into the Gulf. The Euphrates and the Tigris rivers are considered as forming one single transboundary watercourse system. They are linked not only by their natural course when merging at the Shatt al-Arab but also as a result of the man-made Tharthar Canal connection between the two rivers in Iraq.

The discharge, or flow, of the Euphrates and Tigris is still a matter of dispute among scholars and experts. This is not only because the flow patterns have shown great deviations, which impede the computation of a representative average discharge value, but the rapid development on both rivers, which has disrupted the natural flow, has also created difficulties for hydrologists to determine the discharge values. In addition to this, the lack of mutual trust and confidence inhibits the riparians of the basin from releasing the necessary data and information relevant to rainfall and runoff. The annual mean flow of the Euphrates is 32 billion cubic meters per year. Approximately 90 percent of the mean flow of the Euphrates is contributed by Turkey; the remaining 10 percent originates in Syria. As for the Tigris and its tributaries, the average total discharge is 52 billion cubic meters per year. Turkey contributes approximately 40 percent of the total annual flow, whereas Iraq and Iran contribute 51 percent and 9 percent, respectively. It should be noted that the Euphrates and Tigris rivers have extremely high seasonal and multi-annual variance in their flow. Further, the natural flows of both rivers passing from Turkey to Syria, and from Syria to Iraq, change due to irrigation and energy projects, which the riparians have already initiated. The rapidly increasing populations of these countries and the importance given to agricultural development and to food production necessitate further utilization of these rivers. The major problem, however, arises from the fact that the projected water demands of the riparians surpass the actual amount of water that can be supplied by the Tigris and the Euphrates rivers.[16]

Competitive Transboundary Water Relations (1960–80)

Between 1960 and 1980, all three riparian states paid more focused attention to socioeconomic development, based on water and land resources. The central agencies designated the major river basins, with their recorded potential for water and land resources, for large-scale development projects. In this respect, the Euphrates and Tigris rivers were determined to be the backbone of water development. To illustrate, it was the vast development potential of both the Euphrates and the Tigris rivers which, in the 1960s, led to the idea of harnessing the waters in a region where nearly one-fifth of Turkey's irrigable land could be found. In this context, Turkey implemented the Lower Euphrates Project to build a series of dams on the Euphrates to increase hydropower generation and to expand irrigated agriculture. Later on, in the late 1970s, the Lower Euphrates Project evolved and expanded into a larger multi-sectoral development GAP, which includes 21 large dams, 19 hydropower plants, and irrigation schemes extending to 1.7 million hectares of land.

On the other hand, in the early 1960s when the Baath Party came to power, Syria initiated the Euphrates Valley Project. The government set a number of objectives to be met by the project: irrigating an area as wide as 640,000 hectares, generating electric energy needed for urban use and industrial development, and regulating the flow of the Euphrates in order to prevent seasonal flooding. Moreover, the Baath Party that came to power in Iraq in 1968 emphasized agricultural and irrigation projects in order to provide food security for Iraqi people. Hence, a "Revolutionary Plan" was developed.

Due to the competitive and uncoordinated nature of these water development projects, disagreements over transboundary water issues surfaced in the late 1960s. At the same time, water negotiations were held by the riparian technocrats. The main theme of these technical negotiations was the impact of the construction of the Keban Dam in Turkey and the Tabqa Dam in Syria on the historical water use patterns of Iraq. While Turkey suggested establishing a joint technical committee with a mission to determine the water and irrigation needs of the riparians, Iraq insisted on guaranteeing flows and signing a sharing agreement. While Turkey released certain flows during the construction and impounding of the Keban Dam, no final allocation agreement was achieved at the end of numerous technical meetings.[17]

Escalating Transboundary Water Disputes (1980–90)

From the 1980s to the late 1990s, transboundary water issues moved into the realm of high politics when non-water issues became decisive factors that led to greater tensions and disputes. Despite official denials by Damascus, Syria's support of subversive actions against Turkey since the early 1980s have been widely known and documented.[18] Although the regional political environment was not conducive for water cooperation in the early 1980s, at the end of the first meeting of the Joint Economic Commission between Turkey and Iraq, the permanent Joint Technical Committee (JTC) was established in 1980 to discuss and finalize the water issue among the riparians. Turkey's initiation of the GAP was the major reason for Iraq to take the lead to establish the JTC. Syria joined the JTC in 1983 whereupon Turkey, Syria, and Iraq held sixteen meetings up until 1993. Yet, the riparians failed to empower the JTC with a clear or jointly agreed mandate. Instead, they continued unilateral and uncoordinated water and land development ventures. Thus, a series of diplomatic crises over the development and usage of transboundary waters erupted.

Turkish foreign policy circles regarded the transboundary water relations with Syria and Iraq in the context of political and legal relations, which are governed by official treaties, diplomatic correspondence and contacts. Even though the terrorism issue marred the bilateral relations with Syria, official policy of Turkish authorities, particularly that of the Ministry of Foreign Affairs, was to deliberately separate the terrorism issue from water-related matters. However, one significant deviation from this official stance was the signing of two protocols at the prime ministerial level, which linked security and terrorism issues with water sharing arrangements. The Turkish-Syrian Joint Economic Commission met on July 17, 1987 and at the end of the meeting, Turkey and Syria signed the Protocol of Economic Cooperation. It included several articles pertaining to the water issue. According to the temporary protocol, Turkish side undertook to release a yearly average of more than 500 cubic meters per second at the Turkish-Syrian border, which is equivalent to the half of the medium flow rate of the Euphrates river. There was also a security protocol signed concluding that both states will prevent activities against the other from originating in their countries. It is important to note that this protocol was regarded as a temporary arrangement.

These bilateral water sharing agreements did not provide sustainable solutions to the depletion and degradation of the water and land resources in the Euphrates-Tigris river basin. Furthermore, the shortsighted stipulations of these agreements proved to be unsatisfactory to both upstream and downstream riparians, as they kept complaining about the mismatches between their growing needs and the deteriorating water resources in the basin. Syria and Iraq perceived the interruption to the flow of the Euphrates, caused by the impounding of the Atatürk Dam, as the beginning of many such interruptions that would result from the envisaged projects of the GAP. The thirteenth meeting of the JTC, held in Baghdad on April 16, 1990, provided the occasion for a bilateral accord between Syria and Iraq, according to which 58 percent of the Euphrates water coming to Syria from Turkey would be released to Iraq.

New Perspectives in Transboundary Water Politics since 1998

These transboundary water relations were not taking place in a vacuum. A severe political crisis occurred between Turkey and Syria when Turkish authorities' frustration with Syria's lack of cooperation reached its peak in October 1998. High-ranking Turkish military officers and politicians made public statements that they wanted Syria to stop supporting terrorists immediately. This Turkish initiative, the implications of which seemed to be clearly understood in Damascus, produced results and the Syrian authorities deported the head of the PKK, Abdullah Öcalan, soon after. On October 20, 1998, a framework security agreement, the Adana Accord, was signed between the two countries. Meanwhile, Turkish and Iraqi policies have often coincided on the issue of Kurdish separatism. This was extended to tacit military cooperation in the second half of the 1980s to fight the PKK. Turkey carried out cross-border operations into northern districts of Iraq to fight the terrorists. However, the situation drastically changed after the first Gulf War. Turkey joined the Allied embargo against Iraq, and Iraq became less cooperative.

Relations between Turkey and Syria improved considerably after the signing of the Adana security agreement in 1998, and new and promising initiatives have been undertaken since then. In 2001, Turkey's Southeastern Anatolia Project Regional Development Administration (GAP RDA) made contact with Syria by sending a delegation on the invitation of the General Organization for Land Development (GOLD), part of the Syrian Ministry of Irrigation. As a result, a joint *communiqué* was signed between the GOLD and GAP RDA on August 23, 2001. Once again the water issue was relegated to the technical level and was handled by intergovernmental networks composed of technocrats. GAP-GOLD cooperation is based on the common understanding of providing sustainable utilization of the region's land and water resources through conducting joint rural development and environmental protection projects, joint training programs, expert and technology exchanges, and study missions. Syrian and Turkish delegations paid visits to each other's development project sites. During these contacts they had opportunities to exchange experiences pertaining to the positive and negative impacts of the decades' old water and land resources development projects. Unlike the technical negotiations in the 1960s, the GAP-GOLD dialogue included diversified issues such as urban and rural water quality management, rural development, participatory irrigation management, and agricultural research.

Furthermore, the improved political and economic relations among the riparians since the late 1990s have produced fruitful impacts on the water-based development in the region. The significant progress in the economic relations of Syria and Turkey can be observed in the major sectors of sustainable development, such as agriculture, energy, health, and other water-related sectors. A series of government, private sector, and civil society delegations paid numerous mutual visits reaching productive understandings and agreements on trade and economic matters. These culminated in the signing of the Free Trade Agreement in 2004, a real breakthrough in the advancement of bilateral economic relations. The years 2003 and 2004 witnessed the signing of two framework cooperation agreements on health and agriculture, respectively. Both agreements underlined the importance of enhanced cooperation and development in the two neighboring countries. They included, among other things, discussion of water-related issues, such as soil and water conservation in agricultural practices and combating waterborne diseases.[19]

The Future of Turkish-Syrian Relations

At the beginning of the twenty-first century, the future of Turkish-Syrian relations look more promising when compared to the closing decades of the twentieth century. With the signing of the Adana Protocol in 1998 following a thwarted confrontation in October 1998, one of the two most troubling issues between Turkey and Syria is shelved, at least temporarily for a foreseeable future. However, the dispute over use of the waters of the Euphrates and the Tigris rivers remains unresolved. Moreover, another river in the region, namely the Orontes river, which is called "*Asi*" and "*Nahr al-Asi*" in Turkish and Arabic, respectively, is among the controversial issues between Turkey and Syria.

The Orontes river passes through the territories of Lebanon, which is in an upstream position, then Syria, a midstream country on the Orontes, and Turkey, which is in a downstream position. Turkey and Syria provide the major tributaries to the river. The Orontes is heavily used by all the riparians, and there are problems among the three countries concerning the use of the waters. While Lebanon and Syria have settled their differences on water allocation, Turkish-Syrian side of the problem remains to be solved. As has been the case in the Euphrates-Tigris river basin, problems related to usage of waters of the Orontes river as well could not be isolated from larger political issues between Turkey and Syria. Since Beshar Al Assad's ascension to presidency in 2000, even though the two countries have not launched a full-fledged cooperative project regarding the water issue, they have achieved significant cooperation in areas of agriculture, transportation, energy, health, and environment. Thus, the positive atmosphere enabled some developments regarding the prospects for finding a solution to the water problem. The joint dam project which is planned to be built over the Orontes river by the two countries could be noted as a major step toward the solution of the water problems.[20]

Another source of positive impressions for a more peaceful and good neighborly relations between Turkey and Syria in the future is the role Turkey wanted to play between Syria and Israel in the resolution of their conflict over the Golan

Heights, which are occupied by Israel since the "six days war" back in June 1967. Notwithstanding the optimism, one has to be rather careful as well as cautious in not setting the expectations very high regarding the mediation role Turkey can play between Syria and Israel. Problems emanating from the hard core mainstream opposition in Israel toward any peace deal with Syria aside, Turkey may face serious difficulties itself in the process of secret negotiations. At the very heart of the Golan Heights conflict lies the use of the water resources in the Banias river by the Israelis in the occupied Syrian territories for decades. The Banias river is significant in that it constitutes one of the major sources of the Jordan river. Israel looks favorable to the proposal of returning the Golan Heights back to Syria only on the condition of retaining its water rights in the Banias river. For a peace deal to be reached between Syria and Israel, Syria's loss of water from the Banias river will have to be compensated, and Turkey's waters in the Euphrates river, in particular, are seen as the primary candidate. Even if the AKP government that mediates between Israel and Syria agrees to such a deal, the state establishment in Turkey, the Turkish General Staff in the first place, will probably oppose any such proposal. Moreover, the AKP government gave a renewed boost to the GAP, which will probably need more waters from the Euphrates and the Tigris rivers, which will make it all the more difficult from Turkey's standpoint to agree to leaving excessive amounts of waters to Syria. A breakthrough in this complex situation may be possible if the waters of the Seyhan and the Ceyhan rivers in Turkey's Mediterranean region are considered instead of Euphrates river. However, as of the end of the first decade of the twenty-first century, the positions of the parties are yet to be clarified.

For a more promising estimate about the future of the Turkish-Syrian relations with more confidence, Syrian authorities must determine the standing of their country in the global fight against terrorism. So long as Syria remains in the list of the states that sponsor terrorism, as declared by the United States, or use terrorism as a proxy strategy, and so long as the strategic ties between Iran and Syria are maintained, such as the support given to Hezbollah and its activities, the resolution of the Israeli-Syrian conflict may not take place in the foreseeable future. Such a situation will surely have ramifications for Syria's neighbors, including Turkey. Considering Turkey's long-standing commitment to Westernization, Turkey's relations with its Middle Eastern neighbors may improve significantly if they also turn their face to the West and they do enthusiastically care about establishing much better relations with the West. If they achieve to do so, Turkey's place in the Middle East will become an asset, rather than a burden, for the Western world. In such a case, Syria will have more opportunities to exploit from its neighborhood with Turkey, the latter being a candidate country before the EU.

What's left to be done is to approach the remaining conflict-laden issues, such as the dispute over the use of the limited water resources in the region, rationally and also with a genuine desire to solve them, as has been the case in the signing of the Adana Protocol that put a halt to Syria's support to PKK terrorism. In addition to all these, one final step must also be taken by Syria at the earliest date possible, which is to make a formal declaration that it recognizes Turkey's current frontiers, including the Hatay province. Short of such a development, the prospects for a fruitful relationship between Turkey and Syria may lag far behind their potential.

NOTES

1. Extracts from the Web site of the Turkish Ministry of Foreign Affairs, www.mfa.gov.tr; italics added.

2. Richard H. Pfaff, "Disengagement from Traditionalism in Turkey and Iran," *Western Political Quarterly* 16, no. 1 (March 1963): 79–98.

3. The oldest fixed boundary in the Middle East, the Turco-Persian border, was established in 1639 with the Treaty of Kasr-ı Shirin, also called the Treaty of Zuhab. Maurice Harari, "The Turco-Persian Boundary Question: A Case Study in Boundary Making in the Near and Middle East" (PhD diss., Columbia University, 1958).

4. John Calabrese, "Turkey and Iran: Limits of a Stable Relationship," *British Journal of Middle Eastern Studies* 25, no. 1 (May 1998): 76.

5. Richard Pomfret, "The Economic Cooperation Organization: Current Status and Future Prospects," *Europe-Asia Studies* 49, no. 4 (June 1997): 657–67.

6. Calabrese, "Turkey and Iran," 77.

7. The following parts in this section benefited mostly from the article of the author, which was previously published in the *Middle East Policy* journal's December 2008 issue titled "Implications of a Nuclear Iran for Turkey" coauthored with Barış Çağlar.

8. Hootan Shambayati, "A Tale of Two Mayors," *International Journal of Middle East Studies,* no. 36 (2004): 253–75.

9. Author's conversations over a long period of time, especially since 2002, with high-ranking military and diplomatic officials as well as academics and experts in Turkey, many of whom spoke under the condition of non-attribution. Of these, however, Mr. Seyfi Taşhan, founder and Director of the Foreign Policy Institute in Ankara (October 2007); former Commanders of the Turkish Air Force Gen. Ret. Ergin Celasin and Gen. Ret. Halis Burhan (February 2008); Former Minister of State Mr. Vehbi Dinçerler (February 2008); and Prof. Dr. Colonel Taner Altınok, Director of the Institute of Defense Studies at the Turkish Military Academy in Ankara (March 2008), have granted the permission to be cited with their personal views on the subject matter.

10. Nuray Başaran, "Özkök Paşa'dan Duyduğum İlk Mesajlar" [First Messages that I Heard from General Özkök], *Akşam,* April 22, 2005. For more on the official position of the TAF, see www.tsk.mil.tr.

11. Ronald Grigor Suny, "Provisional Stabilities: The Politics of Identities in Post-Soviet Eurasia," *International Security* 24, no. 3 (Winter 1999–2000): 139–78.

12. Stanford J. Shaw, *From Empire to Republic: The Turkish War of National Liberation, 1918–1923* (Ankara: Türk Tarih Kurumu, 2001); Erick J. Zurcher, *Turkey: A Modern History* (London and New York: I. B. Tauris & Co. Limited, 2001).

13. David Fromkin, *A Peace to End All Peace: The Fall of the Ottoman Empire and the Creation of Modern Middle East* (New York: Avon Book, 1989).

14. Countless interviews with leading Turkmen people during the short-term leadership seminars hosted at Bilkent University in Ankara between 1998 and 2004.

15. Tarık H. Oğuzlu, *Turkmens of Iraq as a Factor in Turkish Foreign Policy: Socio-Political and Demographic Perspectives* (Ankara: Foreign Policy Institute, 2001).

16. Ayşegül Kibaroğlu, "The Role of Epistemic Communities in Offering New Cooperation Frameworks in the Euphrates-Tigris Rivers System," *Journal of International Affairs* 61, no. 2 (Spring/Summer 2008): 183–98.

17. Ayşegül Kibaroğlu and Olcay Ünver, "An Institutional Framework for Facilitating Cooperation in the Euphrates-Tigris River Basin," *International Negotiation: A Journal of Theory and Practice* 5, no. 2 (2001): 311–30.

18. Meliha Benli Altunışık and Özlem Tür, "From Distant Neighbors to Partners? Changing Syrian-Turkish Relations," *Security Dialogue* 37 (2006): 232–34.

19. Ayşegül Kibaroğlu, "Cooperation for Development: Emerging Frameworks for Sharing Benefits in the Euphrates-Tigris River Basin," *Boğaziçi Journal* 20 (2006): 135–52.

20. Ayşegül Kibaroğlu, *Building a Regime for the Waters of the Euphrates-Tigris River Basin* (The Hague, London, and New York: Kluwer Law International, 2002).

Biographies

MUSTAFA KEMAL ATATÜRK

Mustafa Kemal was born in 1881 in Salonika, a province of the Ottoman Empire. He attended primary school at the Şemsi Efendi School in Salonika. He continued his education at the Salonika Military Middle School and the Monastir (Bitola) Military Preparatory School. In 1899 he entered the İstanbul War College and graduated with the rank of infantry second lieutenant in 1902 and graduated from the War Academy as a staff captain in 1905. Mustafa Kemal was assigned duties in the 5th Army in Damascus in 1905 and in the 3rd Army in Macedonia in 1907. While he was on duty in Monastir and Salonika, he served in the Operations Army, which suppressed the rebellion (March 31 Incidents) in İstanbul. He participated in the operation to suppress the rebellion in Albania. In 1911, upon the military landing of Italy in Tripoli, he was sent to Tobruk. He led the Turkish Forces in Tobruk and Darnah successfully. He participated with the rank of major in the Balkan Wars between 1912 and 1913. He served in the army corps, which recaptured Edirne from Bulgaria. In 1915, during World War I, he participated in the Çanakkale (Dardanelles) Battle as the 19th Division Commander. He successfully stopped the enemy attacks at Gelibolu (Gallipoli). He acquired fame with the name of "Hero of the Anafarta Heights." He was appointed as the Army Corps Commander at the eastern front in 1916 and rose to the rank of brigadier general. He stopped the Russian attacks and recaptured Bingöl and Muş from the enemies. In 1917 he was appointed to the 7th Army Command that was on duty in Palestine and Syria. The same year he went to Germany with the Heir Apparent Vahdeddin. He made studies at the German General Headquarters and at the German battle fronts. In 1918 when he was reassigned as the 7th Army Commander on the Syrian front, World War I ended. He came to İstanbul after the Mudros Armistice. He departed from İstanbul with the duty of Army Inspector, by keeping secret his aim of saving the country from enemy occupation. He went to Samsun via the Black Sea on May 19, 1919. He published the Amasya Circular on June 22, 1919. He resigned from the duties given by the Ottoman Government and from the military. He acted as chairman of the congresses convened in Erzurum on July 23, 1919 and in Sivas on September 4, 1919. The TGNA (TBMM) started its historical duties in Ankara on April 23, 1920 with Mustafa Kemal's efforts. He was elected Chairman of the Assembly and Head of the Government. It was declared to the world that the Sèvres Treaty, which was signed between the Ottoman Government and the Allies, was not accepted by the Turkish Nation. The Turkish Army, led by Commander-in-Chief Mustafa Kemal Pasha, concluded the Sakarya Major Battle with victory. Mustafa Kemal was given the rank of "Marshal" and the title of "Gazi" (war hero) by the TGNA due to this victory. The Mudanya Armistice was signed on October 11, 1922 and the Allies withdrew from the Turkish territories, which they had occupied. After the National War of Liberation, the Republic was proclaimed on October 29, 1923 by the TBMM and Mustafa Kemal became the first President of Turkey. Mustafa Kemal was given the surname of Atatürk with the Law No. 2587, dated November 24, 1934, and it was forbidden for this surname to be used by other persons. Atatürk was a genius statesman with the reforms he made successfully. During a large part of his life, he worked for the independence and prosperity of his nation, and he emerged victorious from every battle he entered. Mustafa Kemal Atatürk died on November 10, 1938.

İSMET İNÖNÜ

Mustafa İsmet was born in İzmir in 1884. He completed his primary and secondary education in Sivas. After he attended the Preparatory School for Civil Servants, he went to the Preparatory School for Engineering in İstanbul. İsmet then entered the Imperial School of Military Engineering in 1901 and graduated from this school in 1903 as an artillery second lieutenant. He graduated at the head of his class from the General Staff School in 1906 and was appointed to the company command of the 2nd Army, 8th Regiment in Edirne with the rank of staff captain. He became a major in 1908 and served in the Operations Army, which suppressed the rebellion known as the March 31 Incidents (April 13, 1909). He joined in the operation to suppress the Yemen Rebellion between 1910 and 1913. He drew attention with his successful services and professional characteristics in the border problems and the agreements made with rebels in this and previous duties. When he worked together with Mustafa Kemal as the Army

Corps Commander at the Caucasian front, they developed their friendship and joint ideas on the future of the state. Subsequently, Mustafa İsmet fought at the Syrian front and was in the forefront during the National Struggle as the closest brother-in-arms of Mustafa Kemal. He participated, as the Edirne Member of Parliament, in the TGNA (TBMM) opened on April 23, 1920. Subsequently, on May 3, 1920, he became the General Deputy of the General Staff in the Cabinet. Colonel İsmet, despite the fact that he was in charge of the duties of a member of parliament and a minister, was appointed to the duty of Western Front Command. He played an effective role with the regular army during the War of Liberation and in the suppressing of the Çerkez Ethem rebellion and domestic revolts. He stopped the advances of the Greek army into Anatolia in the First and Second İnönü battles in January and April in 1921. Colonel İsmet rose to the rank of brigadier general after the First İnönü Battle. Upon the victory won after the Sakarya Major Battle and the Grand Offensive, he represented the Grand National Assembly at the Mudanya Armistice meeting. He was sent to the Lausanne Peace Conference as the Minister of Foreign Affairs and served as the chairman of the Turkish delegation. İsmet Pasha signed the Lausanne Treaty on July 24, 1923, which provided for the recognition of the independence and sovereignty of the Republic of Turkey. He served as the Prime Minister in the first government between 1923 and 1924. At the same time, he assumed the duty of Deputy General Chairman of the Republican People's Party (*Cumhuriyet Halk Partisi*—CHP). İsmet Pasha was given the surname of İnönü by Atatürk, when the Surname Law was promulgated in 1934. He continued his duty as Prime Minister between 1924 and 1937. After the death of Atatürk in 1938, İsmet İnönü was elected as the second President of Turkey by the TGNA and was also made the General Chairman of the CHP. At the First Extraordinary General Assembly of the CHP, which convened on December 26, 1938, he was elected as "the permanent general chairman" and was given the title of "National Chief." İnönü succeeded in keeping Turkey outside of the war disaster during World War II. He was effective in the transition to a multiparty political regime after the war. After the 1950 general elections, the Democrat Party (*Demokrat Parti*—DP) took over the government from CHP. İsmet İnönü continued his political life as the general chairman of the main opposition party CHP until 1960. He became a member of the Constitutional Assembly after the May 27, 1960 military coup d'état, and he was appointed as Prime Minister on November 10, 1961. After he left this duty in 1965, he continued his political life as a member of parliament. When the group he supported at the CHP Congress was defeated by Bülent Ecevit's list, he resigned from the Party and the Parliament in 1972. İsmet İnönü, in accordance with the Constitution, continued his life appointment in the Republic Senate until his death on December 25, 1973. He married Mevhibe in 1916.

ADNAN MENDERES

Ali Adnan Ertekin Menderes was born in 1899 in Aydın, as the son of a wealthy landowner. After primary school, Menderes attended the American College in İzmir. He graduated from the Law School of Ankara University. In 1930, Menderes organized a branch of the short-lived Liberal Republican Party (*Serbest Cumhuriyet Fırkası*) in Aydın. After the ban of this party, he was invited by Atatürk himself to join the Republican People's Party (CHP) and was elected deputy of Aydın in 1931. In 1945, he was expelled from the party with two other colleagues due to inner-party opposition. On January 7, 1946, he formed the Democrat Party (DP). The DP won 52 percent of the votes in elections held on May 14, 1950. Menderes became Prime Minister and in 1955 he also assumed the duties of Foreign Minister. He later won two more free elections, one in 1954 and the other in 1957. On May 27, 1960, a military coup d'état removed the government, and Menderes was arrested along with some other party members. They were charged with violating the constitution. He was executed by hanging on September 17, 1961.

SÜLEYMAN DEMİREL

Sami Süleyman Gündoğdu Demirel was born on November 1, 1924 in İslamköy, a village in İsparta province. After finishing elementary school in İslamköy, he attended middle and high schools in İsparta and Afyon. He graduated from the Faculty of Civil Engineering of the İstanbul Technical University (İTÜ) in February 1949. In the same year, he started duties at the Electric Works Study Administration. In 1954 Demirel was appointed as the Chairman of the Department of Dams and in 1955 appointed as the General Director of the State Hydraulic Works (DSİ). He worked as a self-employed consultant and engineer between 1962 and 1964. His political life started in 1962 with membership in the Justice Party (*Adalet Partisi*—AP). After he was elected as the Chairman of the Party on November 28, 1964, he facilitated the formation of the coalition government and served as the Deputy Prime Minister in the coalition government, which ruled between February and October 1965. In the elections held on October 10, 1969, his party was the sole winner by a landslide once again. He resigned upon the Generals' Memorandum of March 12, 1971. Between 1971 and 1980, he served as Prime Minister for three more times, respectively in 1975–77, 1977–78, and 1979–80. He was removed from office after the military coup d'état on September 12, 1980, and he was banned from politics for seven years. After the political bans were removed with a referendum on September 6, 1987, Süleyman Demirel was elected as the Chairman of the True Path Party (DYP) on September 24, 1987. Then he again entered the Grand National Assembly as an İsparta Member of Parliament after the

November 29, 1987 Parliamentary elections. After the general elections on October 20, 1991, he served as Prime Minister in the 49th Government composed of the True Path Party and the Social Democrat Populist Party (*Sosyal Demokrat Halkçı Parti*—SHP). On May 16, 1993, he was elected by the TGNA the ninth President of Turkey. Demirel completed his term of duty on the 16th of May 2000. He married Nazmiye Şener in 1948.

BÜLENT ECEVİT

Mustafa Bülent Ecevit was born on May 28, 1925 in İstanbul. In 1944, he graduated from Robert College and later started working as a translator in Press Publication Head Office. He went to the United States in the mid-1950s on a State Department fellowship. There he worked at two newspapers in North Carolina. Ecevit was elected into the Turkish Parliament for the first time in 1957. He was a member of the Founding Parliament between 1960 and 1961. He served as the Minister of Labor between 1961 and 1965 contributing to the acceptance of right to strike and collective agreement. In 1966 he became the Secretary-General of the Republican People's Party (CHP). In 1971 he resigned from the post as a protest to the party decision to support the transitional government established by a military intervention. In 1972, he succeeded İsmet İnönü as leader of the party and became prime minister. This government is most noted for ordering a military intervention in Cyprus on July 20, 1974, in response to a coup engineered by the military Junta in Greece, with the purpose of dividing the island, uprooting hundreds of thousands of people. After the military coup d'état that was headed by the then Chief of General Staff General Kenan Evren, he was also banned from involvement in active politics for seven years. When the ban was lifted in 1987, he became the leader of the Democratic Left Party (DSP). With his comeback in 1999 general elections, he was successful as caretaker Prime Minster. But in 2002, early elections were held and Ecevit failed to put back his party into the National Assembly. In 2004, he made his retirement from politics. Ecevit was a Turkish politician, poet, writer, and journalist. He died due to a respiratory failure on November 5, 2006 in Ankara.

NECMETTİN ERBAKAN

Necmettin Erbakan was born on October 29, 1926 in Sinop. After the high school education in İstanbul Erkek Lisesi, he graduated from the Mechanical Engineering Faculty at the İstanbul Technical University (İTÜ) in 1948 and received a Ph.D. from the Aachen University in Germany. After returning to Turkey, Erbakan became lecturer at İTÜ and he was appointed as professor in 1965 at the same university. After working some time in leading positions in the industrial sector, he switched over to politics and was elected a deputy of

Konya in 1969 general elections. A mainstay of the religious wing of Turkish politics since the 1970s, he has been the leader of a series of political parties that have risen to prominence only to be banned by Turkey's secular authorities. During his long career in politics, Erbakan was well known for his "Islamist" approach to politics. The Constitutional Court in the 1970s and the military coup leaders in the 1980s shut down his parties, the National Order Party (MNP) and the National Salvation Party (MSP), respectively. His unpredicted rise to premiership and his hasty attempts to shift the direction of Turkey's mainstream foreign policy orientation from the Western world to the Islamic world by paying his first official visit as the Prime Minister of Turkey to the Islamic fundamentalist Iran and his second visit to Colonel Qaddafi's authoritarian Libya has generated much reaction in Turkey's mainstream secular circles. He was driven out of the office that he had stayed in only about a year, with a so-called postmodern coup. The Constitutional Court eventually shut down Erbakan's Welfare Party in January 1998 and its successor, the Virtue Party (FP), in June 2001. Erbakan is the leader of the Islamist movement *Millî Görüş*, which he also founded. He received a prison sentence as government allocated political funds into his party were embezzled or improperly spent.

TURGUT ÖZAL

Halil Turgut Özal was born on October 13, 1927 in Malatya. He graduated from the school of electrical engineering at the İstanbul Technical University (İTÜ) in 1950. He then went to the United States in 1952 and received education in economics. When he returned to Turkey, he was appointed as the Deputy General Director at the Electric Works Study Administration. Özal did his military service between 1961 and 1962 as a member of the Scientific Consultancy Board at the Ministry of National Defense. He helped establish the State Planning Organization (DPT). During this time, he also taught courses at the Middle East Technical University (ODTÜ). Between 1967 and 1971, Özal worked as the Member of the Prime Ministry Technical Experts Board and carried out the duty of the Undersecretary of the State Planning Organization. During this period he also served as chairman in the Economic Coordination Committee, the Monetary and Credit Committee, the RCD Coordination Committee, and the EEC Coordination Committee. Özal served as a consultant at the World Bank between 1971 and 1973. After his return to Turkey, he worked in various industrial organizations. Toward the end of 1979, he was appointed as the Undersecretary of the Prime Ministry. In the same period, he also carried out, by proxy, the duty of the Undersecretary of the State Planning Organization. After the September 12, 1980 coup d'état, he was appointed as the Deputy Prime Minister responsible for economic affairs in the military government formed. He resigned from this duty in 1982. He established the Motherland Party

(ANAP) in 1983. The same year, his party won the parliamentary elections and Özal became the nineteenth Prime Minister of the Republic of Turkey. After the 1987 elections, he formed the government once again and served as the Prime Minister. Özal was elected as the eighth President of Turkey by the TGNA (TBMM) on October 31, 1989. He served as the President from November 9, 1989 and until his passing due to a heart attack on April 17, 1993. Turgut Özal married Semra Yeyinmen in 1954 and had three children.

NECİP TORUMTAY

Necip Torumtay was born in 1926 in Trabzon. He graduated from the Turkish Military Academy in 1954. He served as a General at the Turkish Army between July 24, 1987 and December 3, 1990. In the Gulf War in 1991, the Army also strongly opposed the decision of President Turgut Özal to act together with the United States. Being the Chief of Turkish General Staff, General Necip Torumtay did not want to conduct a military operation to occupy the northern Iraq as requested, and he resigned due to deep disagreement on this matter with President Özal. Necip Torumtay is the first and the only Chief of General Staff in the TAF who resigned from this post.

DENİZ BAYKAL

Deniz Baykal was born on July 20, 1938 in Antalya, Turkey. He was educated at the University of Ankara's Faculty of Law. He later studied at the University of California, Berkeley and Columbia University, New York as a research fellow. He finished his Ph.D. in 1963 in Ankara. He became an Associate Professor in the University of Ankara's Faculty of Science where he lectured extensively. He served as the Minister of Finance, Minister of Energy, and Minister of Foreign Affairs at various times throughout his career, as well as Deputy Prime Minister. Later he became the Secretary-General of the Republican People's Party (CHP) in 1988. In 1992, he was elected as the leader of the party. His social democrat Republican People's Party is the second biggest of the country and is serving as the major opposition party in the Parliament. Baykal was elected as the Vice President of the Socialist International in 2003.

RECEP TAYYİP ERDOĞAN

With family origins in Turkey's Rize, Recep Tayyip Erdoğan was born in İstanbul on February 26, 1954. He graduated in 1965 from Kasımpaşa Piyale Elementary School and in 1973 from Istanbul Religious Vocational High School (*İmam Hatip Lisesi*). Erdoğan received his high school diploma from Eyüp High School where he took a graduation exam. Erdoğan graduated in 1981 from

Marmara University's Faculty of Economics and Commercial Sciences. During the late 1970s, Erdoğan worked for İstanbul's municipal transport company, the IETT. He became active in politics with the National Salvation Party (MSP), which was led by Necmettin Erbakan. Turkey witnessed political tension during the late 1970s, which were particularly marked by right-wing and left-wing armed conflicts that led to the 1980 military coup d'état. Erdoğan left the IETT and worked in the private sector. The political party system was restored in 1983. Necmettin Erbakan was banned from politics by the coup authors. The former members of MSP founded the Welfare Party (RP). Erdoğan reentered politics through this new party. He became the party chairman in İstanbul province in the 1985 local elections and stood for mayor of Beyoğlu district. He did not win the local elections. The party nominated Erdoğan as a candidate for Parliament from the central İstanbul area several times during the late 1980s. Erdoğan did not win enough votes until 1991. In 1991, the party passed the 10 percent threshold necessary to gain seats in the Parliament for the first time. He was elected as the Mayor of İstanbul on March 27, 1994. He was convicted by a court for inciting religious hatred and sentenced to 10 months imprisonment, but served only 4 months. He founded the Justice and Development Party (AKP), which won the first general elections soon after its foundation. Tayyip Erdoğan became the Prime Minister of Turkey on March 14, 2003.

APPENDIX B

Chronology

1071	Manzikert (*Malazgirt*) Battle, Sultan Alparslan defeated the Byzantine army which was led by Romanus Diogenes. The Battle played an important role in breaking the Byzantine resistance and preparing the way for Turkish settlement in Anatolia.
1299	Ottoman Empire was established, Osman proclaimed his independence from the Seljuks and sowed the seeds of the Ottoman Empire in Söğüt.
1453	The conquest of Constantinople (İstanbul), the seat of the Byzantine Empire, by Sultan Mehmed II *the Conqueror*.
1639	The peace accord between the Persian and the Ottoman empires reached with the Treaty of Kasr-ı Shirin in 1639 succeeded in reducing tensions.
1683	The Battle of Vienna, it has been a landmark event that heralded the end of Ottoman expansionism into the European territories.
1839	Reform and Reorganization (*Tanzimat*) movement launched by Sultan Abdülmecid I.
1876	Basic Law (*Kanun-i Esasi*), first Ottoman constitution, was enacted and it established freedom of belief and equality of all citizens before the law.
October 30, 1918	The Armistice of Mudros, signed between the Ottoman Empire and the Allied powers at the end of World War I.
May 19, 1919	Mustafa Kemal leaving İstanbul to go to Samsun; he engaged in organizing a nationwide resistance movement against the foreign occupying forces all over Turkey without delay.

June 22, 1919	Amasya Circular was declared by the Turkish national movement under the leadership of Mustafa Kemal. It was the first of such declarations that underlined that the national sovereignty would be regained at all cost with the determination of the Turkish population to fight back the occupying powers.
July 23–August 9, 1919	The Congress of Erzurum was convened. At the end of the Congress, the Association for the Defense of Rights of Eastern Anatolia (*Müdafa-i Hukuk Cemiyeti*) proclaimed the political objective of the national resistance and liberation movement launched by Mustafa Kemal.
September 4–11, 1919	The Congress of Sivas was convened, and the resolve of the Turks to liberate the country was reiterated.
December 27, 1919	Mustafa Kemal arrived in Ankara, which he chose as the seat of the national resistance and liberation movement.
April 23, 1920	TGNA was established and convened its first plenary session and elected Mustafa Kemal as the Speaker of the TGNA.
August 10, 1920	Treaty of Sèvres, signed between the Ottoman Empire and the Allied powers, which partitioned the Ottoman territories among the British, French, Italians, and Greek that had already occupied large portions of lands in Anatolia and the Thrace region.
January 1921	The victory of Colonel İsmet against the Greek in the Battle of İnönü.
March 16, 1921	Treaty of Moscow, signed between the Turkish national movement who were represented by the TGNA and the Soviet Union.
October 20, 1921	Treaty of Ankara, signed between Turkey and France. According to the Treaty, in return for economic privileges that France would receive from Turkey, it would recognize the TGNA as the representative of the Turks, and the French military would soon evacuate the territories that it had occupied since the end of World War I.
August 26–30, 1922	A Grand Offensive was launched against Greek occupying power. The Greek were forced to leave the Turkish territories and İzmir was liberated on September 9, 1922.
February 17–March 4, 1923	İzmir Economics Congress convened in which Atatürk delivered a long speech emphasizing the fact that the new Turkish state would adopt a Western-style economic and political regime.
July 24, 1923	Lausanne Peace Treaty was signed. It settled the Anatolian part of the partitioning of the Ottoman Empire by annulment of the Treaty of Sèvres signed by the Ottoman Empire as the consequences of the Turkish Liberation War between Allies of World War I and Grand National Assembly of Turkey (Turkish national movement).
October 29, 1923	Republic of Turkey was proclaimed in the new capital Ankara.

June 5, 1926	Ankara Treaty was signed between Turkey and Britain. Atatürk had recognized the decision taken by the League of Nations concerning the status of the Mosul district, once an Ottoman *Vilayet* (governorate), which was left to Iraq.
February 9, 1934	Balkan Entente was signed among Turkey, Greece, Romania, and Yugoslavia.
July 20, 1936	Montreux Convention was signed, establishing a new regime in the Turkish Straits with full sovereignty of Turkey.
July 8, 1937	Sadabad Pact was signed among Turkey, Iran, Iraq, and Afghanistan in Tehran.
November 10, 1938	Atatürk passed away. İsmet İnönü became the President.
July 23, 1939	Hatay (Sancak) annexed to Turkey.
October 19, 1939	A trilateral declaration was signed among Turkey, France, and Britain.
December 4–6, 1943	Cairo summit, Turkish President İnönü agreed "in principle" to join World War II provided Turkey received enough military equipment, arms, and munitions.
July 17–August 2, 1945	Potsdam Conference, Soviet Union made claims on the Straits of Turkey and on the islands in the eastern Mediterranean, which were under the Italian control.
1950–53	Turkey's participation in the Korean War.
February 1952	Turkey became member of the NATO.
1953	"Agreement of Cooperation and Friendship" known as the "Balkan Pact" was signed among Turkey, Greece, and Yugoslavia.
1955	Baghdad Pact was adopted by Iraq, Turkey, Pakistan, and Iran, as well as the United Kingdom. In 1958 the United States joined the military committee of the Alliance. Its goal was to contain the Soviet Union by having a line of strong states along the USSR's southwestern frontier.
1960	Republic of Cyprus was created following the Zurich and London conferences under the aegis of the United Kingdom, Greece, and Turkey as guarantor powers.
1960	The military coup d'état resulting in the execution of the then Prime Minister Adnan Menderes together with the Foreign Minister Fatin Rüştü Zorlu and Minister of Finance Hasan Polatkan in the Menderes Cabinet.
1963	Ankara Treaty was signed between the EEC and Turkey; Turkey became an Associate Member.
1963	Turkey reacted with a limited air operation to "show flag" over Cyprus, which was inhabited by both Turkish and Greek Cypriots.
June 1964	U.S. President Lyndon Johnson sent a bitter letter to the Turkish Premier İnönü reminding bluntly that the United States would not side with Turkey in case its intervention in Cyprus prompted a Soviet aggression.

1964	RCD, established by Iran and Turkey along with Pakistan to counter Soviet penetration. It then turned into the ECO to promote economic, technical, and cultural cooperation among members although the organization failed in achieving concrete outcomes.
March 12, 1971	Turkish military intervened in politics for the second time by issuing a memorandum publicly, which harshly criticized the Süleyman Demirel government for its conduct of economic and political affairs in the country. In response to the generals' memorandum, Prime Minister Demirel resigned promptly, with a view to preventing a possible coup d'état similar to the one that took place only 11 years ago.
July 1974	Turkey's military intervention (Peace Operation) in Cyprus against the coup staged by the Greek Cypriot extreme nationalists, encouraged by the military Junta in Athens, who wished to annex the island to Greece.
1975–78	U.S. Senate to impose an arms embargo on Turkey during the Jimmy Carter administration.
September 12, 1980	Military coup d'état staged by the then Chief of General Staff General Kenan Evren and the Force Commanders in response to the deteriorating anarchic situation in the country.
1983	Turkish Republic of Northern Cyprus declared its independence, and recognized only by Turkey.
April 1987	Turkey submitted its formal application to the EC for full membership referring to its right documented in the Ankara Treaty that was signed in 1963 and entered into force in 1964.
July 17, 1987	Turkey and Syria signed the Protocol of Economic Cooperation. It included several articles pertaining to the water issue.
June 25, 1992	BSEC Organization was established.
1996	Israel and Turkey signed an agreement for military cooperation.
February 28, 1997	"Postmodern coup," staged by the military to overthrow a coalition government led by pro-Islamist Prime Minister Necmettin Erbakan. A long list of decisions, called the February 28 decisions, were adopted by the then Parliament, including the establishment of a compulsory eight-year uninterrupted primary and secondary education in an attempt to prevent students enrolling in religious schools after the completion of primary school.
October 1998	Syria signed the "Adana Protocol" with Turkey committing itself not to give any more support to any groups that would damage the national interests of Turkey.
February 15, 1999	The head of PKK Abdullah Öcalan was captured in the Greek Embassy in Nairobi, Kenya.
December 1999	At the Helsinki Summit meeting of the EU, Turkey was officially declared a candidate country for full membership.

March 1, 2003	The TGNA voted on the U.S. troop-basing resolution. The resolution failed with 264 yes votes, 250 no votes, and 19 abstaining, because it required the approval of an absolute majority of the 550-member Parliament.
December 17, 2004	During its summit meeting in Brussels, the European Union has decided to formally start in October 2005 the accession negotiations with Turkey for full membership.
July 13, 2006	BTC oil pipeline, "Silk Road of the 21st Century," which crosses the territory of Azerbaijan, Georgia, and Turkey, started to operate.
October 17, 2008	Turkey is elected to the United Nations Security Council as a Non-Permanent Member to represent Europe for the years 2009 and 2010.

Bibliography

Ahrari, Mohammed E. *Jihadi Groups, Nuclear Pakistan and the New Great Game.* Carlisle, PA: US Army War College Strategic Studies Institute, 2001.

Alantar, Zeynep Ö. "Türk Dış Politikası'nda Milletler Cemiyeti Dönemi" [The Period of League of Nations in Turkish Foreign Policy]. In *Türk Dış Politikası'nın Analizi,* edited by Faruk Sönmezoğlu. İstanbul: Der Yayınları, 2001.

Altunışık, Meliha Benli, and Özlem Tür. "From Distant Neighbors to Partners? Changing Syrian-Turkish Relations." *Security Dialogue* 37 (2006): 229–48.

Armaoğlu, Fahir. *20. Yüzyıl Siyasi Tarihi, Cilt 1–2: 1914–1995* [20th Century Diplomatic History, Volumes 1–2: 1914–1995]. İstanbul: Alkım Yayınevi, Genişletilmiş 13. Baskı, 2004.

Ayoob, Mohammed. "Turkey's Multiple Paradoxes." *Orbis* 48, no. 3 (Summer 2004): 451–63.

Başaran, Nuray. "Özkök Paşa'dan Duyduğum İlk Mesajlar" [First Messages that I Heard from General Özkök]. *Akşam,* April 22, 2005. For more on the official position of the TAF, see www.tsk.mil.tr.

Blanche, Ed. "Israel and Turkey Look to Extend Their Influence into Central Asia." *Janes Intelligence Review,* August 2001.

Bonner, Michael. "Turkey, the European Union and Paradigm Shifts." *Middle East Policy* 12, no. 1 (Spring 2005): 44–71.

Brzezinski, Zbigniew. "Hegemonic Quicksand." *National Interest,* no. 74 (Winter 2003/4).

Bush, George W. "Address to a Joint Session of Congress and the American People," September 20, 2001. For the original script of President Bush's address, see www.whitehouse.gov.

Calabrese, John. "Turkey and Iran: Limits of a Stable Relationship." *British Journal of Middle Eastern Studies* 25, no. 1 (May 1998).

Çevik, İlnur. "The Spheres of Interest of the Military." *Turkish Daily News,* October 14, 2003.

Choi, Kwangsoo. "The Original Turkish Concerns about Developments in Northern Iraq." Master's thesis, Bilkent University, May 2008.

Coşar, Nevin, and Sevtap Demirci. "The Mosul Question and the Turkish Republic: Before and After the Frontier Treaty, 1926." *Turkish Yearbook* 35 (2004): 43–59.

Criss, Nur B. *Istanbul Under Allied Occupation, 1918–1923 (Ottoman Empire and Its Heritage)*. Leiden: E.J. Brill, 1999.

Demirözü, Damla. "The Greek-Turkish Rapprochement of 1930 and the Repercussions of the Ankara Convention in Turkey." *Journal of Islamic Studies* 19, no. 3 (2008): 309–24. Advance Access published on March 18, 2008.

Eldem, Edhem. "Ottoman Financial Integration with Europe: Foreign Loans, the Ottoman Bank and the Ottoman Public Debt." *European Review* 13, no. 3 (2005): 431–45.

Erlanger, Steven. "Israeli Spy Satellite Ditches after Takeoff." *International Herald Tribune*, September 7, 2004, 5.

Falkenrath, Richard A. "The CFE Flank Dispute: Waiting in the Wings." *International Security* 19, no. 4 (1995): 118–44.

Foster, Henry A. *The Making of Modern Iraq*. Oklahoma: University of Oklahoma Press, 1935.

Fromkin, David. *A Peace to End All Peace: The Fall of the Ottoman Empire and the Creation of Modern Middle East*. New York: Avon Book, 1989.

Güneş, Şule. "Türk Boğazları" [Turkish Straits]. *ODTÜ Gelişme Dergisi*, no. 34 (December 2007): 217–50.

Güngör, Uğur. "The Analysis of Turkey's Approach to Peace Operations." PhD diss., Bilkent University, 2007.

Harari, Maurice. "The Turco-Persian Boundary Question: A Case Study in Boundary Making in the Near and Middle East." PhD diss., Columbia University, 1958.

Hersh, Seymour. *Chain of Command: The Road from 9/11 to Abu Ghraib*. New York: Harper Collins Publishers, 2004.

———. "Israeli Agents Operating in Iraq, Iran and Syria." *Democracy Now*, June 22, 2004. http://www.democracynow.org/2004/6/22/seymour_hersh_israeli_agents_operating_in; Seymour M. Hersh, "As June 30th Approaches Israel Looks to the Kurds." *New Yorker*, June 28, 2004.

Hickok, Michael. "Hegemon Rising: The Gap between Turkish Strategy and Military Modernization." *Parameters: US Army War College* 30, no. 2 (2000): 105–20.

Hiçyılmaz, Ergun. "Tarihte 'Gel Kore'ye Gir NATO'ya' Süreci" [The "Come to Korea, Enter NATO" Process in History]. *Sabah*. http://arsiv.sabah.com.tr/2004/07/04/cp/hob114-20040627-102.html.

Cavid Veliev, "Hocali Massacre." *L'Actuel: Online Newspaper*. http://www.lactuel.be/detail.php?id=3103.

Huntington, Samuel. "The Clash of Civilizations." *Foreign Affairs* 72, no. 3 (Summer 1993).

Karaosmanoğlu, Ali L. "Europe's Geopolitical Parameters." In *Turkey, Central and Eastern European Countries in Transition*, edited by Subidey Togan and V.N. Balasubramanyam, 271–89. New York: Palgrave Press, 2001.

———. "The Evolution of the National Security Culture and the Military in Turkey." *Journal of International Affairs* 54, no. 1 (2000): 199–217.

Karaosmanoğlu, Ali L., and Mustafa Kibaroğlu. "Defense Reform in Turkey." In *Post-Cold War Defense Reforms: Lessons Learned in Europe and the United States*, edited by Istvan Gyarmati and Theodor Winkler, 135–64. New York: East West Institute, Brassey's, 2003.

Kibaroğlu, Ayşegül. *Building a Regime for the Waters of the Euphrates-Tigris River Basin*. London and The Hague: Kluwer Law International, 2002.

———. "Cooperation for Development: Emerging Frameworks for Sharing Benefits in the Euphrates-Tigris River Basin." *Boğaziçi Journal* 20 (2006): 135–52.

————. "The Role of Epistemic Communities in Offering New Cooperation Frameworks in the Euphrates-Tigris Rivers System." *Journal of International Affairs* 61, no. 2 (Spring/Summer 2008): 183–98.

Kibaroğlu, Ayşegül, and Olcay Ünver. "An Institutional Framework for Facilitating Cooperation in the Euphrates-Tigris River Basin." *International Negotiation: A Journal of Theory and Practice* 5, no. 2 (2001): 311–30.

Kibaroğlu, Mustafa. "Clash of Interest over Northern Iraq Drives Turkish-Israeli Alliance to a Crossroads." *Middle East Journal* 59, no. 2 (Spring 2005): 246–64.

————. "Good for the Shah, Banned for the Mullahs: The West and Iran's Quest for Nuclear Power." *Middle East Journal* 60, no. 2 (Spring 2006): 207–32.

————. "Impact of the Northern Tier on the Middle East: A Rejoinder." *Security Dialogue* 27, no. 3 (September 1996): 919–24.

————. "Iran's Nuclear Ambitions from a Historical Perspective." *Middle Eastern Studies* 43, no. 2 (March 2007): 223–45.

————. "Kurds Hold the Key for Both Turkey and the US." www.bitterlemons-international.org, March 2008.

————. "La Turquie, les États-Unis et l'OTAN: Une Alliance dans l'Alliance" [Turkey, the US and NATO: An Alliance within the Alliance]. *Questions Internationales,* no. 12 (March–April 2005): 30–32.

————. "New Tests for Turkey's Evolving Security Relationship with Israel." *Terrorism Focus* 5, no. 7 (February 2008). jamestown.org/terrorism/news.

————. "Turkey." In *Europe and Nuclear Disarmament,* edited by Harald Müller, 161–93. Brussels: European Interuniversity Press, 1998.

————. "Turkey and Israel Strategize." *Middle East Quarterly* 9, no. 1 (Winter 2002): 61–65.

————. "Turkey Says No." *Bulletin of the Atomic Scientists* 59, no. 4 (July/August 2003): 22–25.

————. "Turkey's Triple-Trouble: ESDP, Cyprus, N. Iraq." *Insight Turkey* 4, no. 1 (January–March 2002): 49–58.

Kirişçi, Kemal. "Reconciling Refugee Protection with Combating Irregular Migration: Turkey and the EU." *Perceptions, Journal of International Affairs* 9, no. 2 (2004).

Kristensen, Hans M. *US Nuclear Weapons in Europe: A Review of Post-Cold War Policy, Force Levels, and War Planning.* Washington, D.C.: Natural Resources Defense Council, February 2005.

Kuniholm, Bruce R. "Turkey and the West." *Foreign Affairs* 70, no. 2 (1991): 34–48.

Kürkçüoğlu, Ömer. *Türk-İngiliz İlişkileri* [Turkish-British Relations]. Ankara: Ankara Universitesi Siyasal Bilgiler Fakültesi Yayınları, 1978.

Kut, Şule. "Turks of Kosovo: What to Expect?" *Perceptions, Journal of International Affairs* 5, no. 3 (2000): 49–60.

Melek, Kemal. *İngiliz Belgeleriyle Musul Sorunu 1890–1926* [The Mosul Question in British Documents 1890–1926]. İstanbul: Üçdal Neşriyat, 1983.

Memorandum of Understanding between the Government of Turkey and the Government of the United States of America on the Establishment and Implementation of Basic Policy, Principles, Procedures and to Determine the Status of Forces to Be Provisionally Deployed in Turkey for the Purposes of Possible Operations Toward Iraq.

Oğuzlu, Tarık H. *Turkmens of Iraq as a Factor in Turkish Foreign Policy: Socio-Political and Demographic Perspectives.* Ankara: Foreign Policy Institute, 2001.

Pfaff, Richard H. "Disengagement from Traditionalism in Turkey and Iran." *Western Political Quarterly* 16, no. 1 (March 1963): 79–98.

Pollack, Kenneth M. *The Persian Puzzle: The Conflict between Iran and America.* New York: Random House, 2004.

Pomfret, Richard. "The Economic Cooperation Organization: Current Status and Future Prospects." *Europe-Asia Studies* 49, no. 4 (June 1997): 657–67.

Question of the Frontier between Turkey and Iraq. Report Submitted to the Council by the Commission instituted by the Council Resolution of September 30, 1924. Lausanne: League of Nations, 1924.

Sanger, David A., and Dexter Filkins. "US Is Pessimistic Turks Will Accept the Deal on Iraq." *New York Times,* February 20, 2003, A1 and A13.

Sezer, B. Duygu. "Turkey's New Security Environment, Nuclear Weapons and Proliferation." *Comparative Strategy* 14, no. 2 (1995): 149–73.

Shambayati, Hootan. "A Tale of Two Mayors." *International Journal of Middle East Studies,* no. 36 (2004): 253–75.

Sharp, Jane. "Intervention in Bosnia—The Case For." *World Today* 49, no. 2 (1993): 29–32.

Shaw, Stanford J. *From Empire to Republic: The Turkish War of National Liberation, 1918–1923.* Ankara: Türk Tarih Kurumu, 2001.

Shaw, Stanford J., and Ezel Kural Shaw. *History of the Ottoman Empire and Modern Turkey.* Cambridge: Cambridge University Press, 1977.

Suny, Ronald Grigor. "Provisional Stabilities: The Politics of Identities in Post-Soviet Eurasia." *International Security* 24, no. 3 (Winter 1999–2000): 139–78.

"Synopsis of the Turkish Foreign Policy." Republic of Turkey, Ministry of Foreign Affairs, The Balkans. http://www.mfa.gov.tr/sub.en.mfa?91541430-f1dd-41d0-b6eb-e1a6cc3e556b.

Türkeş, Mustafa. "Atatürk Döneminde Türkiye'nin Bölgesel Dış Politikaları 1923–1938" [Turkey's Regional Foreign Policy during the Atatürk Era 1923–1938]. *Atatürkçülük ve Modern Türkiye,* Uluslararası Konferans, October 22–23, 1998, Ankara, 123–41.

Udum, Şebnem. "Missile Proliferation in the Middle East: Turkey and Missile Defense." *Turkish Studies* 4, no. 3 (Autumn 2003): 71–102.

Wohlstetter, Albert. "The Delicate Balance of Terror." In *US Nuclear Strategy: A Reader,* edited by Philip Bobbitt, Lawrence Freedman, and Gregory F. Treverton, 143–67. London: The Macmillan Press, 1989.

Zurcher, Erick J. *Turkey: A Modern History.* London and New York: I. B. Tauris & Co. Limited, 2001.

Annotated Bibliography

Altunışık, Meliha Benli, and Özlem Tür. "From Distant Neighbors to Partners? Changing Syrian-Turkish Relations." *Security Dialogue* **37 (2006): 229–48.**
This article examines both the reasons behind increasing ties between Turkey and Syria since 1998 and the new challenges this rapprochement is facing due to the rapidly shifting international context. It argues that although systemic factors have been crucial in setting up the parameters of the bilateral relationship, these factors gain meaning through the complexities of domestic settings. The U.S. policy of regime change and the Iraq War of 2003 and its aftermath are taken as the main regional and international factors influencing relations between the two countries since 1998. Domestic factors like the process of regime consolidation in Syria under Bashar and rising nationalism, the Kurdish issue, and the coming to power of the Justice and Development Party in Turkey constitute the main lenses through which these systemic factors are evaluated and policy outcomes projected.

Altunışık, Meliha Benli, and Özlem Tür. *Turkey: Challenges of Continuity and Change.* **London and New York: Routledge, 2005.**
The book provides a general framework for Turkey, focusing on the developments in politics, economics, and international relations of the country, mainly for the general reader. It is rich in details of Turkish domestic and foreign policy. Two general perspectives inform the analysis in the book. The first is the dynamic interaction between internal and external contexts. Each chapter makes an effort to establish or at least invoke those links. Second, the book underlines the theme of continuity and change in the politics, economics, and international relations of Turkey. In each realm both continuities and changes at times present significant challenges. The extent to which Turkey has been able to face those challenges constitutes an important part of the volume.

Armaoğlu, Fahir. *20. Yüzyıl Siyasi Tarihi, Cilt 1–2: 1914–1995* **[20th Century Diplomatic History, Volumes 1–2: 1914–1995]. İstanbul: Alkım Yayınevi, Genişletilmiş 13. Baskı, 2004.**
This book provides thorough analyses of the twentieth-century diplomatic history with a background account of the relations of the Great Powers of Europe in the nineteenth century which the author analyzes as the root causes of World War I. In this context, the book provides detailed explanations on the nineteenth-century diplomatic history by referring to the independence of the United States and its foreign policy as well as the British and French colonialism in Africa and Asia. The nineteenth-century Ottoman Empire is also examined with special focus on the "politics of balance" pursued by the Empire vis-à-vis its relations with her rivals in Europe. The main events of World War I are explained year by year, including the peace agreements which ended the War. The period between 1919 and 1939 is analyzed in two main sections under the titles of "temporary peace" and "crises and collapse of the peace." These analyses are also paralleled with the examination of the Turkish foreign policy in the period of 1919 and 1939. The volume provides detailed analyses of World War II with its consecutive periods. Turkish foreign policy during World War II constitutes the subsection of this part. Cold War is examined with its main phases: 1945–60; 1960–70, structural changes in the Eastern and Western Blocs; and the Détente period. Separate parts are devoted to the political developments in Asia after World War II and the Middle East in the period of 1960 and 1980. Furthermore, Turkish foreign policy is scrutinized in the period of 1960 and 1980. The period between 1980 and 1995 is analyzed by referring to the developments in the Middle East and Asia and the demise of the Soviet Union, as well as the analyses on the Turkish foreign policy in this particular period.

Aydın, Mustafa, and Çağrı Erhan, eds. *Turkish-American Relations: Past, Present and Future.* **London: Routledge, 2004.**
This book presents an analytical picture of the many aspects of Turkish-American relations from the early years of the nineteenth century to the post–Cold War era. It devotes much attention to the underlying forces and the effects of the long and rich history on the relationship. The editors assert that though the context, intensity, and the extent of the relations have changed over the years, there are a number of issues discernible for their dividing or uniting effects on the Turkish-American relations that have remained almost unchanged. The volume is divided into three parts. Part I includes analyses on the historical experiences of the Ottoman-American relations. Part II discusses the contemporary issues and tries to shed light on the developments since the end of Cold War. Part III comprises essays which assert that the Turkish-American cooperation will continue, albeit under a new set of rules of engagement.

Bağcı, Hüseyin. *Türk Dış Politikasında 1950'li Yıllar* **[1950s in Turkish Foreign Policy]. Ankara: METU Press, 2001.**
The book analyzes Turkey's foreign policy during the Democrat Party (DP) rule in the 1950s. The book addresses themes such as the domestic and foreign policy factors affecting the DP government under the premiership of Adnan Menderes; contending security interests of Britain, the United States, and Turkey pertaining to the Middle East; Turkey's attitude toward the Cyprus problem; and Turkey's role in the Middle East in the late 1950s. In this context, the intimate relationship between domestic politics of the Menderes government and its foreign policy posture is examined.

Choi, Kwangsoo. "The Original Turkish Concerns about Developments in Northern Iraq." Master's thesis, Bilkent University, May 2008.
This Master's thesis analyzes that there are historical, demographical, political, and geostrategic contexts of Turkey's long-standing interests in the developments taking place in Iraq after the 2003 War. Hence, the thesis scrutinizes the treaties between Turkey and British related to Mosul that go back to the 1920s; the close cultural ties between Turkey and Turkmen or Iraqi Turks who have lived in mostly northern Iraq; and the direct threat of PKK who have stationed in northern Iraq to Turkey and an increased instability of security structure in Middle East.

Coşar, Nevin, and Sevtap Demirci. "The Mosul Question and the Turkish Republic: Before and After the Frontier Treaty, 1926." *Turkish Yearbook* 35 (2004): 43–59.
The article examines the Mosul Question with special attention to the aftermath of the Frontier Treaty of 1926. At the outset, the article provides an historical background of the Mosul Question, beginning from the Lausanne negotiations in which the fate of the *Vilayet* (province) became the key issue on the way to peace. The period between 1923 and 1926 in which the increasing tension between Britain and Turkey dominated the League of Nations negotiations is analyzed. Finally, the article focuses on the period after the 1926 Frontier Treaty, to clarify the payment questions of the Iraqi government's royalty revenues of 10 percent to Turkey.

Demirözü, Damla. "The Greek-Turkish Rapprochement of 1930 and the Repercussions of the Ankara Convention in Turkey." *Journal of Islamic Studies* 19, no. 3 (2008): 309–24. Advance Access published on March 18, 2008.
The Greek–Turkish rapprochement of the 1930s aimed to sort out some problems that Greece and Turkey had to deal with after the Lausanne Treaty. In this context, the article analyzes the discussions that took place in Turkey during the rapprochement. By claiming that information and comments on the Turkish–Greek rapprochement of 1930 are mostly to be found in non-Turkish historical studies, the article aims to give some information about how this period was experienced in Turkey, in Turkey's *vox populi* and in the Parliament.

Eldem, Edhem. "Ottoman Financial Integration with Europe: Foreign Loans, the Ottoman Bank and the Ottoman Public Debt." *European Review* 13, no. 3 (2005): 431–45.
The article examines the financial integration of the Ottoman Empire with Europe between 1854 and 1881 with particular attention to the first foreign loans contracted in 1854 and the establishment of the Ottoman Public Debt Administration that controlled a large portion of state revenues. The article argues that while bringing a much-needed stability to the flailing Ottoman financial situation and thus opening the way to economic development, the new system also radically changed the very nature of the process of integration, by introducing an imperialist dimension that had been lacking in the previous decades.

Fromkin, David. *A Peace to End All Peace: The Fall of the Ottoman Empire and the Creation of Modern Middle East.* New York: Avon Book, 1989.
The book reveals how and why the Allies after World War I came to remake the geography and politics of the Middle East, drawing lines on an empty map that eventually became the new countries of Iraq, Israel, Jordan, and Lebanon. Focusing on the formative years of 1914 to 1922, when everything seemed possible and oil was not a political issue, Fromkin shows how choices narrowed and the Middle East began along a road that led to the endless wars and escalating acts of terrorism that continue to this day.

Güneş, Şule. "Türk Boğazları" [The Turkish Straits]. *ODTÜ Gelişme Dergisi,* **no. 34 (December 2007): 217–50.**
The article deals with the status of the Turkish Straits by analyzing the international law principles pertaining to the international navigational uses of the straits; the changes in the administration and navigational regime of the Turkish Straits from the Treaty of Lausanne (1923) to Montreux Convention (1936); and the recent legal arrangements Turkey has adopted to respond to the environmental protection needs and navigational safety of the Straits.

Güngör, Uğur. *The Analysis of Turkey's Approach to Peace Operations.* **PhD diss., Bilkent University, 2007.**
This dissertation analyzes the motivations that lie at the roots of Turkey's involvement in peace operations, mostly organized under the leadership of the United Nations in the post–Cold War era. It contends that participation in such operations has been an identity-constructing activity in the sense that Turkey has tried to reinforce its eroding Western identity in the 1990s through this particular way.

Karaosmanoğlu, Ali L. "The Evolution of the National Security Culture and the Military in Turkey." *Journal of International Affairs* **54, no. 1 (2000): 199–217.**
The article mainly focuses on the role of military in foreign and security policy making in Turkey. It deals with the domestic political and institutional aspects of the problem to the extent that they concern foreign and security policy making. The article analyzes the evolution of security culture in Turkey by arguing that Turkey has historically displayed a consistent security culture of *realpolitik* which has evolved across centuries from an offensive character to defensive one. The article also puts forward that since the eighteenth century the process of Westernization has left its footprints on the Turkey's national security culture. Finally the article claims that the role of military in foreign and security policy making has diminished gradually.

Karaosmanoğlu, Ali L., and Mustafa Kibaroğlu. "Defense Reform in Turkey." In *Post-Cold War Defense Reforms: Lessons Learned in Europe and the United States,* **edited by Istvan Gyarmati and Theodor Winkler, 135–64. New York: East West Institute, Brassey's, 2003.**
The article argues that in the post–Cold War era, the defense reform in Turkey has been successful to a great extent due to the absence of civilian opposition to the demands of the military and the sustained political consensus about the threats the country has had to counter. The article presents two broad objectives of Turkey's reform policy as improving deterrence capacity against threats emanating from the region by developing a forward defense capability and preparing TAF for the new missions of NATO, EU, and other international organizations, namely peace-support, peacekeeping, peacemaking, and crisis-management tasks.

Kibaroğlu, Ayşegül. *Building a Regime for the Waters of the Euphrates-Tigris River Basin.* **London and The Hague: Kluwer Law International, 2002.**
Over the last three decades, in the works of the international water law community and in a series of international conferences convened by the specialized agencies of the United Nations as well as with the emergence of global water policy institutions, serious efforts have been devoted to developing general principles and norms for achieving effective and equitable

management and use of transboundary water resources. Hence, this book is an attempt to put together a meaningful set of principles, norms, rules, and decision-making procedures of a region-specific regime framework for effective utilization of the waters of the Euphrates-Tigris river basin with a view to promoting cooperation among the riparian countries.

Kibaroğlu, Ayşegül. "Cooperation for Development: Emerging Frameworks for Sharing Benefits in the Euphrates-Tigris River Basin." *Boğaziçi Journal* 20 (2006): 135–52.
The article examines the growing complexity of transboundary water resources management in the Euphrates-Tigris river basin by delineating the hydropolitical history as well as focusing on the recent developments in the region. Overall analyses on the origins and the evolution of the water dispute in the region are followed by discussions on the opportunities for cooperation inspired by the benefit sharing approach. The article argues that cooperation in the Euphrates-Tigris basin needs to be based on wider socioeconomic development concepts.

Kibaroğlu, Ayşegül. "The Role of Epistemic Communities in Offering New Cooperation Frameworks in the Euphrates-Tigris Rivers System." *Journal of International Affairs* 61, no. 2 (Spring/Summer 2008): 183–98.
This article analyzes the politics of water resources in the Euphrates-Tigris river basin, focusing on current developments. The article discusses opportunities for more interactions in the river basin with broader aims for socioeconomic development, in addition to the limited goal of water sharing. In this respect, one significant development in the region is the Euphrates-Tigris Initiative for Cooperation (ETIC) established in 2005 by a group of scholars and professionals from the three major riparian countries. This article introduces the origin, objectives, and activities of ETIC within the epistemic community theory with particular references to new areas of cooperation in the basin.

Kibaroğlu, Ayşegül, and Olcay Ünver. "An Institutional Framework for Facilitating Cooperation in the Euphrates-Tigris River Basin." *International Negotiation: A Journal of Theory and Practice* 5, no. 2 (2001): 311–30.
The paper describes the negotiation mechanisms and processes between Turkey, Syria, and Iraq, as well as the bottlenecks and opportunities that exist over utilizing the waters of the Euphrates and Tigris rivers. Negotiations over the water issues involved, both at the technical level and higher levels, have been suspended since the mid-1990s. The paper asserts that there is a need to revitalize these negotiations. A clear understanding of the respective rights and obligations of the three riparians and an objective definition of such needs are prerequisites for sustaining the negotiation process. The paper concludes by elaborating on the modalities of institution building that would facilitate negotiations over the use of the waters of the Euphrates-Tigris rivers system.

Kibaroğlu, Mustafa. "Clash of Interest over Northern Iraq Drives Turkish-Israeli Alliance to a Crossroads." *Middle East Journal* 59, no. 2 (Spring 2005): 246–64.
The article gives an account of how Turkey and Israel are approaching a crossroads in their strategic relations because of their apparently conflicting views and attitudes about the future political and constitutional restructuring of Iraq. It sheds light on the background of negotiations between Turkey and the United States, which resulted in a failure to secure the approval of the TGNA. It examines the concerns as well as the would-be objectives of Israeli policy

makers with regard to the future of Iraq and puts forward arguments that may explain why Israel may have a potential interest in northern Iraq. It analyzes how and why an autonomous or independent Kurdish political entity in northern Iraq might be extremely crucial for the ultimate security of Israel, a country which perceives itself as encircled by enemies and exposed to existential threats. The article presents a thorough analysis on the degree of possible damage that can be caused to the future of the relations between Turkey and Israel due to their apparently clashing interests over northern Iraq.

Kibaroğlu, Mustafa. "Good for the Shah, Banned for the Mullahs: The West and Iran's Quest for Nuclear Power." *Middle East Journal* **60, no. 2 (Spring 2006): 207–32.**
The article discusses in detail the implications of Iran's nuclear capabilities for regional and international peace and stability. Iran's strategic relations with the United States and the leading European nations such as France and (West) Germany in the 1960s and 1970s are discussed with special emphasis on their nuclear cooperation. It examines closely the ups and downs in Iran's efforts to advance in the nuclear field both technologically and scientifically. It investigates whether Iran intends to develop nuclear weapons with the capabilities that it has now or will acquire in the future. The article presents the views of Iranian scholars, scientists, bureaucrats, and intellectuals who are involved in the nuclear projects. It discusses the possible consequences of the policy options that are available to the United States in its effort to prevent Iran from realizing its ambitions. It also examines whether other states in the region, such as Iraq, Saudi Arabia, Egypt, Syria, and Turkey will seek nuclear weapons to counter Iran's nuclear capabilities. It concludes with remarks on what can be done to find a solution to the crisis between Iran and the United States, both of whom have maintained their positions regarding the major points of disagreements since late 2002.

Kibaroğlu, Mustafa. "Impact of the Northern Tier on the Middle East: A Rejoinder." *Security Dialogue* **27, no. 3 (September 1996): 319–24.**
The article is a rejoinder to the article by Mahmood Sariolghalam entitled "The Future of the Middle East: The Impact of the Northern Tier" published in the same issue of the *Security Dialogue.* The author criticizes four major hypotheses raised in that article, which include issues such as Turkish-Middle Eastern relations, Turkey's relations with the former Soviet republics of Turkic identity, and Iran's relations with the Middle East and the Caucasus and Central Asia. The article emphasizes the role of Russia as the key determining actor in the politics of Central Asia and the Caucasus as well as the Middle East, which according to the author is neglected in Sariolghalam's article.

Kibaroğlu, Mustafa. "Iran's Nuclear Ambitions from a Historical Perspective." *Middle Eastern Studies* **43, no. 2 (March 2007): 223–45.**
The article discusses the changing approach of Western countries toward Iran's quest for nuclear power under the Shah and the Imam. The article provides a thorough analysis of Iran's relations with the successive U.S. administrations in building up its nuclear program in the 1960s and 1970s under the Shah regime. The article asserts that in addition to Iran's strategic relations with the United States, France and Germany have played roles in the expansion of its nuclear infrastructure as well as raising a cadre of Iranian professionals and scientists. It emphasizes that Iran's nuclear science and technology transfer from the United States and the Europeans came to a sudden halt with the Islamic Revolution of February 1979. The article analyzes that after a decade-long effort to revitalize its long-stalled nuclear power projects

and to expand the scope of scientific and technological infrastructure, Iran was left with Russia as the only major potential supplier. In the early 1990s, the United States imposed sanctions when Iran intensified its efforts to expand the scope of its nuclear program. The article concludes with the analysis of the heightening of tensions between Iran and the West in the 2000s by discussing the role of the IAEA and EU along with the United States.

Kibaroğlu, Mustafa. "Turkey." In *Europe and Nuclear Disarmament,* edited by Harald Müller, 161–93. Brussels: European Interuniversity Press, 1998.
The chapter discusses Turkey's attitude toward the nuclear-related matters like a ban on nuclear tests, a cutoff in the production of fissile material, establishing nuclear-weapons-free zones in various parts of the globe, and the post–Cold War strategies of NATO and of the Western EU. The chapter lets the reader view the issues from a wider angle. Accordingly, a special attention is paid to discussing at length the difficulties of formulating appropriate strategies for Turkey emanating from the extremely complex geopolitics of the country.

Kibaroğlu, Mustafa. "Turkey and Israel Strategize." *Middle East Quarterly* 9, no. 1 (Winter 2002): 61–65.
In 1996, Israel and Turkey signed an agreement for military cooperation. The article analyzes the military cooperation by addressing the following questions: What exactly is the real nature of this bilateral relationship? What is included; What is excluded? Does this relationship bind Turkey and Israel to a set of formal or informal commitments in the present? And does the military cooperation agreement imply any commitment regarding future contingencies? It concludes with an analysis that as Turkey looks to Israel to bolster its strategic deterrent, it should expect Israel to seek a strategic depth in return.

Kuniholm, Bruce R. "Turkey and the West." *Foreign Affairs* 70, no. 2 (1991): 34–48.
The article maintains that during the Cold War era underpinning Turkey's role in the NATO alliance was the principle of reciprocity: Turkey would play an important part in the defense of the West and make its facilities available, while the West would provide Turkey with a deterrent against Soviet attack, as well as military and economic assistance. Against this background, the article analyzes the early period of post–Cold War (1991) by asserting that Turkey's relations with its allies continue to be informed by the notion of reciprocity and are colored by shifting security concerns. The only difference from recent years is that, with the Soviet threat sharply diminished and Ankara having assumed an important role in the allied coalition against Iraq in the Gulf War, Turkey's strategic significance is once again being assessed chiefly in its Middle Eastern context.

Kut, Şule. "Turks of Kosovo: What to Expect?" *Perceptions, Journal of International Affairs* 5, no. 3 (2000): 49–60.
The article argues that ethnic Turks in the post-communist Balkans were faced with one of two diametrically opposed experiences in the 1990s. They were either caught between the nationalism of the majority and that of the major minority, as in Kosovo and Macedonia, or relieved of ethnic tension and benefited from the overall democratization of the country, as in Bulgaria and Romania. The article stipulates that in both situations, however, they were able to form ethnic parties and participate in political processes. The article asserts that, again in both cases, especially due to Turkey's position in the region as a major power, more often than not they have gained confidence as citizens of their respective states. It denotes that Turks have been

strongly in favor of the territorial integrity of their new states in former Yugoslavia or elsewhere in the Balkans during the turbulent 1990s.

Oğuzlu, Tarık H. *Turkmens of Iraq as a Factor in Turkish Foreign Policy: Socio-Political and Demographic Perspectives.* **Ankara: Foreign Policy Institute, 2001.**
The paper makes an inquiry into the demographic structure of the Turkmen people residing in Iraq. The discussions are followed by a further analysis as to how the existence of the Turkmen in Iraq might serve Turkey's interests in the region. It also examines the ways as to how Turkey might contribute to the betterment of Turkmen's life. The paper mainly deals with the political aspect of the Turkmen life in Iraq with a view to better comprehending the contemporary history of these people since the establishment of monarchy in Iraq.

Sander, Oral. *Türkiye'nin Dış Politikası* **[Turkey's Foreign Policy]. Ankara: İmge Yayınevi, 3. baskı, 2006.**
The volume begins with a discussion on the methodology in history studies and describes the general characteristics of the twentieth-century diplomatic history. It presents main characteristics of Turkish foreign policy such as Turkey's attachment to the West. The book examines the Turkish foreign policy with its basic features of continuity and change. The main themes of Turkish foreign policy such as the relations with the Balkans, Black Sea, and the Middle East are analyzed by and large. It starts with the general themes and flows through the specifics. In this context, the discussions on Turkey's relations with the NATO and Turkic world provide inspiring analyses.

Sezer, Duygu B. "Turkey's New Security Environment, Nuclear Weapons and Proliferation." *Comparative Strategy* **14, no. 2 (1995): 149–73.**
The article asserts that Turkey has been touched deeply by the geostrategic changes introduced into the international system by the end of the Cold War and the disintegration of the Soviet Union. It presents and analyzes Turkish perceptions of its evolving security environment in the post–Cold War era as it impacts Turkish interests and policies, with particular reference to the implications for Turkish security of the existing nuclear weapons and potential proliferation in regions and countries that are located near its borders. The article describes the impact of the dissolution of the Soviet Union on Turkish security perceptions and policies. It reviews developments and trends in the Balkans and in the Middle East/Persian Gulf region as they impinge on Turkish security. Turkish attitudes toward nuclear energy, the nuclear option, and proliferation are also discussed.

Shaw, Stanford J., and Ezel Kural Shaw. *History of the Ottoman Empire and Modern Turkey: Volume 2, Reform, Revolution, and Republic: The Rise of Modern Turkey 1808–1975.* **Cambridge: Cambridge University Press, 1977.**
It is the second book of the two-volume *History of the Ottoman Empire and Modern Turkey.* It discusses the modernization of the Ottoman Empire during the nineteenth and early twentieth centuries, the spread of nationalism among its subject people, and the revolutionary changes in Ottoman institutions and society that led to the Empire's demise and the rise of the democratic Republic of Turkey. Based on extensive research in the Ottoman archives as well as Western sources, this volume analyzes the external pressures, reform measures, institutional changes, and intellectual movements that affected the heterogeneous Ottoman society during the Empire's last century. It concludes with an analysis of contemporary Turkey's constitutional and political structures and principal domestic and foreign problems.

Sönmezoğlu, Faruk. *II. Dünya Savaşı'ndan Günümüze Türk Dış Politikası* [Turkish Foreign Policy since World War II]. İstanbul: Der Yayınları, 2006.
This volume provides a comprehensive analysis of Turkish foreign policy since World War II. It consists of four main parts, which denote four main historical periods, to analyze Turkish foreign policy with its continuity and change. Each part begins with a discussion on the state of affairs at the international and national setting. Then, Turkey's relations with the countries at her neighborhood as well as her relations with the West (the United States and Western Europe) are explained depending on the leading international actors which Turkey interacts with at that particular period. There are also concise discussions on Turkey's relations with the nonaligned movement within the framework of the United Nations in the Cold War era.

Türkeş, Mustafa. "Atatürk Döneminde Türkiye'nin Bölgesel Dış Politikaları 1923–1938" [Turkey's Regional Foreign Policy during the Atatürk Era 1923–1938]. *Atatürkçülük ve Modern Türkiye,* Uluslararası Konferans, October 22–23, 1998, Ankara, 123–41.
The article examines the Turkish foreign policy during the Atatürk era (1923–38) with a special attention to the regional policies developed in that period to respond to the challenges faced by the new Republic in the Mediterranean, Balkans, and the Middle East. In this context, the article analyzes the objectives and achievements of the Balkan Entente, Mediterranean and Sadabad Pacts by underlining their contribution to the regional peace and cooperation in Turkey's neighborhood. Moreover, the article provides a coherent analysis on how the residual issues from the Treaty of Lausanne had been solved through the methods of peaceful settlement of disputes such as international bilateral and multilateral negotiations and conciliation under the perceptive leadership of Atatürk.

Zurcher, Erick J. *Turkey: A Modern History.* London and New York: I. B. Tauris & Co. Limited, 2001.
The volume focuses on Turkey's continuing incorporation into the capitalist world and the modernization of state and society. It begins with the forging of closer links with Europe after the French Revolution and the changing face of the Ottoman Empire in the nineteenth century. Zurcher argues that Turkey's history, between 1908 and 1950, should be seen as a unity and offers a strongly revisionist interpretation of Turkey's founding father, Kemal Atatürk. In his account of the period since 1950, Zurcher focuses on the growth of mass politics, the three military coups, the thorny issue of Turkey's human rights record, the integration into the global economy, the alliance with the West and relations with the EC, Turkey's ambivalent relations with the Middle East, the increasingly explosive Kurdish questions, the economic crisis of 1994, and the continuing political instability and growth of Islam.

Index

About the Authors

AYŞEGÜL KİBAROĞLU (Ph.D., Bilkent University, 1998) is a faculty member in the Department of International Relations at Middle East Technical University, Ankara, Turkey. She is the author of *Building a Regime for the Waters of the Euphrates-Tigris River Basin* (2002), as well as articles on this and related Turkish security topics.

MUSTAFA KİBAROĞLU (Ph.D., Bilkent University, 1996) is a faculty member in the Department of International Relations at Bilkent University, Ankara, Turkey. He is the author of numerous articles on Turkish foreign policy and security issues, which have appeared in both English and Turkish languages.

15479771R00137

Printed in Poland
by Amazon Fulfillment
Poland Sp. z o.o., Wrocław